Introduction

Easy to understand, deep and profound, Phuong has completely made readers infatuated with his book *Secret Power* – it is about a type of power which could disseminate profoundly and form powerful thought, opinion or knowledge which in turn can be used to shape the attitude and influence the emotion of the crowd, thus directing the crowd's behavior according to the will of the user.

Phuong also shows us quite a few things about dark PR techniques (Dark Art) in business which are being used to manipulate and to mislead public opinion as well as to eliminate enemies, to help us identify and protect ourselves, thus enhancing our ability to control the society.

How to apply the secret power to shape the attitude and to influence the emotion of the crowd will be presented in detail in this book along with many practical examples to help you have an easier time understanding and applying it.

One notable thing about the Secret Power is that it contains power of *the modern doctrine of PR* - a very new approach of PR to the age-old business problems (sales, building and protecting company's reputation). The modern doctrine of PR is more comprehensive than the PR concepts in the past because it contains both value of professional knowledge and value of social contribution.

Regarding the value of social contribution, the modern PR doctrine publicizes techniques which can help people perceive PR correctly and make it become more popular to the public.

In terms of the value of professional knowledge, the modern PR doctrine shows us how to apply the power of 5 Supreme Arts to help enterprises achieve their goals as well as a sustainable development.

As containing in it both the value of professional knowledge and the value of social contribution, this book is considered to be one of the remarkable efforts to bring the PR industry back to its roots and its original mission which is contributing to the building of a healthy information society and a transparent business environment, thus enhancing the society.

Table of contents

Lists

Acknowledgement

"I sincerely thank my father, my mother, my wife and my daughter who have to go through so many difficulties to give me the best condition to complete this book. It was conceived with so much love that I could never repay".

About the author

Le Tran Bao Phuong is known as one of the leading experts of public relation industry in Vietnam. He is fascinated with the understanding about the causes, the deep root and the way people influence as well as be influenced by public opinion. He is also a famous lecturer and currently one of the favorite PR speakers.

Author's words

- *"What is the secret power?"*
- *"It is the power of PR!"*
- *"What about the 5 supreme arts?"*
- *"How extraordinary are they?"*
- *"How to apply the PR power to achieve more success in life?"*
- *"How to know if it works?"*
- *"Who proves it!"*

Before answering these questions, I want to say that I am very lucky because I have a chance to share many good things to help you have a better career and life.

I believe that the title of the book has your attention, because you are looking for a few tips to get out of the un-equability of your current condition.

You have just realized that you are living in a society whose basic nature is the synthesis of all relationships, and you as an individual gets to influence others and be influenced by them.

You realize that this world is unfair. There are people who always obtain benefits from privileges reserved for themselves without any effort. They are not better than you, but with such privileges, they can always torment you.

You have just realized that the major cause of your sorrow was that other people didn't follow your will, they down played and intervened so much into your hope, or even showed up in your dreams. They destroyed all your expectations and hopes.

You know that this was too much and you could not wait any longer to have a beautiful, healthy and balanced life. And since everyone has the right to be happy in this life, your demand is very natural and need to be respected.

So what will it be if you can handle the PR techniques which are capable to help you influence the belief, opinion, attitude and emotion of the crowd, thereby shaping their understandings and behaviors to achieve what you want, and you can make the decision based on your gut feeling without being influenced by others?

My friends, this book is the gift that I want to share with you. It is a secret of powerful PR techniques that are able to make an impact on both individuals and crowds on a large scale. It is an arsenal full of PR tools used to secretly influence the opinion, emotion and behavior of other people. It is a concise guide book that could help you identify the way bad people influence your behavior in order to achieve their goals. This book is going to uncover those tactics.

Now, the first important thing is to determine who you are, what you need from this book and what it can help you.

The objective of the book

- *"Is it for me?"*

This book was written for you, my friends, no matter who you are - an ordinary person, a person running an enterprise, a person practicing PR, or somebody wants to be more successful in life.

Supposed you are just an ordinary person who wants to protect yourself from the impact of the dark propagandizing forces which quietly manipulating the behavior of you and your kids, then this book is the most useful companion for you.

- *"Why?"*

Because you haven't re-legalized yet that the propagandizing forces are adjusting your awareness, attitude and purchasing act on a daily basis. They will always try to describe the useful features of the product that they offer, along with a lot of evidence that guarantee a dreamlike effect. Those dreams are the ones in which you will get rid of your fears and fulfill your needs. They convince you that you should buy that product, and let them take care the rest. Their products will completely solve all your problems. They happen to be everywhere in every moment to do so.

Because you haven't realized that they regularly "inject" into each of your neurons the dream of a resounding success, a happy family, a good health, beauty and respect, and then suggesting you to choose the product or service which can be able to fulfill your urgent needs.

Taking advantage of your negligence, they fire the "magic bullets"[1] straight into things that you are infatuated with, concerned with and afraid of - things that are the weaknesses to your soul - to break down your "firewall".

After your "firewall" has been broken down, you are no longer protected. Bad news would freely change your viewpoint, attitude, and emotion, thus adjusting your behavior.

Your attitude would fluctuate from the state of "disbelief" to "doubtfulness". Your reaction would change from convincing yourself "to believe" in what they said to performing "a specific action" they expected. It is the collapse of "the firewall". My friends, you could see that this happens all the time.

– *"How did they influence my behavior?"*

They used news on TV, press comments, experts' statement, scientist opinion, opinions shared by people with the same thinking, and movie facts etc, to change your thinking, attitude, and belief, thus guiding your behavior respectively. They also do the same to younger target like your kids.

And you begin to notice that the information you receive daily on TV, newspapers, movies etc., which lets you learn of the things happening around you, are always adjusted, censored and distorted products. They themselves are the tool to manipulate

---

[1] The hypodermic needle model or the magic bullet theory supposes that viewers are passive and directly affected by the media. They unconditionally accepted messages they received from the media without consideration. Thus, the message has been fired straight into viewers and penetrated into their minds like a magic bullet.

Although there are debates about this theory, but the "hypodermic needle model" still contains some truths in it. Harold Lasswell (1927) was a leading communications theorist in this category. He said that mass media have an enormous power which can influence and rule public opinion. For example, during World War II, (political) communication activities were always used to manipulate, and to brainwash the crowd.

and to adjust your perception, because bad people would not give you the information that you should know, but the information that they deem beneficial for them only.

And you begin to notice that they also use the Internet and public forums (a virtual world with less discipline) as an ideological weapon to shape your thinking, to create new demands in your sub consciousness, and to evoke a deep and desire that you have not ever imagined of just to influence your behavior in reality.

In reality, the things that are happening are even more dangerous than ever before. The less prepared someone is, there is a higher chance that he gets manipulated. There is no other result.

And if you are a chief executive officer who wants to achieve business goals, then this book is the guide book that you should be passionate about.

- *You are infatuated by this book because you need the power of PR. Why?*

Because you know that the future of a business depends a lot on what customers feel about the business. In fact, what customers think about your business are actually coherent messages have been injected in their heads before, so to build and to maintain your organization's credit, you should have the power of PR.

Moreover, you also have witnessed quite a few situations where many customers are willing to gather to criticize a certain enterprise for harming the interest of one of them.

Hence, when an enterprise creates a negative disposition in just a single individual, it accidentally imprints the same thing upon the entire community. And then it gets back not only one but also a series of retaliations. This means that just one or two really angry people is enough to cause a social media crisis for enterprises.

So in case an individual is a customer, then what should you do? In case it is the government, journalist, supplier, investor, shareholder, internal employees, or people from alliance and association, what should you do? In case it is the competitor, what should you do?

You must manage effectively the relationship with them to avoid potential obstacles in your business. Hence, you need the power of PR.

- You are infatuated by the book because your brand is being forgotten by consumers.
- *"So what should I do?"*

Certainly you will need to determine the cause of the disease and choose the right communication solutions to solve it radically. So, you need the power of PR.

- You are infatuated by the book because modern society is highly democratic and information is disseminated widely, and any comment of customers would directly influence your enterprise.

All business owners know that enterprises must gain public support to prosper and to promote other multi-sided relationships. Therefore, they always try to put a certain positive personality into the relationship between their enterprises and customers

Thus, this book is helpful. It will show you the technique to be able to adjust the distorted understanding of customers about a product or an organization, to spread advantageous information to the market, to help achieve business goals, and to help enterprises get out of the whirlwind of misinformation

If you are a PR practitioner looking for a unique know-how to improve your current job results and to save your time and to be succeed early in your career, then this book is a great read for you.

As you realized that though PR was mentioned many times as an advanced art of public persuasion, a large number of books about PR only reflect incompletely the shadow of PR power, such as the trick to drafting an attractive press release, organizing an effective event, or gaining many benefits when working with pressmen. Well, certainly they are not enough and we deserve more than that.

Everything is totally different and fresh in this book. It does not only help you understand the power of PR, but also show you the way to apply the 5 supreme arts to influence the crowd's behavior on a large scale to develop business activities.

You are about to realize the real value of this book for PR practitioners: it helps you succeed early in your career and save lots of time working. The book is a great inventory of supplemental information for you. The content in this book is very trustworthy, because it has been drawn from practical experiences and authentic studies over many years.

Finally, no matter who you are, you should have this book, because it can bring you many advantages both in work and in life. That is quite certain!

The birth and purpose of the book

This book was born from a date with destiny!

Before publishing this book, I have been through all the deepest passions and fears.

The book may create limitations for the practice of PR, because its content has exposed almost entirely everything there is to know about PR techniques and the application mechanisms to draw and to influence the crowd´s behavior.

– *"Should I publish it?"*

It was written according to my experience during the practice of PR on many projects with national and international organizations, and also through studying and teaching. I'm totally comfortable with this besides the fact that I have been tormented for 3 years because of the question: "Should I publish it?"

– *"Yes!"*

Only until May 2014, I then understood thoroughly that it was very necessary to publish this book, because of three reasons:

First, the book will bring many benefits to people because it is related to things that directly influence their lives. It is because that at present, mass communications in our society is severely distorted.

Second, PR is a kind of power. Each power always has two sides. So does PR. PR could generate both good and bad things depend only on the motivation of the practitioner.

Thus, when commenting upon the impact of mass media on social violence, Eric Maigret (2003) also stressed:

> Mass media itself does not create violence, but it can be misused by killers to build their violent world and sickly thoughts.
>
> The media is rather the storage of forms of action than the instigator of action. If there is any imitation, it would to   choose the method to murder, rather than to murder itself."[2]

Knife can be a dangerous weapon if misused, however it is not prohibited because everyone knows how to use it in a healthy way.

Third, PR is a scientific and artistic industry[3] which remains ambiguous to many people and PR career has not been defined in the right way. Frankly speaking, I do not mean to teach you anything. What I am trying to do is to help people understand more about PR to be able to identify any organization using its power for bad purposes; thus strengthening the ability of the normal people to control and build a healthy information society, helping everyone could enjoy the pure truth in this wonderful life.

> "The truth is always true and powerful. If someone believes that he or she has discovered the valuable truth, then it is not only a privilege for them, but also the responsibility to disseminate it"[4] (Edward L. Bernays, 1928).

There is currently no guarantee that all PR activities are totally transparent, sound and respectful to consumer's benefits. According to a study, even in the US and UK, there is not any specific legislation on the practice of PR.

---

[2] Eric Maigret, *Sociologie de la communication et des médias*, Armand Colin publisher, p. 58, Paris, 2003, according to Tran Huu Quang, *The communication theory and applications in research of communications in Vietnam*, 16/12/2012.

[3] The scientific aspect of PR is expressed in the method of collecting information, analyzing data, setting and deploying propaganda strategies specifically and carefully. The artistic aspect is expressed by creating messages which are likely to touch the emotion and soul of abstract public groups to lobby their support (author's note).

[4] Edward L. Bernays.(1928) *Propaganda* (p. 22), Horace Liveright.

There are several associations such as the CIPR and PRSA that have applied a Code of Conduct for PR professionals, but it is not an orthodox law like the professional law for doctors, lawyers or journalists.

Therefore, I strongly believe in this book. It will surely help you understand more about PR in order to be able to take part in controlling the society. I believe this effort will be welcomed by everybody in order to allow the PR industry to return to its roots and its original mission is to contribute to the building of a healthy information society and a transparent business environment, thus enhancing the society.

Contents of the book

The book is divided into 4 parts with 12 chapters as follows:

Part 1: The invisibly ruling power, includes 2 chapters, explaining why people want to influence their fellow beings' behaviors; is there any invisible ruler, and who is he; what is the secret of this invisible power? What are the ancient ruling wisdoms? How can we put them into practice? What is the power of PR and its ancient origin; why is PR power getting more and more powerful; how can PR power be applied nationally and globally? What is the modern doctrine of PR? How can they help us?

Part 2: Exploring how the 5 supreme arts influence the crowd´s behaviors, includes 6 chapters, you will learn the details of how to apply each supreme art to shape the attitude and rule the emotion of the crowd to achieve your goal.

Part 3: Professional ethics and dark PR, includes 2 chapters, you will be see a tactics system of dark PR which is being used to manipulate and to mislead public opinion and to annihilate the enemy. These disclosures will help you understand more about dark PR, identify and stay away from them, thereby enhancing the ability to control the society.

Part 4: Summing up the 5 Supreme Arts, includes 2 chapters, you will get a structured look on the whole philosophy and key points of each art.

My friends, there are many debates on how to officially define Public Relations (PR) in the world. The debating is completely understandable because PR activities are always changing and varying based on each environment such as press, economy, politics, society, and culture of every nation. They are flexible.

And according to a research, most of debates concerns with concepts and academic perspectives rather than with powerful ruling wisdoms which have been being applied in current PR activities.

Therefore, whether how PR is defined in text, it will remain a great power. Therefore, any academic debate could not influence the power of PR presented in this book.

In addition, the PR industry has existed and developed over the past 100 years, however, many problems still remain.

According to Paul Holmes (2010), the President of Holmes foundation majoring in PR evaluation, the PR industry is suffering from 3 most essential issues, namely the PR industry has not done a good job of hiring the best employees; the PR industry is still not strong in terms of research, evaluation, and measurement; and the PR industry can still not create for itself an image and good reputation. Ironically![5]

I agree with Holmes about these 3 issues. And with a desire to contribute into the PR industry worldwide, I have been solving 3 issues below by:

- Teaching at universities, sharing experiences to help bridge the gap between learning and practicing PR; training new generations of PR practitioners to behave ethically and to have professional capacity.
- Sharing the ways to evaluate and to measure the effectiveness of PR activities;
- Writing and sharing widely useful books about PR to restrict partial prejudices about PR career and to improve the image of the industry.

---

[5]Paul Holmes. (2010). *Interview with Paul Holmes*. at:
http://www.forumdavos.com/interviews/read/3 and
http://www.youtube.com/watch?v=iYRoHhnoQeo [date of access: October 6th, 2013]

Besides, I think PR industry is still suffering from another important issue: it is facing the worst kind of crisis reputation.

Obviously, PR remains a rather vague concept to the community; it is being accused as "Dark Art"; enterprises have not appreciated PR as an essential activity; PR practitioners have not yet proven how PR helps businesses achieve their goals[6]. The professional pinnacle of PR industry is to build and to protect reputation, however PR itself is stuck in its own problems. Ironically!

I am deeply concerned about this issue. And with the desire to contribute to the PR industry worldwide, I have been trying to solve the 4th issue by widely releasing this book around the world.

The book will help people understand more about PR and its positive power in sales promotion, building, and protecting enterprises reputation; thereby helping enterprises grow steadily to in turn contribute to the growth of the national economy.

It is my great pleasure to give you this book as a gift; and I believe that it will help you improve your current work results, save you a lot of time in achieving your goals in career.

It is a significant mission in my life because through the book, I can contribute a little to help the PR industry worldwide develop in a healthy way, hence helping to better people´s lives. This is an extraordinary mission, and I feel happy to know that so many people in this world, including you, do really need this book.

Thanks for the love you have for this book. I sincerely wish you success and happiness in life!

Le Tran Bao Phuong
From Vietnam, August 2014
phuongpr@icloud.com

---

[6] According to PR practitioners in Southeast Asia (including the Philippines, Indonesia, Vietnam, Singapore, Malaysia, Thailand) presented at the ASEAN PR Network Conference taking place from 2nd to 3rd June 2014 in Jakarta, Indonesia.

Introduction

"The PR power (aka The Secret Power) is a type of power which could disseminate profoundly and powerfully thoughts, opinions or knowledge which are able to shape the attitude and to influence the emotion and behavior of the crowd, thus making them follow the wishes of the user." (Le Tran Bao Phuong, 2013)

Before diving into the application of this power, let's find out the mystery of number 5.

The mystery of number 5

- *"Why do humans have 5 fingers on one hand and 5 toes on one foot?"*
- *"Why do people perceive the world through five senses (smell, see, touch, hear, taste)?"*
- *"Number 5 is considered to be the symbol of the mystery and what do we know about this mysterious number?"*

According to Oriental thoughts and many explanations from ancient ages, number 5 contains many mysterious meanings. Some special views of number 5 can be listed as follows:

The five Elements Theory explains that all things in the universe are made of 5 elements: Metal, Wood, Water, Fire and Earth.

The masterpiece manual on military tactics, The Art of War[7] figured out 5 virtues (Wise, Loyal, Humane, Braver, Just) that make up the 5 indispensable qualities of a General.

According to Shu Ching, one has the 5 blessings[8] would lead a happy and complete life. 5 blessings includes: Longevity, Wealth, Health, Virtue, and Fulfilling death.

According to Feng Shui, the number 5 symbolizes 5 directions (East, West, South, North and Center). The number 5 symbolizes longevity and immortality.

In the field of military, "when conducting a powerful force, ancient people divided it into 5 arms: the left, right, front, back and central. In the United States, when Dwight David Eisenhower was promoted to the Supreme Commander of the US army (1890-1969), 5 stars were used"[9].

One more point to considerable, number 5 is the number of Kings. It symbolizes the power of the ruler.

In fact, the US pentagon[10] was built according to the design closely related to the mystery of number 5: it is arranged in a pentagon (five sides), 5 parallel rows of houses on each side, every row of houses has 5 floors. The courtyard in the center is 5 acres in area (2 hectares).

It is believed that the Pentagon represents the determination to rule 5 continents of American people. And the fact also clearly demonstrates that the Pentagon has the ruling power and a vast influence on most political and military issues around the world.

---

[7] The Art of War was drafted by Sun Tzu in 512 BC.

[8] In Shu Ching, a set of books compiled and translated by Confucius and his disciples 2.500 years ago in China.

[9] Nguyen Xuan Vinh, Nguyen Phu Thu, *Number 5*, at http://anhduong.net/Aug06/ConSo5.htm [date of access: May 15th, 2012]

[10] The Pentagon was designed by George Edwin Bergstrom and built from 1941 to 1943.

Picture 1. The powerful Pentagon of Americans (source: wikipedia).

Revealing the secret

— *"Why do we talk a lot about number 5?"*

— *"Because the power of PR is derived from ancient ruling wisdoms related to number 5".*

Since ancient times, ruling forces have learnt that human brain is the only physical thing that can transform things from the metaphysical world into the visible world. It is the only thing that be able to turn the thought in one's mind into action.

The finding of ancient wisdoms has shown that this metabolic mechanism is based on five key elements, that is:

✿ Perceptions and attitudes about an issue (created by public opinion, mass media, ideology, culture, religion, prejudice, personal knowledge);

✿ Personal feeling;

✿ Personal standard;

✿ Time pressure, social pressure, or pressured by the expectation of others;

✿ Herd mentality.

Therefore, in order to influence people's behavior in the visible world, ancient ruling forces used the powerful and mysterious media techniques to shape the attitude, to rule the emotion and to create an action pressure on the mind of the crowd in order to manipulate their behavior, causing them to be loyal, to respect and to worship them in a deep resignation.

I have realized that there are five ancient ruling wisdoms that have the power to influence the crowd's behavior[11].

When applying the 5 ancient ruling wisdoms in the field of modern PR, I called them the 5 Supreme Arts; and deliberately named each of them by a familiar name to make it easier for you to get (see picture 2).

You will notice that each supreme art contained in it the powerful ancient ruling knowledge hidden under familiar name. You will see that, the supreme power of 5 secret arts is still there. They are always powerful.

The most important thing is that the unifying power of 5 Supreme Arts constituting the power of PR (also known as the Secret Power).

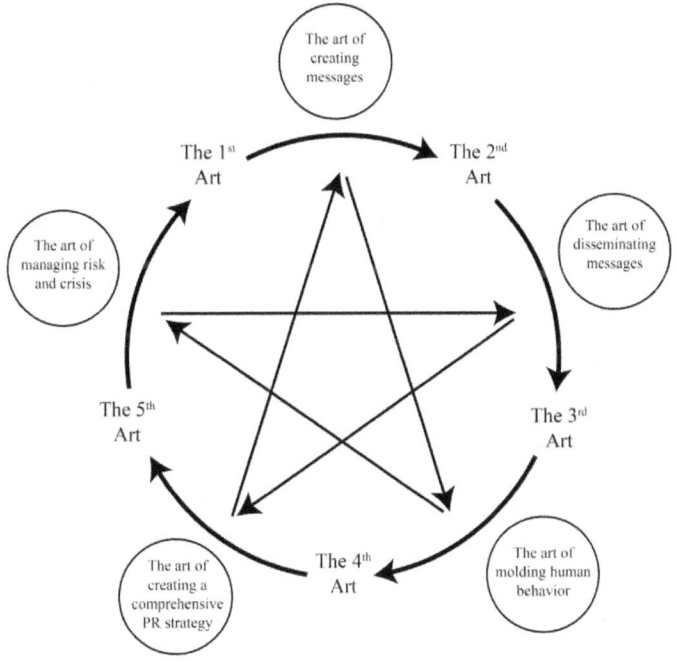

Picture 2. 5 supreme arts to make up the power of PR (aka the Secret Power)

---

[11] See Chapter 1, Section 1.4. Five ancient ruling wisdoms

The 5 ancient ruling wisdoms should be applied on sales promotion in the modern age;

Just by applying the finding of the ancient wisdom (No. 1, No. 4), we can easily realize that there are two key factors in a purchasing decision of human beings *"the attitude toward the product and the purchasing pressure."*

✡ 2 key factors:

1. *Their attitude toward the product*: love / hate / interest / indifference / desire / unclear etc.
2. *The pressure on purchasing an item*: convinced / threatened / forced / keeping up with the Jones/ imitating others purchase / self-rewarding /impulse buying/or buying by snatches, etc.

From the clear perception of 2 key factors in purchasing decision of human beings, you can continue to manipulate the ancient ruling wisdom to speed up sales promotion by the following drawing techniques:

✡ LET'S:

- Use the power of images to create icons stimulating purchases; use the power of words, news, music and movies to wake up the imprint of time, memories of happy childhood (or childhood deprivation), create the buying urge... in the crowd to persuade them to purchase an item;
- Stimulate their natural instinct; and
- Intervene in the self-purchasing decision of the crowd to boost the consumption of the product / service[12].

5 ancient ruling powers have a strong power to shape the attitude and behavior of the crowd.

The attitude of the crowd toward an issue will determine their behavior to it. This attitude is generated from their knowledge and experience. Their knowledge and

---

[12] Please see the detailed instruction and examples in Chapter 3, 4, 5 and 6.

experience are derived from ideology, prejudice and from what they heard, saw, read, or learnt from others, as well as from the evidence and past experience.

When the knowledge and experience of human beings are deep, they will end up fortifying their trust on a decision or a certain option. Their attitude will become assertive and conservative.

Therefore, in order to change the attitude and behavior of the crowd, keep on giving them a large amount of evidence in contrast with their beliefs, as well as creating the opposite evidence that get responses from the crowd to change their old beliefs and form a new attitude and behavior in them.

- *"Can we shape people's belief?"*

Absolutely yes, because one´s point of view depends on what he believes, and because what he believes can be changed, then his viewpoint is going to be changed (Seth Godin, 2008). As their view changes, their belief will also change. And when the belief itself is changed, the attitude and behavior of human beings towards an issue will also be changed accordingly.

Furthermore, just by hearing so much about an unbelievable thing can make us thinking about it, and it is often difficult to second guess a thing that is believed by many people in a long time.

We are not surprised that human beliefs can be shaped and changed. Religious belief of human beings seems to be the strongest one. However, it has been successfully changed (see Box 1).

Box 1:

Religious beliefs can be shaped

A typical evidence for the statement above is the success of the campaign to eradicate smallpox by the World Health Organization (WHO) in 1980 in Asia and Africa after crossing one of the biggest barriers; religious belief.

Have you ever heard of that campaign? The story happened in 1980, WHO announced for the first time that smallpox - a disease that had had threatened human

---

life - has been globally eliminated. The disease had been existed for over 3000 years and had killed hundreds of millions of people. The campaign of WHO to eradicate the disease had gone for 21 years at a cost of more than 300 million USD with the help and efforts of more than 80 countries. The success of this campaign was regarded as the greatest achievement of WHO in public relations (on an international level).

The Campaign had overcome many challenges to achieve the final success, such as the Cold War hostility between many countries, the state bureaucracy, specific medical management in quite a few countries, the diversity of native cultures, and especially the fierce resistance due to religious beliefs...

Religious belief in India

Smallpox was a very popular disease in India since 1500 BC and it was linked to the Gods and Goddesses in the Hindu temple, for example The Hindu goddess Shitala Mata.

Shitala Mata is one of the goddesses that is worshipped vastly in India with more than 32 temples in Calcutta and almost every household worships the image of the goddess. There is a belief that if somebody gets smallpox, it means that they have been visited by Mata Shitala Goddess.

Remember that the Goddess is quick-tempered. Many devotees believe that if they try to prevent or treat smallpox, they would provoke the goddess and get punished. Therefore, they deliberately failed to report the infectious cases and refused to be vaccinated. Besides, the vaccine comes from the cow which is a sacred object of Hinduism, the campaign faced a lot of opposition.

Before such barriers, WHO implemented a strategy to shape the belief wisely. WHO interpreted that vaccination was a form of worship and created the slogan "Worship the goddess and take a vaccination too."

The vaccination was done together with religious rituals and the hymns to be sung in the temple of Shitala Goddess. This strategy has been successful and has reduced the objections from the believers against the vaccination.

Religious belief in West Africa

In West Africa, it is believed that Sapona is one of the sons of God. When he is satisfied, Sapona will grow crops, harvests. When unhappy, he could make grains grow inside human beings, causing smallpox.

Therefore, many people in West Africa refused to be vaccinated because they believed that this would threaten the existence of the God and their lives. This belief was so strong that, in the early 1960s, a WHO vaccination team was killed by furious followers.

Because of this accident, after interviewing consultation and studying the viewpoints of religious leaders and politicians in West Africa, WHO had adjusted the approach. WHO convinced those who were with smallpox in local areas to get vaccinated. WHO also linked the vaccination to religious ceremonies in local areas.

Religious belief in South Africa

In South Africa, some Christian denominations fiercely protested against any form of medical treatment, because they believed that it was offensive to God's will. They lived in a closed community and refused to report any infectious case.

In this situation, WHO members approached the religious leaders to convince them about the necessity of vaccination. The religious leaders pledged to support WHO, however, they continued to preach against vaccination.

Consequentially, WHO requested the President of Botswana to deported those who refused to be vaccinated. As a result, they agreed to be vaccinated, because the deportation was even worse.

In short, religious belief is one of the most common barriers to the campaign of WHO, because believers don't accept any action that threatens the existence of the god or goddess that they worship.

> The campaign succeeded because WHO has been flexible in the approach and known how to adjust the message to make it closer to the existing viewpoint and to reduce confrontation, thus shaping religious beliefs based on the goal of vaccination[13].

The 5 ancient ruling wisdoms can be applied to influence the crowd's behavior by:

⤳ By manipulating the power of words:

Those who manipulate the 5 ancient ruling wisdoms could adjust the way people feel about the world, hence adjusting their behavior because human beings are the result of how they feel about the world.

It is entirely possible because word is the magic controlling the behavior. Since ancient times and till today, word still retain its power (Sigmund Freud, 1915).

⤳ By stimulating natural instincts and childhood beliefs

Those who use the 5 ancient ruling wisdoms could recognize where the deep motivation of human comes from, and what kind of inner instincts prompt them to act. Therefore, they learn how to press the button of human behavior and influence the behavior of the crowd under the press-and-run mechanism.

About this issue, Edward Bernays[14] (1928) gave a very sophisticated example:

⟂0 ————————————————————

[13] Curtin P.A. & Gaither T.K., *International public relations: Negotiating culture, identity and power*, Sage, USA, 2007.

[14]Edward Bernays (1891-1995) was an Austrian American pioneer in the field of PR, also regarded as the founder of PR. He combined the idea of Gustave Le Bon and Wilfred Trotter about crowd psychology with the idea of psychoanalysis of his uncle Sigmund Freud.

Bernays's viewpoint is if we can understand the purpose and motivation of the mass, we can control them without their perception. Bernays used them to influence the thought and behavior of the crowd.

In the 1920s, women were only allowed to smoke in some specific areas and would be arrested if they violated the rule. Bernays was working for the American Tobacco Company back then. To help increase sales, Bernays sent a group of models marching in New York City. Then he told the media that there was a group of women who paraded and lighted "The torch of freedom" for their sake of gender equality, because women smoking were concerned to be a symbol of emancipation and equality with men.

When receiving the signal from Bernays, these women lit up Lucky Strike cigarettes in front of the lens of photographers. The New York Times (1929) reported that these girls smoked to show a gesture to

28

...Being arrogant, people rarely minds the real reasons influencing their behavior.

It could said that a man buying an expensive car for believing it is the best in the market, after having carefully studied the technical details of all other brands.

Actually, he just deceived himself. He bought it because a man he admired bought it, or because the neighbors did not believe that he could afford it, or because the color of the car reminded him good memories of his fraternity in college.

He also thought that he needed this car for traveling purposes, while the truth is that he preferred walking for his health. He wanted it just because it was a sign of high social status, an evidence of success and something that his wife could be proud of.

So to speak, many of his thoughts and actions were influenced by the causes which he himself could not recognize. They induced him to act in ways that could make up for what were persecuted in his heart.

We buy an item not only because of the value of its usefulness, but also because we see it as a symbol of something different, or a desire that always make us feel shaming when looking at it. "[15]
(page 51-52)

Transition

As time goes by, everything around us will change. All products / services, features, characteristics, prices, packages, logos, slogans, technologies, distribution channels ... will also change.

Q ─────────────────

express their "freedom", and a wish for gender equality. This has helped to break the taboo of public smoking for women and greatly increased the sale of those tobacco sellers.

[15] Edward L. Bernays.(1928). *Propaganda* (tr. 51-52). Horace Liveright.

However, the truth never changes, the practical value of the 5 ancient ruling wisdoms never changes, the power of the 5 supreme arts never changes, the power of PR remains as a pristine and tremendous power as it has ever been, because they are closely linked to the soul, the consciousness, the sub-consciousness and human instinct, and because they are closely associated with the ruling techniques existing in all ages.

In all ages, the demand of the 5 Supreme Arts influencing the crowd's behavior is always urgent for everyone. You also are one of them, because you are devouring this book. This illustrates a very natural need.

Again, whoever you are, you need to have this book in hands, because it can bring you many advantages in both work and life. That is quite certain! This book can help you:

- ⅄ Protect yourself from the impact of evil propagandizing forces which are quietly manipulating the purchasing behavior of you and your kids;
- ⅄ Achieve business goals through the power of PR;
- ⅄ Improve the result of your current work, save time and succeed early in your career.

The next 12 chapters of the book will present in detail how we can achieve all of these three requirements.

— *"Do you want to know?"*

So let's start with **Part 1. The Invisibly Ruling Power**.

THE INVISIBLY RULING POWER

Part 1: The invisibly ruling power, including 2 chapters explaining why people often want to influence their fellow beings' behavior; is there any invisible ruler, who is he; what is the secret of the invisible power? What are the ancient ruling wisdoms? How can we put them into practice? What is the power of PR and its ancient origin; why is PR power getting more and more powerful; how is PR power applied nationally and globally? What is the modern doctrine of PR? How can they help us?

1

The invisible ruler

GENERAL CONTENT

Chapter 1 begins with plenty of interesting things. Do you know why? Because in this chapter, you will get to know why people often want to influence their fellow beings' behavior; if there is any invisible ruler, who is he; what is the secret of the invisible power? What are the ancient ruling wisdoms? How can we put them into practice? What are 5 ancient ruling wisdoms?

1.1. Why do we want to influence other people's behavior?

It's obviously a rhetorical question.

Why do people want to influence one another's behavior? It is because most of their life is to cooperate and encounter with one another to complete their duty and to gain benefits for themselves. Influencing other people's behavior is a natural demand, so to speak.

This is a simple way to understand. To answer this question satisfactorily, we should delve deeply into the nature of the ruling need and the motivation of each individual in each particular situation.

You have realized that people of all time influences other people's behavior to satisfy three kinds of individual needs of existence, material and power.

↟ *Satisfying the individual need of existence*

Propaganda, which is to manipulate other people's behavior has existed since the civilization of ancient Greece.

The vicissitudes of politics, devastating wars,, constant raiding and looting are for power and land, had destroyed the lives of so many innocent people. In the age that people had only 2 options to *kill or to be killed*, every party must win at any cost. There is no problem with ethic issues.

Hence, they did not hesitate to use sinister propaganda techniques such as deliberately leaking fake information so that the enemy could make wrong decisions; making up false information to cast a chill over the enemy, thus shaking their determination; giving distracting information then surprisingly attacking; spreading stories causing extreme hatred to incite the determination of their own people todestroy the enemy; as well as creating a sacred belief to undermine the morale of the enemy and encourage the spirit of martyrdom etc. They manipulated the belief and behavior of the mass to achieve the final victory.

↟ *Satisfying the individual need of material*

In the current peacetime, when the strong beats the weak, it is believed that material sources are progressively scarcer and injustice is the course of nature, the need to achieve goals through other people becomes more and more common. The need to know how to influence as well as change attitudes and behavior of others has become more urgent than ever before.

In fact, if life is really fair, if the supply of natural resources is infinite, we will not need any priority over others. However, we are actually living in a fiercely competing society due to the shortage of resources. This means we are always in a state of competing and struggling with one another for better stuffs.

We need a bigger, more comfortable, and happier house. We need more money, a more glorious career, more reputation, and more admirers. Therefore, we need to learn better as well as to work more efficiently and harder, and the most important thing is to always observe with your eyes wide open, focusing on listening to discover and to quickly seize all precious opportunities and things that can make your life more comfortable.

We believe that in order to control our lives, we need to control others' lives. We need other people doing something good for us. Therefore, we should know how to control their behavior.

⋏ *Satisfying the individual need of power*

There is another reason why people want to influence one another. It is to satisfy *their desire of power* because in deep down inside, they know that they are weak.

According to an ancient Oriental philosophy, people often have 3 most intense needs which are *their Achilles heels* which are the need of Money, Sex and Power. People are constantly pursuing these 3 needs in social life to satisfy themselves, among which the demand of *power* is very easy to spot because it is too intense.

The truth is that people always want others to submit to them, they want others to do what they order. To get into that power, the strong uses violence to suppress, the rich uses money to buy off, the beauty barters love away, and the demagogue uses the dark art to achieve his hidden goal.

In summary, the three types of individual needs of existence, material and power have produced in the corner of their hearts a desire to influence and adjust other people's behavior. It reflects the lust for the invisibly ruling power through the 5 Supreme Arts.

1.2. Invisible ruler, who are you?

- *"Who is the invisible ruler?"*

- *"Is he a friend or an enemy?"*

- *"Where is he from?"*

- *"How can I spot him?"*

In the field of modern PR, there are supposedly two kinds of invisible ruler.

- ⅄ Type 1 is the invisible rulers who are capable of scattering unilateral information to gain the sympathy of the mass or to draw their opposition in order to create public pressure on an issue. Why?

Regarding an issue, it is easy for the crowd to be excessively hostile or to exaggeratedly sympathizing, because they are unwise and insecure. They are unwise not because they hardly understand or don't have political views, but because they rarely learn about a controversial topic of current issues deeply enough to judge it in a multi-dimensional way. They simply believe in other people's comment, and duplicate such comment to others. They just lack the insights.

They are also insecure because they are being ruled by a kind of infectiously discontent. They are very insecure because they only feel safein the crowd. They are very insecure, because with internet they can express their personal views and provoke the crowd to action without having to pay much attention to responsibilities. They are insecure due to the herd mentality.

The insecure and unwise of the crowd have created a favorable condition for the invisible rulers to grow.

⅄ In addition, our life is full of options. And the variety of options creates the invisible ruler type 2.

Everyday we have to make decisions and our choices reflect us. Therefore, we need the wisdom to make wise choices. Naturally, most people prefer making the best choices to solve their personal problems, such as what to wear, what kind of car to buy, how to invest money etc. In reality, we absolutely do not want to do so. Why?

Because if all of us had to study the latest fashion trend, the technique to make wheels within wheels, or macroeconomic problems related to each of our question, it would be extremely hard for us to make any final decision.

Therefore, we often voluntarily agree to let an invisible individual or organization disseminate the data and information relevant to our problems to narrow down our solutions to a certain extent, so that we are able to make decisions on our own. At times, we need to buy items that we have never heard of before, hence we need information to educate ourselves, and we need something to compare.

Theoretically speaking, everyone enjoys buying the best and cheapest commodities offered in the market.

But in fact, if everyone bargained, and carefully checked the technical detail as well as the composition of the product before paying (soap, textile, milk powder, shampoo, cars etc), the trades would be hopelessly stuck. To avoid this chaos, we secretly agree to let our choices be determined by the reputation of the brand and manufactures, feedbacks from other consumers, celebrities' advice etc through a variety of information we have been absorbed.

Therefore, there is always a variety of great effort to fill our head with benefits of the product, and the pleasant experience that we would get when owning the product, thus pushing us to buy. We don't often realize this.

Thus, the invisible ruler type 2 is known to be capable of courting the crowd's approval on a thought, an opinion about a kind of commodity. In other words, he is likely to be able to force the crowd to accept his point of view, stance, and outlook on life.

In short, no matter what type, the invisible rulers are those who master the power of PR and use it to create an impact on human cognition andemotion to stimulating human instincts to change their view, attitude and behavior according to the rulers' wishes.

- *"Then are the invisible rulers good or bad?"*

They are good only if they convince the crowd based on the fact, thus helping clear the mechanism of social decision, create business opportunities, and promote the exchange platform of social values and economic development. They are bad and unethical when they give false infomation to serve the selfish interests of an individual or organization.

Though the good always wins, the bad always exists. The good and the bad create a borderline between black and white. It is extremely fuzzy. It is too fuzzy for us to cross without being aware of it.

Thus, before discussing further about this fuzzy boundary, we need to return to the original root of PR to understand it. We need to go back to the origin of forms of the invisibly ruling powers and the ancient ruling wisdom.

1.3. Exploring the secret of the invisibly ruling power

- *"The invisibly ruling power?"*

- *"Where are they? Why can't I find them?"*

- *"Anyone using them?"*

- *"For what purpose?"*

In the religious thought, word and public opinion, there exists the invisibly ruling power.

➲ *Religious thought carries the invisibly ruling power*

According to Gustave Le Bon (1841-1931), a well-known French psychologist, from the very beginning of civilizations, men have been dominated by those who know

37

how to use the appropriate types of thought to control the mass. Those thoughts are represented by Gods and religious beliefs that the mass could not get by without.

As the matter of fact, from ancient time, the rulers have deliberately imposed on their men many kinds of ideological fanaticism to make them find happiness in reverence, obedience, and willingness to devote themselves to Gods' prophesies through the most respected disciples.

Actually, "the rulers of ancient ages have deliberately taken advantage of Gods images, using idols and temples to rule based on indisputable faiths. Le Bon said that the Roman Empire survived not by its power, but by the religious reverence that it created.

He insisted that:

> It is impossible to explain why only 30 legions of the Roman Empire could force 100 millions of people into compliance. If there was any reason, it would be that the Emperor, the very embodiment of the greatness of Rome, was unanimously worshiped as a God.[1]

➲ *The word carries the invisibly ruling power*

The rulers actually used the word to impose faith on their men and guide their actions.

Le Bon revealed that the magic disciples often got their words soaked with a mighty power known to be attached to short syllables, yet implicating the solutions to many problems. That power was so great that they could make the crowd do the most despicable things with just wisely chosen words. A pyramid even higher than Cheops could be built by the bones of the victims of linguistic power.

➲ *Public opinion also carries the invisibly ruling power*

---

[1] The original: La psychologie des foules, Felix Alacan, Neuvieme edition, 1905. Vietnamese version *Tam ly hoc dam dong*, Nguyen Xuan Khanh, pp. 115 and 157-163, 2006.

During the time of slavery and feudalism, the ruling classes (including slave owners, kings, and officials) were the ones making laws and coercing the community into following those laws, and by their desired methods.

To rule the mobs, they used ruthless violence as well as restricted individuals development by blind faith, which was to make people believe that their fates had already been set, and the kings were the incarnations of the son of God.

No wrong doing could be discussed. Nothing said by the King could be challenged. People were merely plants and trees. This rule did not allow for anything like public opinion, or freedom of speech.

But in the modern society, where democracy and human rights are respected, everything has changed completely.

The ruling classes can no longer do what they want without general consent. They have recognized the power of public opinion and that leaders should be the ones getting the largest support from the majority, for they would never get into power without such support.

The strong development of the internet and mass media has definitely helped keeping the power balance between the government and the public. Any word or act of a government official can go viral instantly. All viewpoints of the social life can be exposed, analyzed and dissected thoroughly.

The process of exposing, analyzing and dissecting those viewpoints is the war against the wrong and the bad to defend justice and fairness. That process symbolizes the growth of public opinion and vitalizes the public voice. As the stronger the multi-dimensional communications grows, the more the right of public correspondence will be reinforced, and the faster the arbitrary rule of the government will decay.

In conclusion, the invisibly ruling powers are contained in religious thoughts, words and public opinion – all of which have a great capability to influence the attitude and behavior of the crowd.

- *"How can I use the invisibly ruling power?"*

- *"Please follow the instruction of the 5 ancient ruling wisdoms."*

To control the behavior of the crowd, a rulerhas to be able to use the five ancient ruling wisdoms (ARWs). What are they?

ARW 1.	Wake up the essential human emotion - such an emotion could stimulate people carrying out a certain action. For most people, they make decision based on emotions, yet they often deny doing so.
ARW 2.	To be able to change the behavior of the crowd, we should be able to change their attitude first.
ARW 3.	Hit the human instinct to create a unanimous response.
ARW 4.	By understanding the elements forming the ancient beliefs of people to know what they like and dislike, you could lean on and drive them to a new direction.
ARW 5.	Creating knowledge and understanding in the mobs about a certain issue could help you win great sympathy and support from them.

If we believe in the power of the 5 ancient ruling wisdoms, we will go down the path of light, right and success. The power of the 5 ancient ruling wisdoms has been appliedto the field of modern PR. I call them the 5 supreme arts, and they together made up the power of PR (aka the Secret Power).

Supreme arts 1.	[The art of creating messages]
Supreme arts 2.	[The art of disseminating messages]
Supreme arts 3.	[The art of molding human behavior]
Supreme arts 4.	[The art of creating a comprehensive PR strategy]
Supreme arts 5.	[The art of managing risk and crisis]

- *"How can I implement each type of those supreme arts?"*

You will be shared about how to apply them in the next part of the book. Each supreme art will be presented in detail in the respective chapter.

Through Chapter 1, you have understood about the invisibly ruling power. You also realized there are five ancient ruling wisdoms that can be applied in the field of modern PR under the name of the 5 Supreme Arts, having a power in influencing the crowd's behavior. These 5 Supreme Arts together made up the power of PR (aka the Secret Power).

But when was PR born specifically? Has it changed as time goes by? How should PR be known? Does PR have a specific power in business activities nowadays?

These interesting questions will be answered in **Chapter 2. The power of PR**

–   *"Ready to begin?"*

2

The power of PR

GENERAL CONTENT

Chapter 2 will give you fresh and interesting knowledge about PR, for instance: what is the power of PR, its ancient origin; why PR power is getting more and more powerful; how to apply it nationally and globally.

In particular, you will learn of a modern PR doctrine – one which uses the secret power to achieve three strategic missions: sales promotion, building and protecting the reputation of organization.

2.1. Ancient origin

- *"When was Public relations (PR) born?"*

- *"Can it help me succeed in life?"*

- *"How useful is it?"*

If we know the origin of PR, we also learn how to manipulate its power. Manipulating the power of PR could result in both good and bad. Keep in mind that every power has two faces.

Although PR has been officially recognized as was born in the 20th century, but its applications have started from the civilization of ancient Egypt for about 3500 years.

The first female Pharaoh of Egypt, Hatshepsut (1508-1458 BC) was one of the most powerful queens in the history of ancient world, despite the fact that a woman holding power was a thing of rarity in Egypt. Her reign lasted more than 20 years (about 1479-1458 BC) and it was the longest reign among the Queens of ancient Egypt. She was also admired due to her ability to gain great public support.

Actually, there was no PR firm at the time that could help Hatshepsut build her personal image in people's heart, but she was surrounded by real PR advisers in planning and strategy.

They instructed her on how to use PR techniques to maintain the crown. They advised her to use images and symbols of kingship to represent the power of a Pharaoh. They helped her take the status of a king rather than "being a great wife of the king". They advised her on how to rule people with the characters of a powerful man to be suitable for the patriarchal Egyptian society. Thus, the origin of public relations is just as old as the civilization of ancient Egypt[1].

---

[1] Patricia A. Curtin & T. Kenn Gaither. (2007). *International Public Relations*. Sage.

Picture 2.1. Queen Hatshepsut of ancient Egypt (source: wikipedia)

According to Joep Cornelissen (2009), in the 19th century, in the extremely developing stage of the Industrial Revolution in the UK and US, industrial groups hired journalists, propagandists and press agencies to implement media campaigns for their purposes. Because the majority of people was credulous at the time, so those media workers often exaggerated and distorted facts.

Until the early 20th century, this issue finally ended, when journalists investigated and exposed many scandals regarding finance and corruption. Journalists had helped raise public awareness on unethical businesses. In response to this, many big organizations hired other journalists working as spokesmen for them, and they were actively spreading information widely to gain the support of the mass.

In the 1920s and1930s, due to the economic reforms in the US and UK; as well as the increasing skepticism against large organizations in public, these organizations needed help from the media more frequently.

Therefore, they hired media workers to improve their internal and mass communication activities methodically and professionally. The PR industry was born ever since.

These organizations have used PR to get closer to the public. PR started its development ever since[2].

2.2. Changing over time

After a long period of development, PR has had quite a few definitions corresponding to the number of people speaking about it. There are over 500 definitions of PR. These definitions have been developed in many places around the world and are based on many different ways to approach the issue.

For example, according to Edward L. Bernays, the founder of the first definition of Public Relations in the early 1990s, PR is "a management function which tabulates public attitudes, defines the policies, procedures and interests of an organization. . . followed by executing a program of action to earn public understanding and acceptance."

In the World Assembly of Public Relations Associates *Associations* in 1978, experts defined: PR is the art and social science of analyzing trends, predicting their consequences, counseling organizational leaders and implementing planned programs of action which will serve both the interest of the organization and the public.

That definition not only emphasizes the art and the order of PR in planning and deployment, but also confirms its ethics in not neglecting community's interest.

And, as the definition framed by the Institute of Public Relations (IPR): PR is the planned and sustained effort to establish and maintain mutual understanding between an organization and its publics.

This definition emphasizes the role of PR as a key communication activity which is be indispensable and has to be held methodically. PR is not an advertisement activity.

According to the Public Relations Society of America (PRSA) (1982): PR helps an organization and its publics mutually adapt to each other.

Then, in 2012, PRSA developed a different definition of PR: Public relations is a strategic communication process that builds mutually beneficial relationships between organizations and their publics.

---

[2] Joep Cornelissen. (2009). *Corporate Communication*, (pp. 14-32), Sage.

- *"But why are PR's definitions quite diversified?"*

Because, according to scholars, PR is one of the communication activities. Communication is changing according to the political, economic and culture of each country. Culture is also an ever-changing field. Moreover, communication and culture are influenced each other[3]. So, PR activities also vary in different cultures, in different countries.

2.3. A modern PR doctrine

- *"What is the modern doctrine of PR?"*

- *"What is the outstanding advantage of the modern doctrine of PR compared to old concepts of PR?"*

- *"Is there any relationship between the modern doctrine of PR and the 5 Supreme Arts?"*

- *"How would it be beneficial for my success?"*

There have been many definitions of PR, but nowadays, PR should be interpreted fully and effectively.

By:

a. Studying the ancient origin and inheriting positive values of PR activities from the past to the present;

b. Applying the Secret Power generated by the 5 Supreme Arts in the field of modern PR;

c. Testing, evaluating and summarizing observations from PR projects in many levels (brand, organization, industry and country).

I found out a pretty simple thing: *"The needs for survival and development of an enterprise is similar to those of a country".*

---

[3] Original: *"Communication and culture are influenced each other"* (Hall, 1981; Hofstede, 1980; Sriramesh, 2007).

If any country wants to develop sustainably , it is necessary to implement three key strategies, that are (1) developing the country's economy and improving people's lives; (2) strengthening ethnic solidarities, building a cultural, ethical, and national lifestyle; and (3) protecting the country against enemy forces. Any enterprise wanting to achieve its business goals should implement three strategic tasks, that are (1) boosting sales, bringing adequate income for workers and investors; (2) gaining community support for the products and production activities of enterprises; and (3) building and developing organizations' brands as well as protecting the organization's reputation nationally and internationally.

Based on the idea of three activities [a, b, c] above, I developed the **Modern PR doctrine** - using the secret power as the basic power to achieve the three key strategies above.

This is a very new approach of PR to enterprises' ever present problems (sales, building and protecting company's reputation).

The modern PR doctrine is as follows:

> "PR is the art of building and deploying powerful communication strategies to help enterprise efficiently solve three basic problems, including sales promotion; managing the partnership between parties to remove obstacles in the process of production and trading; as well as building and developing brands in parallel with dealing with the negative effects from the market that can influence enterprise's reputation nationally and globally."[4]

The modern PR doctrine is more comprehensive than the old PR concepts in the past because it contains both value of professional knowledge and value of social contribution.

Regarding the value of social contribution, the modern doctrine publicized techniques to help people perceive PR practices correctly and made it more popular.

In terms of the value of professional knowledge, the modern PR doctrine showed us how to apply the power of the 5 Supreme Arts to help enterprises achieve their

---

[4] Copyright by Le Tran Bao Phuong.

business goals and develop steadily by providing three communication strategies capable of supporting the need of development of any commercial organization.

- *"Specifically, what are those three public media strategies?"*

- *"And how I can put them into practice?"*

My friends, the answer is right below! Those three communication strategies are:

(A)   Sales promotion strategy;

(B)   Strategy to manage the mutual relationship between enterprises and target public groups;

(C)   Risk management strategy, dealing with negative effects from the market.

- *"Come on! Now we will study each strategy in turn".*

(A) Strategy of Sales promotion

Sales promotion strategy includes PR initiatives to help enterprises achieve their goals as well as increase people's awareness of their products / services in the market.

To promote sales, PR is used to create a new form of demand for consumption, or to create a new look for old product lines, or to awaken the innate passion and smoldering desire of a certain class of customers to stimulate their urge to buy.

In other words, in sales promotion, PR is responsible for strengthening the attitude of the crowd towards products / services and for creating inside of them a kind of purchasing pressure[5]. This is necessary because in order to change the behavior of the mass, we should be able to change their attitude first.

The specific application of the ancient ruling wisdom in sales promotion strategy: to encourage clients to choose a product, we should change their attitude towards the product first, then change their attitude from indifferent to interested in, and finally to longing for it.

Often, in order to do so, sales promotion strategy is often implemented in 3 stages.

---

[5] See details in Chapter 6, Section 6.1.

First, enterprises will use PR to spread a hot topic, or a confidence on a product / service aiming to create a positive attitude on items, or to awaken a latent longing in consumers.

Second, when the public opinion has grown and the people is ready to welcome a new brand, PR continues to tell an interesting story about an optimized product line / service which is able to deal with their scare, fear, depression or yearning that have arisen in public opinion recently, hence bringing them inner peace.

Third, a series of positive reviews from consumers, celebrities, experts on the value of products / services will go viral strongly on media channels (online, offline, activation / event). They are launched to assert credibility for products / services among existing clients, while softening the hearts and encouraging the purchasing decision of the group of customers is still hesitating or baffling.

The technique to influence purchasing decisions is extremely sophisticated. In order to achieve the best performance, PR practitioners must be able to identify and to summarize the clients' vague understanding of the product / service, in order to turn their vagueness into clear desires.

On the other hand, he should be able to learn what customers are "thinking about" product / service, and know how to turn what they are "thinking about" into what they "should think about ".

He should be able to help customers realize the kind of products / services that can provide them a style or a certain quality that they long for.

He should be able to sympathize with the public's view in order to tell a nice story using the audience's language, thus creating sympathy and receiving the positive acceptance, then pushing them to make purchasing decisions.

He should also able to persuade business leaders to adjust product design and communication method with the public so that the image of enterprises is acceptable to the market, culture, belief and public expectations.

We will analyze more of this technique of the modern PR doctrine in the next chapter of the book.

(B) Strategy of managing the mutual relationship between an enterprise and its target groups

According to the classification of Ronald D. Smith (2005), target objects of enterprises are divided into four specific groups, such as: customers, pushing objects, objects supporting and limiting the development of the business (see Figure 2.2)[6].

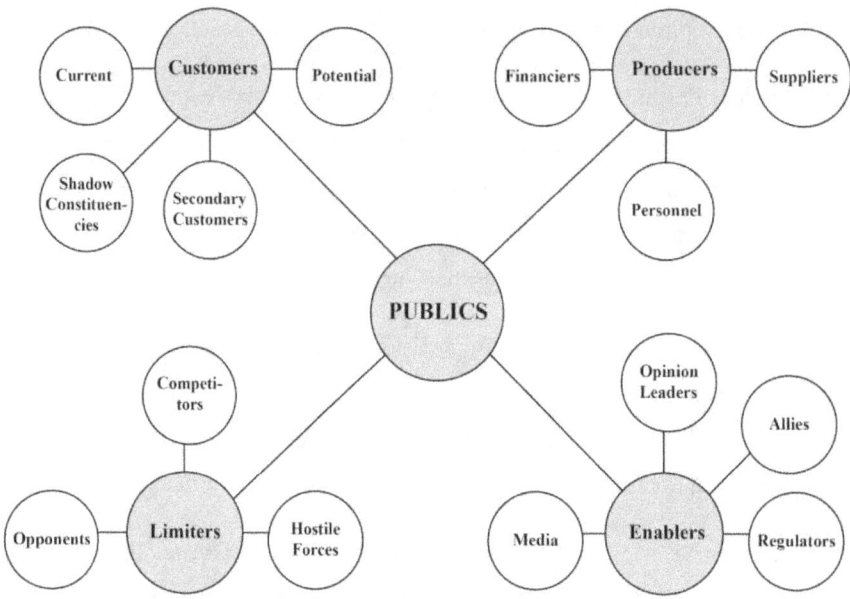

Picture 2.2. Four target public groups

Good management of the mutual relationship between enterprises and target public groups creates favorable condition for production activities, as well as helps build and strengthen the sympathy of key public groups that are capable of affecting the survival and development of enterprises.

It is because the existence of enterprises in the community just likes humans in the society. Both are physically weak and very vulnerable.

We humans cannot live without relationships, cannot grow up well without care and love. In fact, as long as we still keep in touch with our parents, family, friends and relatives, we still feel safe.

---

[6] Ronald D. Smith. (2005). *Strategic planning for PR* (pg. 42-51). IEA.

Also, an enterprise cannot exist without the interactions with the community. It cannot survive and develop without the support of customers, authorities, press men, investors, internal staffs and partners etc.

Therefore, the core mission of PR in the long term is to manage well the mutual relationship between enterprises and key public groups to ensure of their existence and sustainable development.

This is the reason why enterprises often employ a wise policy for foreign affairs: *"We must focus on building and maintaining mutually trustful and respectful relationships with all stakeholders, committing to being a reliable partner through regular communications and meetings, and cooperating in projects serving public interest."*

My friends, since the relationships between enterprises and key public groups present their future value, it's obvious that long term PR activities should be able to build and improve organizations' reputation at least in the mind of key public groups.

You can see that the better the reputation of an organization is, the more competitive its product is; the better the reputation of an organization is, the easier for it to draw investors and talented personnel.

Thus, the function of PR is much more than just a newsmaker for the press. That is the reason why enterprises are trying to establish their own PR department. The function of these units is to interpret exactly the idea, goal, mission, vision and commitment of enterprises to the community, creating an effective communication bridge between enterprises and target public groups.

In other words, PR is to show people who the enterprises really are, what they are doing, how nice they are, as well as to let those enterprises know what does people think about them, hence letting them know what should be adjusted to gain the love and the support of the community.

In addition, through the two-way communication mechanism between enterprises and target public groups, PR helps minimize the gap between how enterprises see themselves and how the public really feels about them.

Ironically, the way people is using PR is rather different from its true nature.

Most of the cases, PR has been used as a mean to conceal and to camouflage negative activities of enterprises. PR is manipulated to exaggerate and to polish the unimportant truth to draw public attention. PR is used to create bogus facts to entice the crowd's behavior for a certain mysterious plot.

Meanwhile, the true function of PR is to interpret deeply the nature, the attitude and the activities of enterprises in society naturally and truthfully to create a right image and a right position in public mind. We will continue to analyze in details this part of the doctrine in Chapter 6.

Box 2:

Analyzing the role and methods of taking care the relationships with target public groups

✿ **General analysis:**

The enterprises that have good interaction relationships with the government will gain benefits from their support. The government recognizes them as good businesses, due to not only paying taxes completely, creating jobs for local people, but also providing the society with good products / services, thus improving and enhancing the quality of people's lives. The government of course will not interfere in or hinder their business. The government will continue to license and support them in their production activities and making profit. This is a win-win situation.

Good interaction with customers will help enterprises to be known and loved, thereby gaining their support for existing and future product lines. More precisely, the purposes of good interaction with customers are to promote sales and to prepare the foundation for long-term growth. You should notice that, in business, there is always a directly proportional relationship between trust and growth.

As for the media (or press men), that enterprises regularly provides information to them will create many benefits. When the media has understaken enterprises exactly, they are immune to unfounded information or PR cheap shots. In other words, enterprises being supported by the media is just getting a dose of vaccine that could help prevent dangerous rumors able to devastate organization's prestige.

For investors and existing shareholders, the periodic feedback on the status of business activities will make them happy. Trusting the leadership helps reduce the

---

unnecessary control. As for potential investors, since PR has the ability to detect and remove hidden biases against companies, it is able to help enterprises successfully call for investment proposals.

As for internal staffs who contribute their labor, having sympathy for companies makes them more connected and loyal. Stable HR condition helps companies retain top talents, save money and time for recruitment and training.

When enterprises have good relationships with suppliers[7]"as friends", they will be accompany enterprises to overcome difficult times when the input supply is scarce, raised price and interest. They may agree to delay the payment and divide it into smaller payments. They will find the best way to deliver on time, in sufficient quantity and with good quality to save production costs and increase the quality of output products.

As for competitors, good interactions with them will help protect the reputation of the industry that all parties belong to and protect each other's interests before customers, thus livening up the commodities market and ensuring a healthy competition. All businesses aware that mutual fights are not only unprofitable but also damaging to each other.

✿ **Methods to take care of relationships:**

To take care of relationships with target groups, enterprises should flexibly select and implement following activities:

For investors and shareholders: enterprises should provide them the product / service of the company to consume, then take advantage of their influence and prestige to promote sales.

For the industry which enterprises belong to: they should actively enter into a league with competitors in the same association to limit unethical businesses and unfair competition that could ruin the reputation of the whole industry.

---

[7] Suppliers of input (raw materials, components and accessories); Suppliers of capital (banks, investment funds).

For dealers: enterprises should often invite them to visit the factories to reinforce their belief in the safety of the manufacturing process and to show that the products are from a clear and reliable origin.

For big merchants, distributors, importers, exporters and important suppliers: enterprises should hold annual meeting appreciating their dedication in the past year, solving problems that have arisen in the process of cooperation and promising a better cooperation in the next year.

For internal staffs, retailers, agents: training sessions on products and sales methods will be the most ideal opportunity to share and to update the information.

For trade union and relatives of employees: give them tours around the office to learn where their family members are working will create a bridge turning an enterprise into a sincere and loyal family.

As for the state management agency or consumer protection association: enterprises should be willing to welcome them visiting the production and technology process from which high-quality products are born.

For the general public: enterprises should make good efforts and publicized their labor policies, wage policies, remuneration policies, and corporate social responsibility policy in order to gather community's appreciation and support.

Enterprises know that "community" including government officials, the press, potential customers, investors, talents, distributors etc., whom enterprises depend on to grow.

(C) Strategy of Retaliation in unfavorable situations

Consumers often make purchasing decisions based on the organization's reputation. Therefore, reputation plays an extremely important role in the enterprise's sales and existence. Therefore, understanding the secret to fighting off negative impacts on the organization's reputation is an important mission of PR practitioners.

But firstly, we need to agree on viewpoints:

- *"What is the organization's reputation?"*

Organization's reputation, mentioned in this book, is considered as the perception that people get from hearing and seeing the brand name of the organization. The perception is often in one out of two states.

1. The first state: " loved, or not loved, or indifference" (peace time)

2. The second state: "hated, abandoned or boycotted" (war time)

In the first state (I call it peace time), the important mission of PR is to build the company's reputation and to proactively prevent any malicious elements that are capable of influencing the reputation and image of the organization (see case study 2.1).

Case study 2.1:

Strategy to build brand advocacy in peacetime

PB is the leading nutrition company in the world with a rich history of more than 100 years of operation in 50 countries worldwide. PB is known for its formula milk powder for children from 0-3 years old.

To limit the barriers and to gain advantage in business, PB has set some big points in its strategy to build brand advocacy in peacetime in 20xx.

Current context:

» Outside the dairy sector:

The mass media agencies are quite critical on the dairy products for children which are overpriced despite of the drastically reduced cost of transportation and raw material.

State agencies, consumers are concerned about the quality of dairy products for children, due to cases of children getting sick by drinking substandard milk.

State agencies are trying to encourage breastfeeding, and to revise advertising and marketing law to restrict communication activities of dairy companies.

» Inside the dairy sector:

Dairy companies are splitting up. There is no sign of cooperation nor alliance between members of the industry. They are struggling alone with the barriers inside and outside the industry.

There are more than 2 cases of dairy companies "playing dirty tricks" on one another. They criticized, mocked each other about product quality and price (indirectly) via mass communication.

Next year forecast:

» Outside the dairy sector:

The topic of price and quality of children formula milk powder will continue to heat up, drawing the attention of the authorities;

Advertising Law will be enacted, creating tremendous barriers for sale promotion of the whole industry.

» Inside the dairy sector:

Enterprises will continue to attack each other to gain an edge in a narrowing market.

PB's goals

1. Gaining essential support of important target groups to help business run smoothly;

2. Limiting obstacles, troubles and potential financial damages.

PB's target groups:

PB understands that if they want to survive and prosper, they must have strong support from important subjects such as investors, authorities, customers, press men, internal staffs, experts, moms and general public.

PR strategy (type C):

Supposed that you are the PR advisor for PB, what should you advise them to do?

You can refer to effective suggestions in Chapter 6 – The art of building a comprehensive PR strategy (Section 6.3).

In the second state (I call it war time), the vital mission of PR is to retaliate unfavorable information and public opinions as well as to address the acts of sabotage the organization's image.

The main task of PR practitioners in this stage is to lighten the attack of the public once his enterprises make mistakes, or to counterblow any false allegation against his organization's existence and development.

In summary, in both peace time and war time, PR always plays a vital role in the existence and development of enterprises. We will have the opportunity to dissect this part of the doctrine in detail in Chapter 7.

2.4. Why is PR getting more and more powerful?

The modern PR doctrine says that PR is the art of building and deploying powerful communication strategies.

This is reasonable, because PR itself has long been a powerful communication field and its power is getting stronger thanks to the interactive relationship that is growing deeper between enterprises and their public groups.

The current competitive trend does not allow the existence of small and weak retailers. It speeds up the establishment of large-scale organizations by merging smaller ones. Thus, the merger has created a larger enterprise, while increasing the number of objects that the company must interact with.

This has strengthened and multiplied many times the need for good management of the relationships between enterprises and their target public groups, to minimize the obstacles that could influence their business and production activity. This has multiplied the power of PR.

Another reason for the growth of mutual relationships between enterprises and their target public groups is the extraordinary development of mass production from the 19th century.

Mass production is only profitable without a break, so the plant has to produce as many products as possible in a same unit of time. In other words, if the enterprise can maximize production capacity, it can both reduce the production cost to increase price competitiveness, and to provide enough goods to dominate the market.

In ancient time without modern production technologies, handicraft and small production dominated; supply often didn't meet demand, hence sellers had a very big voice. Sellers had no reason to compromise with buyers.

Nowadays, everything has changed; sellers' voices have become weaker since market supply replaced goods. Just a single plant can provide enough one kind of products to one region or province. Sellers cannot wait until customers ask for products. Sellers has to maintain constant interactions with customers and the market to ensure of constant sales and to make sure that the factory is profitable.

Unsold goods can influence the existence of the business, while the power of advertisement suffers, and its persuasiveness is becomes blurrier. Like performance of hand painting cannot be compared with the performance of a camera, ads only exist as a pure form of art. Advertisement can no longer convince people to buy. Will you really trust in ads? This leads to the need of a new form of a more effective persuasion. Thus giving PR a supreme power.

On the other hand, along with the boom of mass production, the mass market also develops strongly.

At this time, the direct relationship between producers and buyers has been broken and replaced by a force of intermediate distributors (general distributors, chains of general agents, retail stores, supermarkets, markets). These intermediate forces have quite a strong power. They decide what goods should be sold and which one should be detained. They advise customers in choosing the brands that they themselves consider to be good. Simply put, they have the ruling power over commodity markets.

However, when a series of new intermediaries was born, they compete intensely for the position of "the sovereign" in the field of intermediary distribution. So how do they compete with each other?

They have attempted to distinguish their goods to those of the opponents. They named each product differently and built in them their corporate identity (CI). They promoted their goods to target customers sophistically. They use PR as a powerful tool to create and spread their interesting stories about their product everywhere.

They did so only because of a very simple desire. They wanted customers to fall for their products at first sight, and to buy those products immediately. This expectation remains its value so far. It assign an important responsibility to the role of PR. It increases the power of PR.

PR is getting more powerful because of the rapid development of the mass media, and the internet that allows a tremendous amount of information to disseminate regardless of geographical distance, space or time. Millions of copies are released in just a day, a news goes viral around the world in seconds by just a click.

The rapid development of the media has increased people's opportunity to interact with enterprises as well as the chance to question businesses. It increases enterprises' need of good governance with those multidimensional questioning interactions. It has enhanced the power of PR.

PR is getting more and more powerful because the era of information is being gradually replaced by the era of conversation.

Humans tend to be talkative. Talking makes them happy and comfortable. It also gives them the feeling of being listened to, being attached to a group.

PR created a story to talk about. PR creates masses that have the same way of talking and thinking. PR creates social perspectives. PR contributes to the creation of the flow of life. PR has an extensive and immense power.

In short, you've realized the super power of PR. Moreover, PR companies have been used by authorities as a new tool of "soft power" (see case study 2.2).

Case study 2.2:

The power of PR firms[8]

American public opinion heated up because of an article from Russian President Vladimir Putin published in the New York Times. This 1068 words article was placed in the "Opinion" section of the 11/9 NYT issue, in which Mr. Putin explained why Russia opposed the use of force against Syria.

---

[8]Lam Hong. (2013). *The power of PR firms.* At: http://www.doanhnhansaigon.vn/online/quoc-te/su-kien/2013/09/1076771/quyen-luc-cua-cac-cong-ty-pr/ [Access date: April 2nd, 2014]

He said that a military attack may increase violence in the region, "opening up a new wave of terrorism" and taking more lives of innocent victims.

The article immediately had American officials reacted strongly. Speaker of the House of Representatives John Boehner told reporters he felt "humiliated". Senator Robert Menendez said that the article made him "nauseous", while Senator John McCain said that "the intelligence of every single American person was insulted" in the article.

Mr. Putin's spokesman, Dmitry Peskov confirmed the mentioned article was the idea of Putin: "Basic content was written by Mr. Putin, which was then completed by his assistants". However, according to well-informed circles, Ketchum Communications, an American public relations firm working on a long term contract with the Russian government, was behind the article causing diplomatic troubles.

Ketchum Communications is a subsidiary of Omnicom advertising agency since 1996. This company has a long association with the Russian Government to put articles on the American media, and to consult how to interact with Western media. In 11/2012, according to records from the US Justice Department, ProPublica had published details of Ketchum putting articles praising Russia written by "independent experts" on American news media outlets like CNBC and Huffington Post.

Ketchum also has a contract with Russia to promote the country "as a favorable place for foreign investments." Even the image of a powerful president in the adventures of Mr Putin is also rumored to be "directed" by Ketchum. In the first 6 months of 2013, Ketchum received $ 1.9 million USD from Russia and $ 3.7 million USD from Gazprom, a state energy corporation of Russia.

One noticeable thing is that, Ketchum has also long been a hidden "communication tools" of the US government in a series of programs. In 2004, Ketchum produced of a series of news programs to mobilize public support for the Medicare prescription drug plan from the former President George W. Bush'.

In 2010, Ketchum was awarded a stimulus contract from the Obama administration to promote its push for electronic medical records. Ketchum used to be accused by the US Congress's Auditor to be involved in "secret" propaganda activities for the government.

Since late 1990, Russian government has been aware that the US and other countries look them as a weakened super power and being a bad influence towards the world.

The US media including the Hollywood often describes the Russians as "stupid thugs". Since then, the diplomatic mission of Russia has been seeking out every single opportunity to rebuild the image of Russia as a useful and constructive nation. Its international communications agency RIA got heavily invested and expanded offices in 80 countries around the world. Russia Today, an English language TV channel was launched in 2005.

In particular, since 2006, the Kremlin has hired Ketchum to fight against foreign media, especially the American media.

The Wall Street Journal said, at the time, the current Chief of Staff of Dmitry Medvedev's administration was Sergey Naryshkin, who was in charge of the public relations issue of Russia, along with Foreign Minister Sergey Lavrov. This shows that the Kremlin appreciated the role of PR activities.

However, some analysts doubt that the new Russian government can alter the way that the world, especially the West, evaluates Russia and Russian politicians. "It is difficult to change! The image of a country is not something that can be changed by bureaucratic red-tape", said Fyodor Lukyanov, editor of the Russia in Global Affairs magazine in Moscow.

For instance, the conflict with Russian southern neighbor Georgia in 2008. Then came the territorial dispute with Ukraine in 2009. More recent was a series of international corruption scandals revolving around Gazprom, an oil company. Also mention to Pussy Riot, a Russian feminist punk rock group jailed for daring to protest the Russian government.

Therefore, the Russian government are carrying out "PR" activities actively to the world outside in order to "solve communication problems" regarding the strategy of rebuilding the "soft power" along with the hard power of weapons. Writing articles published in US newspapers is not new to the Russian government.

In 3/2009, before the G-20 meeting with President Barack Obama, Russian President Dmitry Medvedev had had an article published in the Washington Post. He skillfully cited French philosopher Alexis de Tocqueville, the author of "Democracy in

America" predicting "a great future for two countries," based on the common interests that Russia and America have built. The article also had a positive effect on tightening the relationship between Russia and the US in international matters.

Also appreciated the role of media companies, in 2007, the Thai Ministry of Foreign Affairs hired an American PR firm to help them in a PR war launched by the former Prime Minister Thaksin Shinawatra.

The move came after the leaders of the Democratic Party Korbsak Sabhavasu had revealed that the lobbying force of Thaksin in America were writing to express their views on the Washington Times, causing scandals for the new government.

Thaksin was supposed to pay $ 200,000 USD / month for lobbying groups, including Edelman PR firm to build his image and write negative articles about the new government and the military council in Thailand.

Therefore, in order to "counter-attack" using the media, the Thai Embassy in Washington signed a contract with an American PR firm to provide the truth, and details against misleading information about this nation. Reportedly, the diplomatic authority of Thailand in the United States had to pay $ 55,000 USD for this three month campaign.

2.5. The power of PR: on national and global scales

The modern PR doctrine says that PR plays an indispensable role in the formulation and development of corporate brands on both national and global scales. This is reasonable because:

Considering on the national scale, with the strong development of information technology nowadays, the flow of information is increasingly overwhelming almost everywhere. Too much information makes people fall into a real deficit, panic, and inability to distinguish which one is right and which is wrong.

False information may disturb the consumption market, causing harm to reputation and financial loss to enterprises. Thus, enterprises need a professional information management. In other words, they need PR.

More and more people have realized that, a company whether large or small, domestic or foreign, should be responsible for its product / service and manufacturing operations. In other words, it should contact more frequent and have better interactions with target groups (customers, investors, suppliers, authorities, press men...). Or else this will cause distrust, and discredit on the market. Enterprises need a good communication management, therefore they need PR.

Whether a business is thriving or not, it still needs a PR team ready to act and respond to the risks that may occur unexpectedly.

For example, before an adverse rumor against enterprises, customers may become hostile to them, simply because customers do not understand what is happening, nor the real reason of the problem. This is understandable because naturally human beings often overreact to a potential damage, and when they believe that they are in dangerous situation, people often tend to be less conscious and more desperate.

Enterprises need to explain the situation in a transparent manner to turn the hostile attitude of customers into understanding and acceptance, so they need PR.

All the changes within an enterprise, whether small or large (such as policies, regulations, working processes, new technologies, new management or reforms), often influence internal staffs, for they have to struggle to adapt to new process, new way and new behavior or they would lose their jobs. Therefore, naturally, the staff will create negative internal rumors to resist the change. Resistance and rumors will cause confusion inside the organization, leading them to be distracted and less productive. The change should be applied comprehensively in an organization, so enterprises need to implement internal communication activities effectively, thus they need PR.

If any unfortunate incidence actually occurs, good PR practitioner would take advantage of the sympathy of the staff to establish a solid rear. Workers will continue to stick with the company in difficult times. Maybe they know that they would lose some benefits, but in return they understand the value of teamwork, the value of loyalty and they realize that they are not only employees, but also key members that are really important for the survival of the organization. Enterprises should develop this faithful culture, so enterprises need PR.

Even when enterprises decide to perform an action that can cause damage to customers (ex: raising the price), informing customers in advance will help them feel that the decision is fair, transparent and professional. Enterprises are still loved, so enterprises need PR.

Considering on a global scale, the rapid development of the Internet and satellite television has disseminated information on goods all over the world (Sriramesh & Vercic, 2003). Also, because people have become more liberal in the democratic system, the demand for global goods has increased significantly. They can shop anywhere, anytime. This has led to the significant increase in the number of global goods suppliers.

Besides, African, Asian, Middle Eastern, Eastern European and Latin American countries have become, or will soon become, the major centers of both producing and consuming goods. This requires enterprises of these countries to trade and to communicate with global audiences for sales' sake.

Moreover, the formation of the multinational organizations such as NAFTA, EU, ASEAN, APEC, ASEM, AEC and TPP has also shrunk the global market, and strengthened the interactions between enterprises in each organization and between organizations with each other.

These factors have created a demand that PR practitioners should be the leader in the management of the relationships and the interactions between people of this country with people of other countries. This shows the strategic role of PR.

In summary, on the national scale, PR is an essential tool for the development of enterprises' brands at present. Also on the global scale, PR is a key task in the management of the relationship, the interaction between enterprises, between organizations and between people of this country with people of other countries.

Transition

My friends, through chapters 1 and 2, you have had some understandings about the 5 ancient ruling wisdoms, as well as understand thoroughly the nature, important mission of PR to the existence and development of institutions in modern society.

But how can we apply those ancient wisdoms effectively in the 21st century? What are the 5 Supreme Arts, and how can we apply them successfully according to our purpose?

Good questions! Please find out the answer in **Part 2. Exploring 5 Supreme Arts Influencing The Behavior Of The Crowd**.

- *"Ready to begin?"*

EXPLORE 5 SUPREME ARTS INFLUENCING THE BEHAVIOR OF THE CROWD

Part 2 includes 6 chapters, you will be shared in detail how to apply each supreme art to shape the attitude and to rule the emotion of the crowd to achieve the goal.

As for the 5 Supreme Arts, we will start with the first one - *The art of creating messages*.

The basic power of the first supreme art is the power of words, because words have a strange and magical power. Its power is much bigger than what we know about it.

Words can cause heavy mental damages to people for a long time. It influences the way people makes decisions. It has the ability to turn them into the kind of person that it attributes to. Words are a top ranking weapon that is always used in all the wars of perception.

3

The art
of creating messages

GENERAL CONTENT

The first art is the art of creating messages. This art uses the power of words to establish beliefs and influencing human behavior.

The first supreme art was developed from the first ancient ruling wisdom: Wake up the essential human emotions - such an emotion could stimulate people carrying out a certain action, because most people make decision based on emotions, and they often try to justify the reason for doing so.

You might think it is challenging, but it is actually quite easy. In this first art you will learn techniques using the power of words to create a powerful message that can stir public opinion. It will reach the innermost part of human beings to influence their attitudes and feelings that will entice their behavior.

You are going to get specific instructions to apply it:

» **7 key factors** to touch people's heart through: message structure, clarity, citation, bold outlines, the power of words, the power of numbers and the power of images;
» **5 techniques to draw public opinion** to create an extreme impact on the perception, attitude and behavior of the public, through: elicit the permanent loss, create reliable social proofs, bring your writing to life, say what the listener want to hear and tell an interesting story.
» **12 human motives** forcing them to look for, select and consume the information that you spread. That is the overarching philosophy designing contents that strongly attracts readers' attention.

My friend, you've noticed that, because enterprises currently continue to produce a series of mediocre content with a growing number of releases, rather than creating compelling contents that public is interested in and appreciates, therefore, Chapter 3 is extremely important.

Every decision we make, every action we perform often springs from a particular feeling, desire or purpose.

Therefore, the key issue is how a PR practitioner can create a necessary feeling, plant an appropriate desire in the masses' mind to get them reacted the way he wishes and to make them believe that they really want it.

"But how to do so?"

- Actually, they use the power of words.

Because words can create or change human emotions and the very emotions will generate the equivalent actions. Why?

Since the majority of people can be mature physically, physiologically, intellectually, but often lack of emotional maturity. A respected professor can still get mad in a debate. Emotion has a very strong power to control people's behavior. Emotions make people lose their self-control.

You may notice that, with the same problem, different words will bring out different feelings, from which different attitudes and behaviors will be formed in audiences.

- Actually, they used the power of words.

Because words are the mean transmitting messages and the clarity of an issue. Words have a strange, magical power. It can make a gleam become blazing, tell dreadful truths in a less bitter way. It can make bad things look less pathetic. It can cover up the villainous truth wisely. It can turn a curve into a straight line, distorted into circular, ugly into pretty. It is capable of gaining a collective acceptance of something unreal that is often defended as an "invisible value", could not be measured by money.

The reason words have such a great power is that we human beings often tend to be dominated by words rather than existing truths surrounding us (Ivan Pavlov, 1927)[1]. We see the world through words.

---

[1] Original: Men are *"who often are apt to be much more influenced by words than by the actual facts of the surrounding reality"* (Ivan Pavlov, 1927).

- Actually, they used the power of words.

Because words can make a happy man suffered heavy damage mentally and gradually wither during a long time. Words fill in them with an invisible power that could be able to affect our choice of the way we go. It has the ability to turn people into the kind of person that it attributes to. Words are the super weapon used in all perceptional wars. "Words are, of course, the most powerful drug used by mankind." (Rudyard Kipling, 1923).

Just imagine.

On a Friday afternoon the 13th, your boss yells in front of everyone that he has made a serious mistake trusting on you. How would you feel?

World suddenly collapses, you hate that guy. It hurts you so much. You feel like your life and dignity are chilled in bitter anguish.

Ever since, your attitude towards the company becomes dissatisfied than ever before, you would rather not give a damn than respect, rather be depressed than enthusiastic. Your behavior towards the organization changes ever since. You become more dangerous than ever before; you are more likely a destroyer than a contributor.

On the contrary, if your boss recognizes that the company could not succeed without your contribution, you will really be a precious one of the organization. Please note that, since then, the praises will gradually penetrate into each of your neurons. You are forced to behave worthily. It makes you work hard, constantly struggling to protect the prestige that others have imposed on you.

So, whether you realize it or not, the words have touched your ego and created a highly adaptable behavior. Words have a really strong influence on your attitude and behavior no matter what the fact is.

In this life, you have realized that words rule our feeling, form our attitude and behavior. Words have a great power. No wonder why Mark Twain has stressed that: "A powerful agent is the right word. Whenever we come upon one of those intensely right words, the resulting effect is physical as well as spiritual, and electrically prompt."

Therefore, a great artist of words needs to deeply understand the ego or psychology, culture and educational background of each target group. This allows him to see more clearly into: what make people act like that, what would motivate them to attack or forfeit. Hence, he will have an easier to choose appropriate words, expression to create messages that are likely to shape the attitude and rule the emotion of the masses, leading their behavior the way he wants.

- In the art of using words, there are many different applications.

For example, in the domain of literature, writers and poets often use emotional words to describe subtly the mood of the characters, from sorrowful to effusively happy. They also use pictographic words to help readers visualize the space, location, scene of sensational circumstances.

Meanwhile, to the press, words are selected to be the language of information, having a unique meaning to report accurately an issue that needs to be reflected. The media language should not imply any subjective commentary of the writer.

In the field of PR, everything blends together. PR practitioners often use words in the ways of both writers and journalists. This means not only should they write about social issues that media is paying attention to in term of good messages, but also give useful information to readers.

This is such a great challenge: telling an informative story to readers. However, in business, we need effective messages like that, so we should master the art of creating messages to build trust and to influence human behavior. And according to many studies, there are 2 ways to create powerful messages: *verbally* and *nonverbally*.

- *"To be specific, what are they?"*

3.1. Creating verbal messages

Creating verbal messages is the art of creating and skillfully conveying persuasive messages to target groups through words or texts to achieve a particular purpose.

To win people's hearts by verbal messages, we should apply effectively the **7 key elements** to create messages such as: message structure, clarity, quotation, highlighting outstanding traits, the power of words, numbers and images.

These 7 key elements help get your message to be closer and more sympathetic to the readers/audiences. They make them find themselves in it, removing the suspect or hinder in their minds to care and trust your information.

Moreover, you also need to skillfully apply the **5 techniques to draw public opinion** such as: create a fear of loss, create reliable social proofs, bring your writing to life, say what the listener want to hear and tell a good story.

These five techniques have an incredible power. They make the readers feel the urge to act immediately according to your guide.

In addition, you also need to know what the **12** human motives are for seeking, picking up and consuming information on the media. By understanding their motives, PR practitioners easily create appropriate messages to attract their attention.

Now, let begin with **7 key elements**.

3.1.1. Understand thoroughly 7 key elements

Table 3.1. 7 key elements to create a powerful message enticing people's behavior

1. Message structure (7 types)
2. Highlighting outstanding traits
3. Quotation
4. The clarity

5.	Using the power of words
6.	Using the power of numbers
7.	Using the power of images

1. Message structure plays a very important role in the impartation of opinion to convince the public.

Message structure includes 7 types: single-point structure, parallel debate structure, interpretation – inductive structure, open conclusion structure, repetitive structure, problems – solutions structure and now – then structure.

> ⅄ The single-point structure: is to present the one-sided belief of the writer or speaker, without referring to any contradictory belief.

This structure has been proven to be less persuasive in changing public belief, because they might be convinced at the time of receiving the message but will soon change their views when receiving contradictory information. However, it has been proven quite useful in emphasizing the view of the senders for not confounding the recipients in other aspects of the issue.

Business leaders often use single point structure since it helps them communicate clearly what they want their employees to fully grasp. The loyalty of employees has picked off their right to reject or question whether or not they could see the unreasonable things in the message of the leader.

Besides, we can use this structure for groups of people whose level of understanding is limited; or in situations / contexts that has no other unit discusses the problem; or for groups of people who are willing to support and comply with us.

> ⅄ Parallel debate structures: is a clever way to present the pros-cons of the product / service or a problem without having to be completely objective.

Particularly, by commenting on the pros and cons of the products / services that do not affect the need of buyers, we can gain their sympathy, trust, affection to sell the product. This structure is very effective in achieving the purchasing decision of the recipients, especially when they are unable to make up their mind when dealing with too much contrary information.

We should use this structure with public groups that have great knowledge and consideration; or with customers who are still wondering, or with groups of customers that are confused about the pros-cons of the product.

E.g. a paragraph of an article promotes purchasing decisions of those who crave for a glamorous tablet but do not have enough money to buy a decent iPad.

> Although not from Apple, tablet X has been greatly popular thanks to its low price, high endurance and ultra-sensitive multi-touch keeping up with the expensive iPad. Many people believe that tablets X is a rational and affordable choice to those who enjoy watching movies, listening to music, reading books, surfing net by a slim, sturdy, stylish and long lasting battery tablet.

You have realized that this message handled quite well the issue of those who long for a tablet but do not have much money. It mentioned several benefits of the product that can meet their maximum demands. It solved their financial problem. It motivated them to purchase intensely.

> ⋏ Interpretation – inductive structure is presenting information by raising the issue - then interpreting it /or interpreting first - then drawing the conclusion.

Regardless of the kind of structure you are using, you should remember that in an article, the last sentence should be the thesis statement summarizing all of the issues. Without this statement, your call becomes confusing and vague. Just apply this structure to the less savvy who tend to be strongly persuaded by the most dramatic conclusion.

> ⋏ Open conclusion structure is to present relevant evidences that are reasonable enough for the reader/listener to draw the conclusion themselves according to the intention of the writer/speaker.

This structure is quite useful to gain listeners' support and sympathy, without getting criticized for saying straightly something bad.

⋏ Repetitive structure: is to confirm a unique viewpoint time and again using different words, examples to raise the problem.

The repetition has an impact on the domains of human unconsciousness, affecting their stream of thinking, even their intuition. After a long time being affected by this type of repetitive message, we do not remember exactly who say so, and just completely trust in them.

It seems that someone has told you that studying well could earn you more money, success and happiness. So far you have not resisted this belief though you know it is not entirely true.

⋏ Problem - solution structure: the logical way "to make something" a big problem is to attract the attention of the audience, then offering solutions ingeniously to draw and to push their action.

This structure is often used in "sermons" of product sales. For example, after getting to know how to prevent domestic burning and explosion when using electric and gas cookers, we often get suggested what kind of voltage regulators, gas stoves and fire extinguishers are the best.

⋏ The now – then structure: is to give the reader the comparisons, collateral evidences to gain their belief and to guide them to make necessary decisions.

In other words, by offering multiple perspectives and data to reinforce the viewpoints, the structure of now – then is very effective in guiding the decision of the listener.

E.g. an excerpt calls for study abroad based on the now and then structure.

2-3 years ago, the majority of parents, students often chose to study in the US, UK or Australia to get benefits from advanced education. However, recently many people tend to choose Canada as a destination because of the highly practical curriculum, reasonable tuition, with a dynamic, friendly and safe living environment.

Mrs. XYZ, Director of the Representative Office of ABC Corporation of International Education, said: "In addition to general concerns about the curriculum, tuition and living environment, when being asked why they choose Canada, the majority of parents explained that Canada has a high quality educational environment of which practice makes perfect, low tuition, friendly people, and a safe living environment.

Grads have more opportunities to get job offers from large, multi-national companies right in Canada or in other developing countries."

You've realized that at first, the message above gives 3 options of studying in the US, UK, Australia, 2-3 years back then. Then, it discusses key concerns such as the cost of studying abroad, the quality of education, living environment, safety etc., to attract the attention of the readers.

Next, the message has discreetly said that studying in Canada is better than in other countries at the moment. This intentionally hits the comparison habit of consumers when choosing products / services.

Finally, the message has provided advices of experts to choose to study in Canada. This creates a reason to trust, thus stimulating the natural habit of always looking for better things of everyone.

In short: the now – then structure manipulates the technique of stimulating 2 types of human habits (comparing, and preferring the better). The writer is able to convince and guide the reader to believe that their choice of studying in Canada is the right decision[2].

2. Highlighting the outstanding traits is the effort to emphasize the distinctions of product / service that other enterprises' counterparts do not have, as well as to explain in detail to customers how these distinctions provide them the convenience and comfort in life.

---

[2] Content is only for technical illustration of creating messages effectively.

Highlighting here is to clarify the existing prominence, rather than to fabricate unique features that products/services do not have.

These functions should belong to the nature of the product / service, not PR. Why does the features of the product belong to PR?!

3. Quotation from reliable sources in the article is the technique with intermingling words and opinions of authorities attached with reliable statistics to argue for a matter of concern. Quotations should be easy to remember, concise and unambiguous.

4. The clarity helps recipients quickly and properly get the implication of the message. To achieve the clarity, PR practitioners should say no to jargon and should use terms appropriate to life and level of target audience, since we should not use experts' terms talking to workers, authorities' ones to customers.

E.g. To illustrate, in below press release, you will realize how the three elements "highlighting outstanding traits, reliable quotation, and clarity" can be used to make a deeper and more appealing article.

Box 3.1: A noteworthy press release

THE FIRST VIETNAMESE PR COMPANY JOINED THE GLOBAL ALLIANCE FOR PR FIRMS

(Vietnam) dated 06/21/2011. At dawn, Public Relations Organization International (PROI) with international headquarters based in the US officially announced about company X, a Vietnamese PR company, formally joins PROI.

This event, first Vietnamese PR firm admitted as a member of the oldest, largest PR organization in the world – PROI, had marked an important step of the development of mainstream PR profession in Vietnam and promised to establish international standards for this profession.

On this occasion, Mr. ABC - CEO of Company X said, "This is a great honor for us to become a member of PROI, the world's largest PR alliance including PR firms had gotten regional rewards.

From now on, we commit to apply international standards for public relations on all the projects that X have deployed to ensure the highest professional efficiency."

"We have the ambition to become the first bridge, transmitting these exemplary standards to Vietnam, contributing to the development of this profession in our country, especially when its conception is still limited."

Bob Frause, Global Chairman of PROI Worldwide headquartered in the U.S, stated to welcome company X: "With a strategic vision, PROI will continue to develop and expand selectively, by only admitting members who meet the standards that we have set, to serve global customers and regional customers in Asia that are growing across the world."

Reportedly, the admission of the Vietnamese member is to enhance the power of PROI in the Asia Pacific, so company X will be a strategic consultant for the customer network of PROI in Asia Pacific starting from June this year.

The final decision to admit the Vietnamese PR firm was made according to PROI stringent standards of the ability to strategically consult for global customers as well as Asian customers.

This assessment was made by Mr. Allard van Veen along with Mr. Jean Leopold Schuybroek - Chair, Global Development Group, PROI Worldwide, then finally by Mr.Bob Frause, Chairman CEO of PROI in last April in Vietnam./.

* Note: To protect the privacy of clients mentioned in the case study, I have changed their names and revised some details.

My friend, you might realize three elements to create an appealing, trustworthy message:

- Highlight outstanding traits: X is the first Vietnamese PR firm admitted to PROI.
- Quoted from prestigious sources: Bob Frause, chairman of PROI and CEO of company X.
- The clarity:

    - Date: 21st June, 2011

- The significance of company X being admitted to PROI: marks an important step of the development of mainstream PR profession in Vietnam.

- The reason to admit company X: to serve both global and Asian customers.

- The market served by company X: in Asia Pacific since 6/2011.

- Appraisal standards: strict standards of PROI on strategic consulting for global and Asian customers.

- Examiners: Mr. Allard van Veen and Mr. Jean Leopold Schuybroek - Chair, Global Development Group, PROI Worldwide, and Mr.Bob Frause, Chairman CEO of PROI.

In short, for applying three elements "highlighting outstanding traits, reliable quotation, and clarity", the content become reliable and attractive to the readers.

5. Using the power of words

Words have a tremendous power because it has the potential to touch human emotions that would dismiss all the doubts in people's minds and makes them easily believe in the suggestions or hints.

Hints motivate them to perform appropriate actions. Because people are often feel the most vulnerable when they lack something so important that anyone else has (such as a mother, education, food, ability to see the sky), so one of the secrets causing human emotions is to bring these fundamental sorrows out by words.

> Example 1. "... Being scolded by mom can be frustrating to many people, but to poor T, it is a wish never comes true. He lost his mother since birth..."

> Example 2. "Please have a compassion to unfortunate children abandoned by their parents. Every night, for years, they prayed for their parents coming back, but it seems that their prayers are unheard.

They are currently cold and starving. They are weak and need to be fed. Just get flower, then you can donate small amount of money to the shelter."

Do you buy it? Why not? Since with only a small amount of money, I can do something meaningful for poor children, let alone that I was lucky to always have my parents' love.

Don't be so touched! These two examples above are just the assumption by which you can imagine the significant power of words. You see, just a few short lines have a great impact on your emotions.

That is why the effective application of the power of words always plays a decisive role in the success of every PR campaign. That is why I will give you two specific guidelines that you can use to manipulate the maximum power of words.

1. Basic guideline

Instead of using "say" we replace it with "speak / confirm"; "fun" with "happy / perfect"; "Bad" with "poor / powerless / pathetic"; "Childish" replaced by "immature / foolish"; "disparage" with "criticize / attack / censure" etc.

If you really want to master the power of words, please buy the Synonyms & Antonyms dictionary. It will give you an abundant source of vocabularies in appropriate contexts.

2. Advanced guideline

1st Mood. Use simple words containing a hidden insight from old experiences, to evoke a viewpoint, emotion that people have experienced before.

The power of words will be dramatically touching, able to reach the deep emotion inside their hearts, then leading them back to life with the experiences they have. They will completely forfeit.

> For instance. "There is no class since everyone's blood is red and everyone's tears are salty. Because of one's action, he can either is noble or abject." (Buddha)

You have realized that: This question is short but it has a huge educational power and call. Words belonging to experience (like class, noble, abject) have a strong influence on human beings, because they have already known how social classes, noble, abject and despicable are; because they themselves used to be the victim of discrimination.

They may even be their own victim for feeling ashamed, complex of their poverty, difficulties in life.

Meanwhile, simple words (like tears, blood) have been touching them, because they know that social status, assets, reputation are things that they cannot bring along to the grave. Therefore, we are not better or worse than any other. Thus, we should aware of that and act equitably, without class distinction.

To be proficient the first mood of creating messages, PR practitioners should practice observing in term of philosophy, innermost feelings and knowledge of life. This is neither easy nor difficult. It depends on the qualification and practice of each person.

2nd Mood. Using the power of words to hit the deepest concern of public mind and to express your sympathy to their personal issues that are not easy to show, then crystallizing them into sympathy and understanding to make them surrender and act according to your suggestions without any resistance.

Second mood is illustrated by the first paragraph of an article calling for studying in Canada.

> "When family life becomes wealthier, parents have better economic condition to invest for the future and the career of their children, they often decide to send their kids abroad to study.
>
> According to them, study abroad not only gives their children good opportunities to develop their talent, confidence, and self-sufficiency, but also helps them gain more advantages applying for a job. Evidence has shown that the income of people with foreign diploma are still higher than those with domestic diploma.

Some send their children abroad believing that they will be more mature, confident and no matter what the reason is, sending children abroad to study is worth it, and meaningful.

However choosing a country to study abroad is not easy, especially when there are too many options today.

When referring to this issue, experts of consulting company ABC shared: "According to students who have experiences studying in Canada, it is a multi-cultural environment, secure society, with friendly people and beautiful sceneries. Therefore, more and more people are choosing Canada to study and work, especially in the city of Victoria, the capital of British Columbia. "

You might realize that:

About writing method: first, the article intentionally crystallized implicit views about the benefits of study abroad, such as talent development, honorary degrees and high salaries.

Then, it convinced readers that it's worthwhile to invest into studying abroad. Finally, it suggested reader choose Canada because there were a lot of people appreciated it.

Perception of the reader: First, the message clearly revealed inner feelings showing that the writer's argument is entirely reasonable to what readers believe.

It creates the necessary sympathy and unconditional faith. Next, the logical data was pointed out to convince the reader to make decision; the earlier sympathy at the same time paralyzed all the doubts about this information.

Finally, the belief and the fact will haunt and draw the reader's decision, getting them acted according to the will of the writer.

The power of words generated from the second mood has a very strongly drawing value. Do you know why? Because when people have enough sympathy towards each other, and want to trust in something, the facts and logical arguments are just procedures.

6. Using the power of numbers

The statistical figures in the research and market forecast of a prestigious organization always have a great persuading force and often contain an interesting story.

This is important, because those reliable numbers in the interesting story are always what the media looks for every day.

For instance. "Does using mobile phones cause brain cancer or not?"[3] is an issue that many people are interested in.

According to the latest research conducted by scientists from the University of Manchester (UK), the exposure to mobile phone signals does not increase the risk of brain cancer. Researchers have analyzed data provided by the Office for National Statistics to study the growth rate of brain cancer cases in the U.K from 1998 to 2007. If you think that mobile phone signals increasing the risk of brain cancer, then at least there would be more 100,000 people to have with this disease in the past decade. However, there was no significant change from 1998 to 2007.

Certainly, you've realized 3 elements generating an appealing and trustworthy article:

>> Good story: the story of mobile phones and brain cancer had hit it mark, right between the consideration of health problems and the indispensable communication need of society.

>> Reliable source: the University of Manchester, and the Office for National Statistics (ONS)

>> Detailed statistics: " 1998-2007 research", "added at least 100,000 people"

To apply the power of numbers in the fields of business, enterprises can use statistics from their researches, and in-depth investigations of market, industry, as well as of products / services to create an interesting, reliable story, establishing and improving company's position, or boosting customers ' confidence, and updating valuable information for the community.

---

[3] To Nguyen (2011). *Mobile phones do not cause brain cancer?* At: http://vietnamnet.vn/vn/cong-nghe-thong-tin-vien-thong/9899/dien-thoai-di-dong-khong-gay-ung-thu-nao-.html [Access date: Feb 15th, 2012]

The problem is how can business owners get the numbers containing good stories that could benefit their reputation, sales, or business plan?

The answer is: there are 2 solutions.

    ⅄ *The first one.* PR practitioners should conduct research or associate with a prestigious university to investigate.

The result will be interpreted in terms of statistics, and reliable data forming a good story related to the product / service of an enterprise.

    ⅄ *The second one.* Take advantage of the result of researches that other organizations have announced to benefit our story.

Two wonderful solutions!

However, it's not easy for enterprises to implement intensive researches, because this requires a lot of effort, time and money. And taking advantage of the research results of other people to make up our own story is also not easy. It seems that we get stuck here. How can we get over it?

There is still the 3rd solution which can help businesses find the numbers containing good stories (angle) without spending a lot of money and effort. The 3nd solution has 6 steps as follows:

Step 1. Enterprises search for a particular anxiety/issue that people are worried or concerned about. These issues should be related to the story or the strength of the product / service to people's lives.

For instance.

The issue will cause public anxiety: few mothers know how to take care of the brain, the immune system of the baby right from the fetus.

The strength of the product: milk powder X can help children's brain fully develop, strengthen their immune and digestive system even from the womb.

Step 2. Build up the research topic and design the questionnaire.

For instance.

Research topic: "How many mothers are aware of taking care of baby right from the womb to allow them to develop a comprehensive brain, gastrointestinal system, immune system?"

Step 3.

- Launch the online survey by sending questionnaires and receiving answers from target respondents (the community of pregnant women) through the internet to save money and time, or
- Create Opinion Polls[4] on a large online publication or forum to get feedbacks and opinions of people about the issue.

Step 4. Handle the investigation results in term of impressive numbers. If the result coincides with the story that enterprises is aiming for, those impressive numbers will be the basis story of the upcoming sales campaign of brand X.

For instance.

"The survey has shown that there are very few women (under 10%) that aware of the importance and know how to take good care of their kids right from the stages of pregnancy.

Step 5. Make up good stories and make them scientific, because people trust deeply in science since science has always been correct in many things.

For instance.

Nutrition expert A said: "Even in the womb, children should be provided DHA, choline, micronutrients including zinc, iron, iodine, folic acid, vitamin B12, calcium etc.

DHA is a major component in forming the structure and function of the brain during the last 3 months of pregnancy.

---

[4] Opinion Polls is a survey, getting people's opinions on a particular issue, launched on an online publication (or an online forum) with the expected amount of feedback should be around 1000 - 2000 (depending on the number of readers, the response rate, the hot topic of research). Opinion Polls presents a questionnaire so that people can choose the appropriate answers based on their views towards the issue. The feedbacks will be processed statistically to represent the opinions of the masses on that matter (author's note).

Choline is an important nutrient that supports the brain's development and helps synthesize acetylcholine- an important neurotransmitter concerning memory and learning ability.

Micronutrients, including zinc, iron, iodine, folic acid, vitamin B12, and calcium support the formation and development of the fetal brain. Folic acid helps prevent the risk of Fetal Neural Tube Defects. Calcium helps bones and teeth grow strongly and healthily.

Product X with the optimal nutrient composition is an important option in preparing for your baby the best start in life.

Step 6. Transmit the powerful numbers through two stages.

Stage 1. Press agencies have heated up public opinion with serious investigation results showing that over 90% of the women are not aware of and do not know how to take care of the baby's nutrition right from the stages of pregnancy. Soon, the remorse of moms will be widely spread to become a public concerned opinion.

Stage 2. Milk powder X appeared very timely to sate the pressing need of society and to solve the matter of nutrition during pregnancy.

What a great strategy using the power of numbers. This is a classic positive PR strategy that was used to promote sales ever.

My friends, there is one thing you should notice that, while enterprises always need the beneficial numbers for their business, the majority of people tends to believe most numbers without any doubt.

Therefore, when using the power of numbers, professional ethics of PR practitioners will be challenged. They will be standing in front of the thin line between black and white.

Box 3.2: Note

To be a smart consumer, not get manipulated in term of perception and behavior, you should be wary of numbers with unclear origin such as "a study shown

---

that," "the majority of women said that", "the report suggests that", or "the experts said that."

As receiving these numbers, we should wonder that:

» Which organizations published these figures? Whether they are trustworthy or not?

» How did they find out the statistical figures representing a real problem in society?

» Did they hold a mock research as a front to hide the origin of the dishonest numbers?

» Did they just fabricate the numbers to persuade us to buy without any truth to them?

Once you have mastered the technique to avoid dark manipulation, you will contribute to the assessment, feedback about the published figures of enterprises, thus warning and reminding PR practitioners to respect the real figures.

7. Using the power of images

Image is the effective description of the contexts, people, events, and facts that are recorded through the vision, emotion, perspective and angle of the beholder.

It likely helps viewers get to know deeply and accurately the contexts, emotions, actions and incidents. Therefore, it is capable to have a very strong impact on the cognition and emotion of the viewers, thereby enticing their behavior.

In PR, images used in messages often satisfy the following three basic factors: authentication, information and enticement.

(1). The authentication of images reflects the true and accurate movements of the event or incident.

(2). The information of images transmits fully things that need to impart to the viewers.

(3). The enticement of images affects the emotions and behaviors of the viewers. It affects the loving or fighting instinct lying in the deeper levels of human reason[5]. It entices people to speak, to defend or to fight for something based on the appeal.

People often borrow the power of images to denounce, stigmatize, defame, cause misunderstanding or undermine the reputation of an individual, group and party.

In dark PR activities, to take down opponents, organizations often post on the Internet many images that lack authenticity (made up), but containing a full range of information detrimental to competitors. Such as opening a jar of yogurt with maggots crawling inside, or a cake with the mouse inside.

We should know that, because on the internet, people are very easy to get angry, to join a majority passing judgment unilaterally about an issue, hence these type of stigmatized images have a strong power to entice consumers' behavior. It makes consumers hate, eschew and boycott the products.

Also in white PR activities, to call for the social consensus and conformity to traffic rules, a series of large format billboards were set up across sidewalks.

They describe how perfect a dream is, "I want to be a doctor" said a little girl died in a traffic accident. An image depicts a little girl lying on the street, holding medical instruments and dreaming of becoming a doctor. Traffic accidents have ruined both her life and her dream.

Who does not get affect by that image!

You can see that images have a great influence to human emotions.

- *How about 5 techniques to draw public opinion?*

---

[5] The techniques to stimulate 18 types of human natural instincts will be presented in detail in Chapter 5.

3.1.2. Master 5 techniques to draw public opinion

Table 3.2. 5 techniques to draw public opinion

1. Create a fear of loss
2. Create reliable social evidence
3. Breathe life into the article
4. Say what the listener wants to hear
5. Tell an interesting story

1. Create a fear of loss

Only when we have already lost something (opportunity, love, health, liberty or part of the body), we know how precious it is. This means, something taken for granted will becomes valuable when the owner is aware of the pain of losing it.

Creating a fear of loss is widely used in the art of enticing, motivating people in various fields. In the field of PR, there are 2 ways to create the fear of loss to get customers acted urgently.

⊿ *The first one.* Publicize that your prominent products are very scarce.

Shortly, the volume of goods in the market will be reduced proving the scarcity is real. Being sold out very early confirms that item is really hot.

Then, shortly after, when the pain of missing a good purchase has tormented them enough, now the producer releases the second round with limited amount. At the time, you can witness a (Black Friday), people will flock to purchase. They are in a hurry to buy.

⊿ *The second one.* Make customers act immediately, because the opportunity will be lost forever if they don't.

Example 1. In the 3 first months of pregnancy, more than 70% of pregnant women are with morning sickness and eating difficulty, but this time is very important because the brain of the baby is developing.

If you do not provide enough the necessary nutrients during this period, this will affect the baby's brain development.

The necessary nutrients for brain development include DHA, ARA, Omega 3, Omega 6, vitamin A, vitamin E, folic acid, iodine, iron, zinc, essential amino acids and especially Taurine.

These nutrients should be provided to pregnant women from the beginning to the end of pregnancy. If it's too late, the mother will not have any chance to take best care of the forming brain of the child.

According to Nutrition Research Institute A, dairy products X is considered the optimal choice for mothers to supplement an adequate amount of nutrition for the baby. It helps strengthen the baby's brain development right in the womb.

Do you want your child to be a dimwit from the very moments after birth? No, certainly not!

So you should buy milk X to provide all the nutrients necessary for your kid in "the first 3 months of your pregnancy." Buy it right "now or never", because if you do it too late, you will permanently lose this unique opportunity.

Do you know that the above is a message generating the fear of lost in the sales promotion PR campaign of a milk powder manufacturer? You got it!

And yet, still another example:

Example 2. Most infants are infected with Rotavirus in the first 5 years of life. The less the age is, the higher risk they can be infected.

On the other hand, because they are too small to tell their pain and they can only cry, it makes parents extremely distressed. Diarrhea by Rotavirus may last up to 3 weeks leading to rapid weight loss and nutritional deficiency in children.

To protect them against this condition, according to doctors X - Director of Nutrition Center A, we should give infants the first dose of vaccination as soon as possible starting from 6th week and we should complete the vaccination within 6 months of age.

All children over 6 months old are recommended not to drink this vaccine to prevent dangerous diarrhea caused by rotavirus[6.]

Most children around the world are infected with Rotavirus. So are our kids and others might be tortured by the disease.

Do you want your kids to get Rota virus vaccinated immediately? Definitely yes, because children older than 6 months are not allowed to drink this vaccine.

Do you know this is the article skillfully used in a sales promotion campaign of a renowned pharmaceutical firm? Do you that know this message target to the fear of losing opportunities to prevent diarrhea for children of parents? Now you know it!

2. Create reliable social evidence

There are two very good reflections of human psychology we often believe that the quality of the product / service is always associated with the number of consumers and we often judge something to be true because many people suppose so.

For instance. There are 2 restaurants located side by side on the same road. One is so crowded that you have to wait quite a while to be served, and the other doesn't have a single customer, or if it is waiting for only you.

How do you think? The crowded one must be better and you are wise enough not to get into the deserted one and get annoyed leaving later.

If you have the same thought with me it proves that we tend to believe something is true when everybody else just thinks the same and if more people believe it, then the

---

[6] Two examples above just technically illustrate for the art of creating convincing messages, do not represent doctor's advices or recommendations.

truer it is. Appling these two psychological reflections in the field of PR. If enterprises want to sell more goods, they must know how to convince people to buy their products.

The best evidence is not the dry statistic figures or a series of analytical certificates, but the satisfaction of other people that has used it.

For instance. An article of Ms Tham, Ho Chi Minh City, Vietnam.

> "I heard millions of intelligent women have used shampoo X resulting in soft and shiny hair. I do not really know anything about this shampoo, but if everyone feels good, I thought it must be effective for sure. I will try it."

This is an effective enticement because Ms. Tham (like many other women) will be excited with the item that her friends or many people prefer.

This is the reason why consumers' feedbacks in testimonials and experience sharing on TV interviews with non-fiction plots are doing very well in drawing customers to enterprises.

This is an effective enticement because people tend to imitate other people who know the secret that they do not know. They believe that follow others decision can help them avoid the risk.

3. Breathe life into the article

To generate the sympathy to change the view of the crowd about a certain issue, PR practitioners should focus on a story telling expression, not just empty words.

For instance. Kind of boring, dry idle talk:

1. The enterprise X has fallen into a financial hardship.
2. Y's PR service has given customers better business results in the last quarter.

No matter where it is used (an article, lecture, speech, or comment on press release), this idle talk, will not achieve expected goals.

If they are written in a narrative combining business news and stories of life, the ideas above can be rewritten as follows:

1. Being unable to pay the workers for months, constantly dodging phone calls, refusing debts, and dealing with a runaway director are the real evidences reflecting the dire financial situation of company X.

2. The total number of products sold in the market increased 3 times, the number of new customers increased 2 times, and profit rose more than 40% over the same period last year. They all brought a new outlook for the future of company A. People said the miracle was created by the PR campaign planned by company Y, a consultancy, and had been implemented over the past 3 months.

You see, for the two reviews that have been rewritten in an expressive way that readers can visualize things clearly, understandably and reasonably like a movie, unfolding from one scene to another.

In that way, the breath of life is blown into the article naturally. Meanwhile, the attitude of readers towards the issues is formed, their reaction is led and their behavior is drawn, from indifference to anger or love.

4. Say what the listener wants to hear

Whether we write or speak, deliver a speech or give a lecture, the essence of sending a successful message should abide the two following criteria:

1. Prioritize the biggest concern of the audiences above all, it means to say what they expect to hear, what are related to them or appropriate to their qualifications. Then,

2. Send messages calling for their support in order to achieve our desires.

For instance. You will see these 2 following messages which have successfully applied two criteria above:

- *Step 1.* By sympathizing with the audience's fears, the first paragraph of the article will strongly attract the attention of the reader.

   "Currently, studying abroad has become a popular trend and is the choice of many students wishing to study in the new, dynamic and professional environment.

However, how to study abroad efficiently is always a common anxiety since the students themselves and their parents do not have much experiment studying abroad. They do not know where is good, where is bad.

Moreover, it depends on many factors that should be considered carefully such as the financial situation of families, choice of careers, tuition, foreign language proficiency, studying capacity, the ability to live far away from home.

Besides, both parents and students understand that the wrong decision will cause serious impacts on their children's future."

You see, the first paragraph has really gained your attention and sympathy. This is a golden time for the writer to entice your behavior.

> ⅄ *Step 2.* By using the sympathy created in the previous step, suggest readers to attend to the event to learn about studying abroad in order to make the best decision.
>
> "Learning reliable sources of information and referring to practical experience through the event "Real Experience of Study Abroad", held from May 3rd to 4th at Times Square, is the most practical solution for the above anxiety and worry.
>
> Just when we have an accurate feeling and understanding about the country and learning environment firsthand, we can compare, evaluate, and make the right decision.
>
> At this particularly useful event, parents and students can communicate directly with school representatives to clarify their anxieties, as well as to be provided useful information about study abroad. This helps parents and students make good decisions in choosing the appropriate curriculum."

You see, the second paragraph continues to entice your behavior strongly. You think that the event is exciting and you want to take part to see how it is.

The technique "Say what the listener wants to hear" has a tremendous power. Its power lies in 4 points that you should keep in mind:

- The information that it provides is useful to the listeners. It lets them know what is happening. It's not an offer. It turns the listener into a person involved in the issue.
- The impartial information is reliable, so it easily "passes" the defense of the recipient.
- Unbiased information does not trigger any public resistance. Only the understanding and sympathy for readers could entice their behavior.
- Information stimulates the want in recipients about the unique value of product / service.

5. Tell an interesting story

Since ancient times, telling and hearing stories have been the essential need of human beings and this still holds true until today, because through telling and listening to others, we are connected, shared, gossiped, expressed, released and entertained. This makes people's lives better.

I predict that the technique to draw public opinion that will be used the most in the 21st century PR is telling a good story, because good stories really help people make decisions faster.

In fact, telling an interesting story has shown its great ability to attract human attention and to draw their behavior, so much that some renowned PR practitioners even believe that it is the soul of PR, or PR itself is to tell a good story.

They describe that telling an interesting story is turning ordinary things, even the old ones into something different and unique. It's a good idea, but I suppose that it is the work of creative people (such as designers, advertisers). It is not the work of a skillfully PR practitioner. To me, telling an interesting story is not like the method described above. It is not to coat a normal thing with a veneer to attract the attention of the masses, or to create public curiosity, but it is to tell a story as well as possible:

1. Attract the community's attention and turn their understanding of the product to their own knowledge, at the same time
2. Awake inner feelings of people to get their sympathy and create an openness to the product / service, thus making it is easier for them to make purchasing decisions.

My friends, please keep in mind that, in this century, people do not need what enterprises are selling, they buy what they really care about. Their main concern is the solution offered by the product, rather than the product itself. Their concern is the feelings (secure, pleasant, and comfortable) that the product provides them, rather than the product itself.

» For example, an interesting scientific story of producing milk from happy cows on sunny green meadows, from a sterile close production process with more than 2,000 strictly independent checks for each milk can before being sold in the market, to the process of distributing products to consumers in person.

This scientific story makes consumers trust that milk cans containing special, magical, reliable and valuable nutrients. This interesting story makes consumers feel more confident and comfortable with their choices and of course they will purchase the milk.

There is another way to tell an interesting story. It is to tell a touching story promoting family happiness in a bustling and unscrupulous market economy.

» Take the story "Go home for Tet holiday, Family First" as an example. It is the type of story we're talking about.

The story evokes contrition, and directly hits the concern of entrepreneurs who are constantly busy with work and have missed sacred moments with their families in new year's eve.

The images of products are appearing at the same time with images of the man returning home to reunite with his little warm and happy family.

The message of the story is "do not ever look for happiness in elsewhere, but here, in your family, with your wife and children." The story did not tout or brag about the product, but paid attention to elicit the deepest desires of human. It is to get rid of the frivolous life, getting people to go back to spend time with their most beloved people in the warm new year's eve.

The touching story has upgraded the level of closeness and sympathy from viewers for the products. And with this feeling, consumers will easily love and pay attention for to our product. They will buy it because they want to have it, not because they need it. The purchase makes them feel pleasant.

» For example, the story "Bring happiness home" is the type of story we're talking about.

The story "took place a couple of days before Lunar New year in a rural area of China".

A single father of three was expecting his children. One was currently a student, the others were a movie star and business man - who were so busy with their own plans, that they could not able to visit their father. His waiting was almost hopeless. The lonely man was supposed to deliver joyful messages to everyone while he was all alone in the year-end meal.

But it had a truly happy ending out of the blue. His great love and tolerance brought the kids home. In a simple little house in a rural area, they gathered together warmly and happily like the old days.

It ended with a picture of the happy family reunion. And a conclusion opens a rhetorical question: "We have already been on the way home. How about you?"[7]

The story is emotional touching has really caught the attention millions of viewers worldwide.

- *"So what do touching stories have to offer to enterprises?"*
- *"Of course, it is to increase sales."*

---

[7] Source: Hai Thanh. (2013). *Bring happiness home*. At http://cafebiz.vn/quang-cao-thuong-hieu/quang-cao-pepsi-dem-hanh-phuc-ve-nha-2013122414361955718ca110.chn [Date of Access: October 6th, 2013]

- *"Why?"*

Because "whatever is being sold (a religion, a candidate, a widget, a service) is being purchased because it creates an emotional want, not because it fills a simple need." (Seth Godin, 2009).

- Still, another way to tell a good story is to tell a personal experience of consumers about a product / service to persuade others to change their thoughts and views toward it.

This storytelling technique is extremely effective in saving the product / service that has caused a big disappointment to consumers.

In fact, when people feel uncomfortable using a product / service, they will have enough reasons to refuse all messages praising the product / service, and even to encourage other people to boycott the product / service.

Therefore, to avoid rejection, criticism and to rescue bad situations, PR practitioners should use the story of personal experience of a number of customers on the advantages of the product / service to save its image. Personal story will face less challenges because it is personal feeling. However, it is extremely reliable because of the vivid, emotional and intimate details.

- Still, there is another way to tell a good story which is a technique called "on the crest of a wave"
  - *What is "on the crest of a wave"?*

Riding on the crest of a wave in the field of PR is to take advantage of an event, a movie or a particular character that has strongly attracted the attention of public opinion to benefit oneself. To help you easily visualize this subtle technique, please refer case study 3.1 below.

Case study 3.1:

On the crest of a wave

The New York Times has just publicly issued a denial of an article published 161 years ago about Solomon Northup - who owns a memoir lately modulated into a script of *12 years a slave*.

In the article, Northup was typed wrong into Northrup. Certainly, nobody cares this if Solomon Northup's memoir was not modulated into an Oscar-winning movie in 2014.

Rebecca Skloot - author of the blockbuster novel *The Immortal Life of Henrietta Lacks (2010)* - was supposed to be the first person that accidentally discovered the error described above. Stories about the New York Times' typing error quickly spread on Twitter[8].

Discussion Question:

1. According to you, who is on the crest of a wave in this situation?
2. Does this story skillfully promote for the movie *12 years a slave* or the novel *The Immortal Life of Henrietta Lacks*?

- My friend, there is still another way to tell a good story, it's "what goes round goes round" storytelling technique.

This technique in accordance with the law of causality has a unique power to change human behavior on a great scale.

Stories of karma will make people think carefully before doing something. That is why since ancient times, people have manipulated stories of "one good turn deserves another" to guide human behavior to the good.

---

[8]According to Nguyen Pham. (2014). *Because of 12 years a slave, NYTimes edited an article after 161 years.* At http://tuoitre.vn/Van-hoa-Giai-tri/596557/vi-12-years-a-slave-nytimes-sua-bai-bao-sau-161-nam.html [Date of Access: March 8th, 2014]

In the field of PR, telling a story according to this philosophy is not rare, but often it is used in dark PR for evil purposes. "You could be the next victim unless you take a timely action" is a classic story illustrating this manipulation.

For instance. A pharmaceutical company wants to increase sales of vaccine X that would prevent breast cancer for women. They realized that, in order to increase sales, they should increase the number of consumers. They know that their target customers are women of 40-59 years old that will spend money to get vaccinated.

To cause their fear and make them get vaccinated proactively, they deliberately create and spread stories of miserable victims of breast cancer.

The story has implied "you could be the next victim of breast cancer unless you take an immediate action" and that is the most powerful warning to make women of 40-59 years old actively get vaccinated with the said vaccine X. The story is told in a poignant way.

To make it worse, they continue increasing the frequency of this scary story all over the media (TV, press, internet) to create a high urgency as if it is going to happen to you immediately. This help drive up sales. Do you support this approach?

> You have noticed that dark PR messages can assimilate people with troubles that do not belong to them earlier. These troubles suddenly belong to them as soon as they get the message. How reluctant it is!

In summary, the product / service of the enterprise will be rising if it is the embodiment of something genuine, friendly, dedicated, secure, and reliable. And its image should be in line with the culture, lifestyle and feeling of the buyers.

The most basic way to build up the "embodiment" is to tell a good story manipulating the 4 powerful techniques above. However, applying it for bad motives should be under controlled of and criticized strictly by the community and society.

3.1.3. Twelve human motives when we are searching, selecting and consuming information

- *"Why are they looking for information?"*
- *"Is information an indispensable demand to humans?"*

Studies have shown that people search, choose and consume information in the media to satisfy their urgent need in life. And only the message that contains the information sating the need of seekers, is likely to attract their attention and entice their behavior.

According to McQuail (1994), people often desire to get the kinds of information that can help them:

1. "Get information and advice for a particular problem,
2. Reduce personal insecurity,
3. Learn about the society and the world,
4. Find support for one's own values,
5. Gain insight into one's own life,
6. Experience empathy with problems of others,
7. Have a basis for social contact,
8. Feel connected with others,
9. Escape from problems and worries,
10. Gain entry into an imaginary world,
11. Fill time (minimize downtime),
12. Experience emotional release"[9]

Therefore, to create an effective message, PR practitioners should create contents that is appropriate to the product while also meet the information motives of readers.

In total, knowing how to manipulate the 7 key elements to create a powerful message enticing people's behavior (3.1.1), the 5 techniques to draw public opinion (3.1.2) and how to satisfy 12 human motives (3.1.3) give us an artistically panorama of the art of creating an effective message capable of attracting the attention, establishing trust and enticing human behavior.

---

[9] McQuail, D. (1994). *Mass communication theory (pg. 320)*. Sage. London.

This painting will be more beautiful if it is supplemented with colors, images, sounds etc. in the art of conveying non-verbal messages.

3.2. Creating a nonverbal message

- *"What is conveying a non-verbal message?"*
- *"How can I create a nonverbal message?"*

Creating a non-verbal message is to create and to deliver subtly speaker's views through the contexts, colors, images, background music, costumes and expression of manner, eye contact, tone, mood to clarify a particular request, and appeal or order.

Conveying nonverbal messages plays a standard role in creating appropriate emotions in the listeners to help them accept the idea that PR practitioners need them to remember and follow, through two main ways:

» *The first way:* create emotions and atmosphere favorable to entice and stimulate action in humans.

This is not different from producing the sounds of chanting in the practice sessions of religious rituals to create spiritual atmosphere especially for reaching a particular spiritual state.

To understand this, you can go to churches, temples, or pagodas to experiment. And to experience it in everyday life, just try to feel the sound in theatres, to see how it affects your feelings.

Just try to have dinner with your lover at a cozy table of a 5 star hotel to see how the elegance, serenity, and warmth influence your happiness. Try listening to spiritual music of inspirational speakers to see how you love your life and deal with failures.

My friend, please understand that, whatever they see, hear, smell, and touch outwardly also creates the echo inwardly. This echo shapes their emotions, attitudes and behavior.

» *The second way:* create empathy to entice human action.

Empathy is a special language that everyone can feel, and it is very lively and sincerely. In today's fiercely competitive society, most people always long for empathy. Who give us sympathy, we will dedicate to them. Therefore, PR practitioners should create empathy in communication to achieve the goals.

Transition

After finishing chapter 3, make sure you understand how to manipulate the power of words to create a message with the ability to touch people's hearts, and strongly dominate the emotion and behavior of the recipients. Congratulation!

But how can we spread this inspiring message into the market wisely to create advantageous public opinion favorable to our businesses?

To enjoy this joy, let's move on to **Chapter 4. The art of spreading messages** to find the answer.

- *"Ready to begin?"*

4

The art
of spreading messages

GENERAL CONTENT

Dear friends, the second supreme art is the art of spreading messages.

The art of spreading messages was developed from the second ancient ruling wisdom: "Create a common awareness of a particular problem in the masses according to the will of the convincer to achieve a series of similar responses".

To create a common awareness, the message should be conveyed profoundly and accurately. Therefore, this book gives you more than 100 powerful PR tools to disseminate message.

This art can be very valuable if you are a corporate executive or a PR practitioner. It would be a useful knowledge source completing your wise ideas and PR expertise.

And if you are just an ordinary person, this art is a useful that helps you identify the tricks bad people can use to manipulate and influence your behaviors.

The art of spreading messages is applied in the field of modern PR through 114 PR tools, which is divided into 6 groups sorted by the purpose to influence the masses' behaviors, including:

Group one, 64 tools to create public opinion, influences awareness, knowledge and public's belief;

Group two, 16 tools to draw attention to a product / service and to stimulate purchases;

Group three, 11 tools to build trust for a product / service;

Group four, 5 defense tools;

Group five, 13 tools to protect enterprises' reputation during crisis;

Group six, 5 supreme PR tools.

The name of each group also clearly expresses its function.

B efore starting this chapter, we should understand what is a PR tool.

– *"What is a PR tool?"*

I definite that "PR tool is the mean used to spread and to convey the message of PR practitioner to target recipients (individuals, groups, organizations and the masses), influencing their perception, attitude, feeling and behavior[1]."

And throughout this book, if I use the term PR tool, it has the above meaning.

– *"How many kinds of PR tools are there?"*

Regarding categorization, people often put PR tools into 2 groups: offline and online PR.

Accordingly, offline PR uses conventional media channels such as newspapers, magazines, TV, radio, events, exhibitions, sponsorship etc. And online PR uses new digital channels such as websites, forums, blogs, facebook, youtube, linkedin and twitter etc.

This classification is, though very common, quite limited, for the boundary between online and offline is quickly disappearing. In addition, this classification is unable to express the power of PR in impacting the masses' attitude, emotion and behavior. Therefore, we need a better way of classification.

But before going into the new classification, we need to know how:

– *"How many PR tools that can be used?"*

If "Music has just under 5 phonetics but unfathomably flexible, too many notes to hear; There are only 5 basic colors but their combination is unlimited; There are also only 5 main tastes but you can't taste all of their combination"[2]; and then "PR tool has

---

[1] Copyright by Le Tran Bao Phuong.

[2] Lo Trung Kiet (translator Duy Hinh). (2008). *The Art of War & 36 stratagems (chapter 5)*. Thanh Hoa Publishing house.

also only 5 basic components (TV, radio, books, events and internet), but their applications are limitless"[3].

To prove this point, I will give you over 100 PR tools with diverse applications developing from the 5 basic components mentioned above.

I put more than 100 PR tools into 6 groups according to the goal that needs to be achieved in order to influence the crowd's behavior (see Figure 4.1).

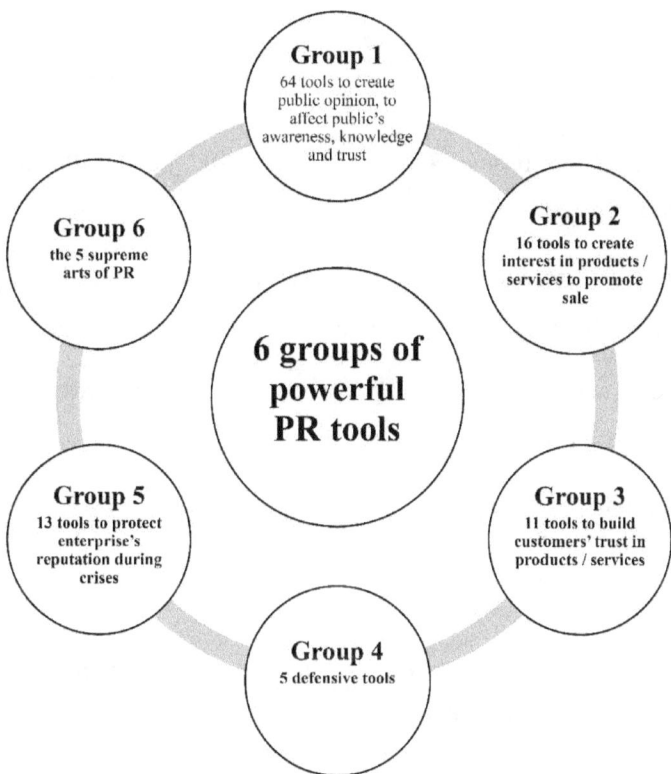

Picture 4.1. 6 groups of powerful PR tools
Copyright by Le Tran Bao Phuong.

– *"Can I combine these 6 groups of tools in a PR campaign?"*

Of course you can! We even have to focus on how to combine them together for the best effect. When combined together, they create a greater power.

---

[3] Copyright by Le Tran Bao Phuong.

- *"So how can we combine them logically to achieve the best communication effect?"*

I save the answers for Chapter 6 that will be dedicated for the art of combining PR tools.

For the time being, what we should do is learn more about the characteristics, the usage and power of each group of tools, because only with a thorough understanding we will know how to apply them in the most effective way, bringing the most benefits to us.

Box 4.1: Note

My friend, before specifically presenting each powerful group of PR tools, I would like to share 3 important things:

1. You are about to reap many valuable supplementation about magical tools that are able to generate strong influence over public opinion thus affecting their actions.

2. The results may be good or bad depending on your motive. You must take responsibility for what you do.

3. No exception.

- *"Come on! Let's get started!*

Group one, 64 tools to create public opinion, influences awareness, knowledge and public belief

Table 4.1.   64 tools to create public opinion, influences awareness, knowledge and public belief

1.1. When target groups are customers or clients				
Editorial	TV program	Celebrity interview	Forum seeding	Picture webpage
Expert editorial	TV documentary	Conference	SEO	Website
Advertorial	TV series	Contest	Social network	QUIZ
Pictorial	TV short interview	Online consulting		

Regular release Expert advice corner		Blog	Webcasts	
1.2. When target group is the media or the press				
Editorial Calendar Press release Photography data Audio tape	Press kit Media alert Angle idea	Media tour Media workshop Media training	Media briefing Media special program	Media intelligence Media annual meeting
1.3. When target groups are experts or consultants				
Consultant contract	Expert tour and meeting	Expert product trial		
1.4. When target groups are local authorities, state agencies				
Authorities tour Authorities sponsor	Authorities product trial Authorities relations	Policy seminar		
1.5. When target groups are organizations, associations				
Activities sponsor	Pamphlet sponsor			
1.6. When target groups are a set of key public groups				
Special event	Video story			
1.7. When target groups are investors, shareholders				
Investor news release Credential Investing presentations	Profit & Lost report Q&A meeting Annual report	Shareholder conference		
1.8. When target group are internal staff				
President message Internal newsletter	Video Direct meeting BOD & Employee	Extra benefit		

Internal bulletin board	party			
1.9. When target groups are distributors, agents, suppliers				
Partner conference	Troop ceremony			

1.1. When target groups are customers or clients

For any commercial enterprise, its survival depends greatly on sale. Therefore, customers is always the most important target group deciding the survival and growth of an enterprise.

This seems obvious, but how enterprises can influence customers to get them to buy.

– *"Why do customers buy your item?"*

My study has shown that, to make a person purchase an item, traders should meet the 5 most critical requirements:

⅄ First, their product / service must be really safe and it has the potential to improve the quality of the buyer's life.

⅄ Second, the price must be reasonable.

⅄ Third, the product must be available in the market so that consumers can easily find it.

⅄ Fourth, enterprises should go in with some of the strongest distributors in the field of distribution to make sure for everywhere delivery.

⅄ Fifth, traders must be able to convince consumers that their product is worth the payment, and how unique and outstanding it is compared to products that customers already have.

My friends, for the first, second and third thing, it depends on the nature of products, on pricing and distribution channels. The fourth depends on the alliance between enterprises and distributors.

The last one depends on the talent of PR practitioner. He must take the responsibility of transmitting the message of products / services to the right target groups to convince them to purchase.

– *"But why it is the responsibility of PR practitioner, shouldn't it be advertisers?"*

Because you know that the analyses on TV, advices on the newspapers and comments on forums always have the greatest impact on your purchase.

This information contains two kinds of meaning - literal and figurative. Literal meaning is information about the benefits of the goods, and figurative one is the purchasing enticement.

Designing this powerful message is PR's business. Transmitting the appealing message effectively is PR's business – the business of convincing the masses subtly.

– *"What if the enterprise have only a bad product?"*

If the enterprise unfortunately has nothing special, or attractive, PR practitioners should not do anything. They should not use PR tools to "make up" some advantages for the commodity to entice people buying.

My friend, you should take notice that, PR practitioners are neither the makers of sensational information, nor a researcher / developer of the prominence of products using words. If the product / service does not give customers a better, more comfortable life, its sales cannot be well, even if it has been polished significantly. The value of the product / service is always the determinant of success.

Therefore, no wonder founder and CEO of Amazon Jeff Bezos (2013) has warned us: "In the old world, you devoted 30% of your time to building a great service and 70% of your time to shouting about it. In the new world, that inverts."[4]

No wonder Steve Jobs, the legend of Apple, referred "branding" as a bad word. According to him, "branding" means forcing someone buying something. It's

---

[4] Jeff Bezos. (2013). Original in *Forbes: "In the old world, you devoted 30% of your time to building a great service and 70% of your time to shouting about it. In the new world, that inverts."*

unreasonable unless enterprises can create valuable products for customers, or help customers use products in a best way, or get a great experience.

Well, you have realized that if PR practitioners deliberately manipulate PR tools to boast about a bad product, they will ruin the product itself, and destroy the reputation of the whole industry at the same time. Therefore, I have to say that with a bad product, you do not need to do PR for it, since doing nothing brings you more benefits.

My friend, you should also notice that each product / service provided to consumers is the most reliable evidence verifying the message of enterprise's promises. Is there any guaranty from a celebrity, or a leading expert that can dispel the feeling of disappointment and frustration of a consumer from a bad product? Surely there aren't! Because the trust for the product / service is not a requirement, but the result after experiencing such product/service.

Furthermore, customers are not just buyers, they are also journalists. They can comment on your products / services, then "publish" those comments on their forums, facebook, linkedin, blogs, youtube to widely spread views on the internet. The important thing is that, currently journalists are coming in flocks to the internet to exploit those negative stories.

In short, the success of a business depends on the quality of products / services. Enterprises have to produce good and valuable products for consumers before considering about PR. With such a consensus, if we have already had good products / services and are keen to promote them widely to buyers to help businesses grow sustainably and strongly, I am eager to share the followings 22 special PR tools.

– *Come on, let's start with the first tool:*

Editorial: Editorial is an objective article posted on the main contents of the newspapers, or major categories of online newspapers. It often contains valuable information for readers and rarely implies any product branding.

– *When should we use Editorial?*

Because the reliability of Editorial is quite high. In terms of media strategy, PR practitioners often use it to create an awareness of a certain consumption trend, creating more favorable conditions for these types of products that are being sold, or making room for incoming new brands.

Expert editorial: Expert editorial is the extension of Editorial that is purely scientific. Expert editorial is usually expressed in the form of specialists' articles about a hot issue concerned by the society (economy, health, education, consumption and security).

– *"When should we use Expert editorial?"*

Expert editorial is usually financed by anonymous organizations to attract the attention of the community on a particular social issue to "pave the way for public opinion" for a product that is about to hit the market and is capable to solve this problem.

Advertorial: Advertorial is an article paid by enterprises (also called purchased article) with the hope of sending the exact information that they want to announce to the market. Advertorial is the advertisement in the form of an editorial (*adver*tisement + edi*torial* = adver-torial)

Typically, depending on the severity of the advertisement, the editorial board will decide where to post it. It can be either within the content pages, introduction pages, advertising pages or pages dedicated to advertorials.

The reliability of Advertorial is lower than that of Editorial. Its effect depends greatly on the writer's technique of telling the story, because readers today are quite perceptive and they tend to disregard and distrust in Advertorial.

– *"When should we use Advertorial?"*

When enterprises do not have an interesting enough story, or when they want their messages to be completely transmitted to the target public groups without any intervention of the editorial office.

Pictorial: is presented by the intentionally united chain of images, reflecting or reporting a particular event or issue.

Pictorial (aka photo article) derived from the art of storytelling, is the top secret of PR, because to tell a good story, people can either use texts or pictures.

Since pictures can be assimilate feelings easily, the Pictorials easily blend the viewer's emotions with the feelings of the characters in the story, so Pictorial has a great power in arousing the feelings of the crowd.

– *"When should you use Pictorial?"*

When you want to spread stories with feelings (such as excitement, happiness, empathy, compassion, or regret) rather than with educational information; and when you want the public to witness enterprise's practical actions rather than words.

Regular release: Regular release is a form of news, or articles that are published periodically in the newspaper or on enterprises' homepages to update information on an issue for a target public group.

– *"When should we use Regular release?"*

Regular release is usually used in a long-term PR campaign with many activities and events taking place throughout the year.

Expert advice corner: Expert advice corner is the angle of expert advisory posted one newspapers or online publications.

It includes 3 parts: the questions, the answers given by experts and the presentation of sponsored logo.

For instance. Advisory corner on the forms of loans in banking and financial publications; or advisory corner of reproductive health in women's daily newspapers; or advisory corner of physicians on a certain rare disease in children, etc.

TV program: TV program is broadcasted periodically (weekly, monthly) on the theme of everyday life, including finance, education, health, consumption, etc.

TV program is not a self-introduction program. It is the official program of TV stations, in which businesses are allowed to promote their brands.

TV program helps enterprises build public understanding about its product on the market. The key to effectively implement this tool is having products supported by

114

many parties (manufacturers, scientists, consumers, authorities), to increase its reliability.

The effect of TV program is often measured by the effect of the channel, airtime, column, message transmission and sales turnover.

TV documentary: TV documentary is a report on TV that reflects a particular social problem causing public concern.

Professional PR practitioners often cleverly integrate into the TV documentary some ideas or signals of a particular brand, implying that the product can solve the existing problems in our social life.

For instance. A popular TV station reports about "melamine - tainted milk harmful to children", the general director of milk company X had cleverly answered the interview that the milk cans X is selling in Vietnam have the same quality with the ones sold in the US due to the same production technology.

Thus, by officially stated on a TV report, the quality of company X's products were confirmed "as good as the products sold in the US" hence gaining the trust of the audience.

We should know that while the TVC is gradually losing public confidence, TV documentary with the ability to spread valuable information to the audience is becoming a persuasive communication tool.

TV series: TV series are broadcasted on television periodically (daily, weekly), such as news programs, morning breaks, market news, press reviews, game shows or music shows.

Enterprises fund TV series as sponsors to have their logos appeared on the program's background and their products viewed at visible angles. With the appreciation to the sponsors of MC, TV series help customers recall the brand and its prestige.

Please note that, when going shopping, customers often buy the products that they have heard before and trusted.

TV short interview: is a type of brief interview with some pedestrians to learn about their views on a particular issue in life.

PR practitioners often use this tool to lead public opinion in favor of their brands.

For instance. Quickly interview pedestrians about the importance of taking care of their feet, and ask their opinions about how to choose a pair of shoes that is not only suitable to individual needs (work, sport, training, etc.) but also is healthy and fashionable. Also in that interview, a health care professional will advise audiences how to choose a pair of shoes scientifically. And then, a celebrity, when being asked, will provide her smart advice about a pair of shoes that helps her stay fashionable and healthy.

You see, all these questions and answers in the TV short interview have generated positive backing for the sales activities of shoe X.

Celebrity interview: Celebrity interview uses a celebrity's perspective to mold the masses' view on certain issues in life, such as work, family, children, health, etc.

Celebrity interview creates a natural, and credible story of celebrities supporting a particular commodity.

For instance. An excellent scenario of Celebrity interview for a milk product for elders is often as follows:

The year-end schedule of a popular actress A is pretty busy. But her family will not be happy without her indispensable role of a dutiful child.

To show her gratitude to her elderly parents, aside from living a useful life, the actress A takes great interest in their nutritional issues. She choose milk Y to ensure a reasonable diet for them and recognize that this product works very well.

She also add that the milk Y company is organizing a meaningful program "Show your gratitude to parents" on behalf of pious children showing gratitude to their parents on the first day of New Year. This is a meaningful program that pious children should take advantage of.

You see, Celebrity interview is quite a sophisticated and effective PR tool due to its natural, emotional way as well as the existing public's love for their figures.

Conference: Conference, such as workshop, press conference or seminar, is an effective communication tool that has the ability to stir public opinion about an issue in order to promote sales for enterprises.

To organize an effective conference, enterprises must create a good story or take advantage of a particular topic of current issues to make up a story throughout the conference.

In fact, there are 5 types of conference as follows:

> ⅄ Type one, enterprises actively create a certain issue of social concern, then organize the conference to align their product value to the solution.

For instance. For pharmaceutical companies, to sell a kind of drug, they often organize conferences on disease prevention, or to announce an advanced treatment for a particular disease.

As for TV game shows organizers, they usually hold press conferences to publish new contents, and forms of the program to attract spectators.

> ⅄ Type two, enterprises take advantage of current social issues to polish their product / service.

Example 1. Melamine contaminated milk has a very negative influence on children health. This is a terribly urgent matter among parents.

Taking advantage of this situation, dairy company X has published widely on the media that its products are safe for children due to a closed production process proven by prestigious rating agencies in the world.

Example 2. Currently, motion sickness patches are causing dangerous side effects such as losing consciousness, nausea, insomnia, etc.

Taking advantage of this issue, drug-maker Y extensively used the mass media to promote that its pill helps prevent motion sickness very effectively, while does not cause any side effects.

My friends, reading each example, you might have realized that a conference could be manipulated by enterprises as "an excuse" to tell the masses their story. If the story gives helpful information, the "excuse" will be accepted. But if the story is only an attempt to entice purchases, we should consider carefully.

- ↗ Type three, enterprises hold product promoting conferences to promote their products /services in new markets to look for new customers, or in old markets to retain old customers.

- ↗ Type four, customer conferences are set up to tighten and strengthen long term relationship with key customer groups. Key customer groups contribute 80% of the revenue of the company. They consume a very large number of products.

For instance. The instant noodle manufacturers buy hundreds tons of glutamate (MSG) for seasoning; fish sauce firms buy hundreds tons of fresh fish for production; construction companies buy thousands of stone cars, thousands of cement bags, hundreds tons of steel for large projects. They are key customer groups of monosodium glutamate makers, aquiculture companies, construction companies.

- ↗ Type five, consulting conferences held to evoke the need in target customer groups to push their purchases.

For instance. "Currently, the IT managers plays a very important role in the enterprises, because they can improve the effect of risk management and administration, helping enterprises run methodically, transparently to achieve the highest profit." (*evoke the need*)

"To meet the needs of improving the professional capacity of the IT Managers, IT Institute hold the *consulting conferences* to improve administration capacity using information technology, and give scholarship up to 100% at the beginning of the new course "professional IT manager" in this May. For all information about applying for a scholarship, please contact us via email: cio@it.com. (*push up the purchase*)

Contest: Contest (online or offline) is a competition with an attractive awards organized by enterprises to attract public attention to their product / service.

For example:

- Photo or testimonial Contest about the recently launched smart phone X.

- 01 million USD prize for the winner of the competition looking for defective, substandard products according to the manufacturer's commitment.

- Baking contest of celebrities has used wine Y as the main spice.

- The contest to mix wine X for world famous bartender that is first held in Vietnam.

You may have noticed that these four competitions are held by enterprises themselves to promote their products. There are various ways to apply this tool.

Online consulting: Online consulting is an online consulting program that broadcasted in the internet, TV, radio with the participation of experts on a particular topic of current concern, to provide and to supplement necessary scientific knowledge to audiences.

In Online Consulting, experts will answer some direct questions from the audience, or questions that they received before, or they prepared in advance.

Content of these questions and answers can be re-published at the *Expert advice corner* on mainstream newspapers, or popular websites with high rate of access to widely spread enterprises' message.

Blog: Blog is a tool to spread messages and personal views of bloggers through the internet. The purpose of a blog is to leak and spread sensational information to entice public concern on a certain issue, or event.

In reality, enterprises usually pay bloggers to spread their message naturally, deeply and widely to thousands of friends through their opinions and/or autobiographies.

My friends, please take note that the blogger can be an ordinary person, a mother, a lonely guy, a gourmet, or a celebrity.

Forum seeding: Forum seeding is to disseminate information on the internet to attract public attention and to influence their decision on a particular issue.

How to implement forum seeding: information seeders disseminate information or notable events on the forums, social networks, yahoo answer, wikipedia, or facebook to orient the story or the idea that they want the masses to support.

SEO: SEO stands for the word of search engine optimization. SEO is the pinnacle tool of online PR practitioners.

SEO helps enterprises' websites get the best position in natural searching results on the search engine (such as google, bing), thereby attracting more visitors to their website.

Social network: Social network including social pages like facebook, linkedin, twitter, google plus, myspace, youtube, pinterest, etc.

Social network represents a miniature society with a lot of information, images, videos that are shared, exchanged and spread by members.

For instance. An enterprises create a Facebook Fanpage (like a newspaper for themselves) to update their activities for those who are interested in and to collect members' ideas.

Social network has the advantage of low cost and rapid spread. However, because members are free to comment, so PR practitioners should be in control to avoid social networks manipulation to smear organizations' reputation.

Webcasts: are websites allowing users to upload and share videos, and TVC on the internet like youtube and/or vimeo.

PR practitioners often use webcasts to enhance the appearance of the brands on search engines to catch the attention of netizens.

The effect of webcast depends a lot on the content, pictures, humor and information of the clips.

Using Webcast is quite simple: PR practitioners will create a free account on youtube or vimeo. Then, uploading their clips (as TVC, TV documentary) and participating in a hot debate in the comments of the clips to catch the attention and views of many people.

Picture webpages: Picture webpages are sites that allow posting, and sharing images such as instagram, photobucket, flickr and bebo. Picture webpage increases the chance of the product appearing on search engines.

Using a Picture webpage is similar to video webcast. This means users will register a free account, then uploading beautiful images of the product to share and spread.

Picture webpage has not been exclusively used in PR industry, because it is only suitable for certain groups of people that have more concern about the images, such as car lovers, fashionitas, jewelry, gemstone, diamond or flower lovers.

Website: is the information portal of enterprises in the internet.

The key role of website is to show the professionalism and reliability of enterprises towards concerned individuals and organizations.

Websites often convey a large amount of information about enterprises such as their mission, vision, core competencies, financial capacity, organization structure, leadership, shareholders, products and services, prizes, activities, etc.

The effect of website depends greatly on the quality of the content, aestheticism, professionalism, and update pace.

QUIZ: Quiz is the survey that analyzes public opinion on an issue using questionnaire. Quiz can be deployed both offline and online. It is often to answer these following questions:

- How do users feel and understand about our product / service?

- What are some of current competitors' messages?

- How could we change the buying behavior of customers?

Quiz provides PR practitioner a good story to tell to catch the attention of the masses on a certain issue. Moreover, it provides them a survey result proving that the value of product / service is trustworthy.[5]

------

[5] Quiz should be used in combination with a technique called "Using the power of numbers" (Chapter 3).

1.2. When target group is the media or the press

The media refers to individuals such as journalists, reporters, and organizations also known as press agencies (in general, the press).

According to an old belief, enterprises must watch out and stay away from the media, because they can be able to destroy their reputation by public opinion. Fear and alienation are their natural demands.

However, that belief is outdated. According to new belief, obtaining mutual understandings between enterprise and the media is an essential need. That is the important task of PR practitioners.

The media is the bridge transmitting the message of enterprises to target public groups. It is considered as an objective third party. They check the information before allowing them to be published. Censorship of the media is the reason why people trust in the information that is published.

However, there is one point that denies this view. It supposes that the public has less confidence towards the information from the press, and prefers information from online community to which they belong. The public has realized that the information from the press (newspapers, online media, television, radio) is often paid by enterprises. Meanwhile, information sharing among members of the online community tends to be impartial comments and / or experience about a product / service.

But whether social network can fully or partly replace the conventional media, managing good relationship between enterprises and the media has always been necessary.

Therefore, we have 8 PR tools to manage interactive relationships with this important public group.

 - *"Let start off!"*

Editorial Calendar: Editorial calendar is a list of topics planned in advance of the deployment of newspaper publications and magazines by year, quarter and month.

The Editorial calendar of each newspaper house is constantly updated and edited depending on the current social and political condition.

Catching up with the Editorial calendar, PR practitioners can brainstorm good stories beforehand to raise their voice in common public opinion. In other words, catching up with the Editorial calendar is a golden opportunity for PR practitioners to integrate their messages into common stories of the society.

Editorial calendar is not a big secret, but newspaper houses never want to publicize it. Their unwillingness is a challenge of PR practitioners.

In fact, it's hard to catch the Editorial calendar. It's so difficult that it has been forgotten in the messy daily work of PR practitioners. It received too little attention to be mentioned in most PR curricula and training materials. And that is the failure of the PR industry for not grasping the flow of public opinion that has been planned before.

   – *"So how can you catch up with the Editorial calendar of each newspaper house?"*

The general rule to have prior relationship with them, gaining their trust. You should actively contribute useful information to their readers based on the topic they want to exploit and take time to invest seriously to this. That´s all!

Press release: Press release is the official text issued by enterprises to inform, or to update their activities to the press, such as the inauguration, opening day, launching new products, changing the board, explaining the cause, or status of the crisis. It can be posted originally on the corporate website to publish information and / or sent directly to journalists by fax or email.

To make a good draft of press release, in addition to practicing writing an article in scientific journal style and format, before writing, PR practitioners should determine 2 core things: which press agencies it will be sent to, what kind of information you should provide them so that it will not only benefit their readers, but also bring positive value to company's image.

Photography data: is an informative image / visual content storage likely to help the public feel positive about enterprises.

Photography data is used to describe the operational activities of the staff; images of new products, affiliates, agents; map of the distribution system, transaction, etc.

Photography data brings greatly effective communications, because when our visual contents are used to illustrate positive editorials, our brand is also regarded as the typical example of this positive angel. Or else, it is a disaster. Every cloud has a silver lining. The most important thing is how skilful the PR practitioner is.

Audio tape: is the recording of the statements of the CEO (or spokesperson) of an organization about a social issue. Audio tape may be considered as the audio press release.

Normally, when there is a topic of an interesting to exploit, journalists will call the CEO to interview and take a private audio recording. However, if PR practitioners want to actively spread the beneficial statements for enterprises, they can send audio tapes to journalists.

For instance. When dairy companies are escalating the price for dozens of reasons, a milk company sends its audio tape to more than 40 journalists stating that they are willing to support the price stabilization program of the government for the interests of millions of children since it is their mission.

Press kit: is reserved for the press to fill their informative need of an event. Often the press kit is used in press conferences, conferences and seminars.

Press kit often includes press release, event schedule, speeches of the board, annual reports, picture CD, company's brochures, product samples, etc.

Media alert: is a concise piece of news about significant issues in the industry. Media alert is drafted by PR practitioners and sent to the media to help them recognize potential topics to exploit.

Media alert is different from Press release. It does not need to show up in the newspapers since it means to be tacit sources for the media. The relationship between PR professionals and the press often relies on media alert to nurture and to develop.

Angle idea: is an outline of a good story sent to the media in order to catch their attention, exploitation and promotion for enterprises subtly.

For instance. Before Vietnam joined WTO, I had sent journalist of the Banking Times the draft of an article named "the advantage of Vietnamese banks as the market split into pieces due to the entry of powerful foreign banks".

As the result, the article was published in the cover in the form of an interview with far sighted CEO of bank X. Journalist L was glad that she had won the editorial office's heart thanks to a great new perspective of the WTO. I myself was glad because the article had provided valuable information to the public, thus naturally enhancing the reputation of the bank.

Media tour: is the factory tour organized for a group of journalists to learn the factory's scale, technology, manufacturing process, wastewater treatment system, quality control process, etc.

Through the tours, enterprises actively highlight the message of their commitment about product quality, prestige and long-term business, as well as building good understandings for the media by real evidences.

With such understanding about the organization, the media will have faith in it. Therefore, they will be very vigilant over negative rumors against it that are contrary to their belief.

Words and similes, Media tour has vaccinated the enterprises against rumor, a virus from unhealthy competitions in the market.

Media workshop: is the direct exchange between enterprises and key journalists in order to gain more understanding and support for the enterprises' mission, goal and business.

Media workshop is an opportunity for enterprises to emphasize the advantages of their products / services; their policies and the way that they contribute to society; as well as clarifying misunderstandings to gain support.

PR practitioners often suggest journalists to retransmit what they understand about enterprises through Editorials.

Media training: is the training course to update new information about an enterprise and its industry to a group of key journalists.

Media training has two benefits.

- ↙ First, it provides journalists specific knowledge that benefits to their career.

- ↙ Second, it helps enterprise prove their position as the leaders in the industry; and show that they are highly professional organizations with methodical operation.

For instance. Enterprises combining with The Bar Association held a training on "Information and Competition Management Law on the Internet" to help journalists get better understanding about the legislation and regulations, and sanctions over unhealthy competitions in the internet, to avoid being taken advantage of as a tool to stigmatize other enterprises.

Media briefing: Media briefing is a short press conference (30-45 minutes) dedicated to the press only.

At Media briefing, the media will have the opportunity to discuss directly with corporate representatives about issues that they are interested in.

Media briefing is usually held before or after the event. As far as I am concerned, the media would prefer media briefing before the event opening, because they do not have much time to attend all events.

Media special program: is a special program for enterprises' favorite journalists.

In fact, enterprises will give them preferences to use free their products / services such as cell phones, computers, bikes, coupons, medical services, etc.

It is to help the media experience the features and advantages of their product / service, thus to enlist their support through testimonials that are disseminated widely in the community.

Media intelligence: Media intelligence is a supreme tool in the field of public relations, in which PR practitioners ask their close group of journalists to share their topics that they are interested in to exploit so that they could take advantage of the coming flows of public opinion that are going to be created by the press.

Knowing such information, PR practitioners can be able to prepare a strategic message consistent with the editorial's viewpoint, then sending them at the right time to make sure that the content is useful.

You should take notice that, a veteran PR practitioner has good relationship with the press can take on this task, maybe even he becomes their source of information, hence saving a lot of promotion cost. However, PR practitioners should avoid exploiting them excessively.

Media annual meeting: is often used to strengthen and to deepen the relationship between enterprises and the media, such as organize intimate parties to meet and talk with journalists as friends.

As far as I am concerned, when sending the invitation to the press for Media Annual Meeting, PR practitioners should have a goodwill and practical reasons to create a sense of comfort to all parties.

Do you notice that the media often ask one another:

- *"Is there any intention behind this intimate party?"*

- *"Well, it is just a chance to meet and talk with journalists as friends".*

1.3. When target groups are experts or consultants

If enterprises need a confirmation from a third party, a prestigious expert is the best choice, because people tend to trust in his opinion.

- *"Why?"*

Because the amount of human knowledge is well beyond the comprehension of any individual. A single person could not master a thorough knowledge of everything. Therefore, we have to trust in experts who have in-depth knowledge of a particular field. You may have noticed that, we rely on their knowledge to solve our personal problems. We also rely on their advices as a guidance when choosing our own directions. We follow them just like students listen to teachers, patients to doctors, or defendants to lawyers.

Therefore, to PR practitioners, establishing interactive relationships with prestigious experts in the industry is very necessary. Building those relationships shoud be deployed with wise and subtle PR tools. Here are 3 of them.

Consultant contract: is a long-term consulting contract signed between experts and enterprises, under which enterprises agree to pay experts a fixed fee each month, to get their initiatives like improving the productivity of the plant, saving energy, environmental protection, etc.

In addition, it is a binding contract. It helps enterprises easily contact with experts to take advantage of their voice, reputation and relationships in the process of communication and crisis management.

As far as I'm concerned, enterprises should sign contracts with experts who are the recently retired leaders of the industry.

– *"Why?"*

Because they are erudite, highly experienced professionals of the industry. Since retired, they have more free time to consult, and already had their students taken over top positions. Dear friends, their voices is a hundred time bigger than yours to the incumbent leaders.

Expert tour and meeting: is the factory tour organized exclusively for experts. The tour is either an opportunity for enterprises to get the advices of experts. Expert tour and meeting create a chance for experts to get to know an enterprise better and trust in its manufacturing business.

Expert product trial: is a program providing experts free product / service, so that they can experience and give feedback about them.

The profound purpose of this is to take advantage of their prestige and influence to promote corporate brands in many community groups that they interact. Expert product trial seems to be normal at first glance, but its effect is extremely high actually.

There is one important thing you should keep in mind that we should not to use health specialists (or doctors) in PR activities, or sales promotion because this approach has been criticized severely.

1.4. When target groups are local authorities, government agencies

The relationship between local authorities and enterprises is a mutual one. In which, the authorities create favorable conditions like the administrative procedure, license, security, and infrastructure for enterprises to produce and get profit.

And enterprises return by paying income tax, consuming local raw materials, creating jobs, as well as stabilizing local people's lives.

Furthermore, the relationship between enterprises and state authorities is also a win win situation.

In particular, the state authorities are responsible for disseminating and guiding the execution of the legislation, monitoring production as well as product / service quality of local companies, and protecting good enterprises by sanctions against fake products, or unlicensed or low quality ones.

As for enterprises, they are responsible for business efficiency and the growth of the industry, increasing local competition and offering many products / services while improving the quality of community life.

Two analyses above on the mutual benefit between a typical enterprise and local authorities has shown a significant link.

This link not only affects the survival and development of enterprises, but also influences the employment of local people, as well as increases the stability of political and social condition in that place.

Therefore, we need 5 PR tools to reinforce this profound relationship. Authorities tour is the first one.

Authorities tour: is a factory tour organized for the leaders of local and state authorities. They can explore and evaluate the technology, manufacturing process, waste treatment, as well as perceptibly evaluate the impact of the plant production of the plant to the surrounding environment.

This is a great PR tool to build corporate reputation, and commitment for an upright, long term business in authorities minds.

Authorities sponsor: is financing the working equipment, costs of promotional activities of the local government, as well as funding their construction of health centers, schools, bridges, and roads.

Authorities sponsor represents enterprises' goodwill about building a long lasting relationship with the government and their commitments for long-term business locally.

Authorities product trial: is to provide free products / services to state leaders; helping them understand, experience the features of product /service, as well as improving the reputation of the brand.

Authorities relations: is the annual meeting between enterprises and the authorities, of which company's representatives report about operation status, wage rate, appreciation to the government for taking care creating favorable conditions for them over the past year, and note the information shared by the government about management policies, tariffs, and draft law about to be issued in the near future.

A person will be in charge of government relations to take more advantages of things. However, because the amount of knowledge in this field is quite large, I will present it in other books.

Policy seminar: is an official seminar for a group of enterprises in the same industry, with specialized organizations in charge of drafting a policy, a new code or regulation.

Enterprises use policy seminar to deepen the rationality and feasibility of policy, law code or regulation about to be issued, thus restricting the damage to their businesses.

Policy seminar is an advanced PR tool that its effect depends a lot on relationships, legal knowledge, professional knowledge, as well as skills of information investigation, persuasion and professional ethics of PR practitioners. This tool is also a part of the professional of lobbying.

1.5. When target groups are organizations, associations

Activities sponsor: Activities sponsor is a program of an enterprise to sponsor operating costs for social organizations and unions, bringing real benefits to the community.

For instance. Red Cross, Association for the Blind, Consumer protection organizations, Study Promotion Association, or housing for the elderly and disabled children.

Funding these organizations' operation shows the corporate responsibility towards society, while increased public sympathy for the organization's image.

Pamphlet sponsor: is a program funding for printing, and issuing propaganda publications serving for community interests, such as handbooks of reproductive health, family planning, prevention of petechial fever in children, university entrance exam, etc.

In sponsored pamphlet, the acknowledgement to enterprises usually comes in a priority. This does not mean to promote them, but to show the appreciation of social organizations to the company's goodwill by bringing useful information for those who need.

1.6. When target groups are a set of key public groups

When enterprises need to publicize certain significant thing (new business strategy, initial technology, or a major new product), the Special Event and Video story are the two most appropriate PR tools.

These two tools are capable of transmitting the message strongly to key public groups such as governments, partners, customers, distributors, agents, press, internal staff and the overall public at the same time.

Special event: is the press conference with the expanded participants, this means the press conference is not only for journalists but also for the government, partners, customers, distributors, agents as well as employees.

The purpose of Special event is either convey important information to target audience right at the event and disseminate messages through the mass media.

The script of this special event is often varied, but it typically includes: exhibition of new products, opening speech, the trial, lucky draw, promotion, music and a feast, or giving souvenirs. The effect of special event depends on the quality of the message, pre and post event as well as propaganda planning skill.

Video story: is telling interesting lofty stories related to the origin, the uniqueness of the product, or business philosophy of the organization by video to attract the attention of the public and to entice purchases.

The power of video story is tremendous, because:

- Video story is created by inspirational soundtracks, and lively visual images revolving around a touching plot full of humanity.

- Video story is the easiest to get message because stories are easy to go viral on social network (youtube, website, blog, facebook, etc).

1.7. When the target group are investors, shareholders

For a company, the informative interaction between the board and investors, shareholders have a very important meaning, because it directly influences the mobilization and liquidity of their shares on the stock market.

Therefore, to ensure the informative interaction between the board and investors, shareholders, PR practitioners have three important missions.

- First, transmit information equally, completely and transparently to all parties (about the operation, business result, profit, deficit, and upcoming business plans of the organization.

- Second, develop and implement communication programs to strengthen the conversation and to persuade existing shareholders, analysts, investors, as well as investment funds on the potential development of enterprises in the future,

- Third, change the existing negative stereotypes about enterprises to create a favorable condition to raise capital and to maximize stock prices of enterprises as much as possible.

132

To help you manage well the informative interaction between investors and the board, this book is going to give you 8 effective PR tools as follows:

Investor news release: is news that are exclusively for shareholders and investors. It is for them to easily understand the operation of the organization.

It is often posted on a company's website at *Information for investors* and only people who have accounts and passwords can access it.

Investor news release is an important tool because it not only meets the information needs of investors in order to effectively control the company's operation, but it also helps the board avoid hindrances from investors in administration task, especially in large projects, or in making important decisions.

Credential: is the company profile. Credential is often sent to customers, shareholders and potential investors to help them understand more about enterprises.

It should demonstrate the enterprise's core competencies, financial capacity, professional team and key members, as well as sharing information of opportunities and potential profits when enticing investors to make investment decision.

The common order of a credential includes: about us, mission, vision, core value, activities, products and services, the board of director biographies, strategic partners, existing customers, implemented projects, achievements, branch network, and contact info.

Investing presentations: is a series of meetings between the board of director (BOD) with the group of potential investors to discuss about the feasibility of capital investment.

Investing presentations provide an opportunity for the board of directors to raise capital from potential investors.

Profit & Lost report: is a report about the profits and losses on monthly / quarterly basic with the explanation about the pros and cons and solutions for the next month / quarter.

Q&A meeting: is the meeting in which investors and shareholders can question the BOD about capital efficiency.

Q & A meeting is also an opportunity for the BOD to answer the questions of owners, as well as to enlist their support.

It is usually held monthly (quarterly) after the owners have received the Profit & Lost report from the BOD.

Annual report: Annual Report is to provide official information about business performance, profit and loss in the financial year to shareholders and investors.

In the annual report, the most notable things is the profit and loss analysis; the objective, and subjective factors that impact on the whole industry and enterprise; prospects of growth forecast, the challenges and outlined strategies to achieve business goals in the coming year.

Due to its public release, annual reports usually do not mention potential projects, or key investment activities that the organization is pursuing.

Shareholder conference: is an annual meeting of shareholders and investors in order for:

- The BOD to report about the business management, profit, ratio of bonus dividend and also to propose next year's business strategy.

- to decide the issues that are beyond the power of the chairman. Such as voting the new executive committee, making decisions on the acquisition, or merger with other organizations.

1.8. When the target group is internal staff

In general, there are 6Ms that contribute to the development of a company:

- man

- money

- machine

- material

- method

- market

The man is the most important factor in 6Ms. And it has reinforced the concurrency of the importance of talent retention.

In fact, the loyalty of the employees is often shaky.

- *"Why?"*

An employee will choose the employer that can bring him as many benefits as possible, such as high salary, full social benefits, comprehensive insurance policy, comfortable working environment, job match, friendly colleagues, regular training and promotion policy.

However, neither can every company give employee full benefits nor every employee deserve these values. Hence there are many job changes to meet the development needs of employees from time to time.

In addition, enterprises could not retain talents when employees want to leave the organization to conquer higher peaks.

Anyway, keeping people staying is a respectful need of business owners. If you're a business owner, you will be optimistic because shortly I will give you:

- 5 effective PR tools to help employees feel comfortable, be highly productive; and

- Philosophy of assimilating the staff to their duties, ensuring the best productivity.

- *"Come on! Let's start immediately with 5 PR tools for employees."*

President message: is the message of the President sent to all employees with the primary purpose is: through the welfare package (travel, compensation, insurance), on behalf of the organization, he would like to thank for their contribution and silent sacrifice and encourage their working spirit.

Regarding their role, PR practitioner should understand the feelings and aspirations of the staff to suggest leaders creating touching message along with adequate working procedures and rewards.

Internal newsletter: is the internal newspaper issued monthly (or quaterly) by the internal PR department.

It is to disseminate, and to update information to all employees about inside activities of all departments and outside activities of the organization. Internal newsletter helps create an identical and adequate understanding about organizations for all staff, so they are proud of their company.

Internal bulletin board: is the internal information board that is used to post written articles about the enterprise, magnificent marketing images for employees to read. That will make them proud of their company.

Internal bulletin board is usually located in busy places with many staff, such as company entrance, or cafeteria entrance. This tool has been proven to be quite effective in the factories, where workers are not allowed to use computers, emails or internal chat.

Video: introduces about the organization, lasting from 4-6 minutes.

The content of the video is often: the origin of the company, business philosophy, production processes, products and services, the size of business, growth, subsidiary system, market share, achievement, social responsibility, and commitment to sustainably develop at the local area.

Video helps all employees grasp the big picture of the whole system and recognize their role and position in it. This awareness helps them feel better about the organization and become more responsible for what they are doing.

Direct meeting: is a direct open exchange between administrators and employees (eg between supervisors-workers, managers-employees) to listen to each other, to discuss on how to deal with problems at work. PR practitioners should oversee the implementation of direct meetings in all departments.

In some enterprises, quite a few managers still ignore the opinions and aspirations of workers, as well as neglect supervising their daily work. Therefore, there is a high risk of occupational accidents, fires, explosions, or waste leak. That is why the application of direct meeting is extremely important and necessary.

BOD & Employee party: is an intimate, cozy party held by PR practitioner to establish a close, and friendly relationship between the leadership and members of the company, to reduce dissent.

The party should be held at the end of the year in a beautiful resort, right after employees have received their full compensation, and benefits.

Extra benefit: is the additional benefits boosting morale of employees after a hard period of working overtime.

Extra benefit may be the additional annual leave, free eating, cinema coupons, supermarket, travel tour vouchers, or simply an email announced that the year-end bonuses will be given two week earlier for the staff to shop enjoyingly, before going home for new year's eve.

My friend, you can apply immediately 7 PR tools for internal staff above. Next, I would like to share with you some important dominant philosophies of PR power in order to make employees more focused in their commitment and responsibility at work through internal communications (see box 4.2).

Box 4.2:

Techniques to assimilate employees to their duties

There are 2 kinds of techniques to assimilate employees to their duties. Specifically, there are techniques to make employees see their duties as an important part of their lives.

They attach more importance to their responsibilities than individual values. Even if they had to choose between work and other values (such as relationships, health, family, leisure, love), they would choose their work over the rest because "This is my responsibility!" There is no other choice. They do not feel comfortable when their work has not been done perfectly.

To implement these two techniques comprehensively, PR practitioners should organize internal propaganda activities and pass at least two kinds of obstacles.

"What are these 2 kinds of obstacles?"

First, because employees will assimilate themselves to their duties if and only if they feel the job matches their future orientation, when they feel themselves valuable to the organization, and when they are appreciated and have the right to respond to the decisions of their superiors. However, not all organizations are able to provide these values. This is the first obstacle.

The second one is regional cultures, leadership style and the satisfaction of employees towards organizations. Employees are just satisfied only if they are actually consistent with the existing culture of the company, or they themselves are adaptable. Or else, they are more likely to leave the organization.

Thus, you might realize that there are three necessary conditions for workers to assimilate themselves to their duties: job match, respect and satisfaction of company's culture.

You should understand these 3 conditions and apply them creatively based on the context of your company. Of course, you can also refer to some assimilation ideas as follows:

↟ Organize periodical meetings (3 or 6 months / time) for BOD to directly share business strategy, opportunities and challenges that company is dealing with. These kind of information will be assigned to each member in term of a liability, or commitment for the development of company.

↟ Organize picnics to explain the benefits that employees are getting from the company, and call for their dedication.

↟ Organize internal communications team to coordinate deploying, and monitoring each performance improvement program that company wants every department to apply.

↟ Organize a freedom forum that all members (including anonymous) can comment, give feedback, and criticize the thoughts, attitudes and behaviors of other members, regardless of their positions, divisions, departments, etc.

1.9. When target groups are distributors, suppliers, agents

Distributors, suppliers is an important target group having a great impact on the development of enterprises. If the company has been producing good products, it should keep its mass production with the lowest cost to distribute products to customers in the most cost-effective way.

It means businesses need a source of raw materials, components and input accessories with full quantity and quality, competitive prices and a strong exclusive distribution network.

This means enterprises need good cooperation with suppliers, distributors, and agents. So, we should take care to study two important PR tools to establish, and to maintain good interactive relationship with this important group of partners. Those tools are Partner conference and Troop ceremony.

Partner conference: is a strategic partner conference dedicated to distributors or suppliers of company in national or provincial scale.

During the conference, business leaders communicate openly and directly with distributors, and suppliers to resolve thoroughly problems arising in the process of cooperation (such as administrative procedures, price, commission policy, or input quality assessment methods), and to find ways to save cost, and time, increasing business efficiency for both parties.

Having been through pressures, I boldly assert that upgrading the relationship between enterprises with distributors, and suppliers to a new level that surpassed the role of a seller and buyers is imperative, because of two following reasons:

- ⌖ Firstly, good relationships with distributors, and suppliers will help enterprises push back their speculation when input raw materials become scarce.

- ⌖ Secondly, good relationship with distributors, and suppliers will help businesses retain them and beat all the activities sowing dissent of competitors aimed at businesses' distributors and suppliers.

Troop ceremony: is to encourage distributors, and agents committing to complete the sales target in the launching campaign of a new product.

It is to arm distributors, and agents with knowledge about the features of new products, or pricing policy, and sales policy, list of answers to common questions, as well as to supply them sales materials, brochures, flyers, banners.

Troop ceremony is important, since it not only helps provide information about new products to distribution channels, but also creates the sacredness in the responsibility of the distributor in "supply useful products to improve the quality of people's lives."

Group two, 16 tools to draw attention to a product / service and to stimulate purchases

My friends, if we do a good thing, please share it with other people. If we have a good book, share it with our friends, colleagues and relatives.

If we know a good product / service, introduce it to everyone, because sharing helps replicate compassion. Sharing knowledge helps us supplement our own knowledge, so sharing good products helps society consume more effectively, and sharing consumption experience together will help us realize the deception to avoid being cheated. .

Therefore, using powerful PR tools to create excitement about the brand and to stimulate purchase of high quality product/service is always advisable.

With that, making an effort to study the following 16 PR tools is an important task.

Table 4.2. 16 tools to draw attention to a product / service and to stimulate purchases

Press conference	Exhibition	Online placement
Massive placements	Discussions online	Hot facebooker
Info poster	In-dept article	Mobile application
Unboxing product	Media center	Movie ad-in
Unboxing service	Fact corner	Consumer handbook
		Consumer disc

Press conference: is to announce outstanding features of a new product to attract attention and entice purchases from the community.

Massive placements: is posting breaking news in all media channels (newspaper, online media, TV, radio) to maximize the spread of interesting information about the new product in a period of time (usually within a week).

Info poster: is the large print advertisements of products / services that are hung / put / pasted at crowded places like markets, schools, airports, hotels, or shopping malls.

For instance. Posters of drug information located at major pharmacies; posters of information about study abroad posted on the bulletin board at the youth culture house, etc.

Info poster is a traditional form of propaganda. Currently it has gradually been replaced by a system of fixed TV commercial at shopping malls, supermarkets, office buildings, railway stations, hospitals, train stations, airports, hotels, or even taxi.

Unboxing product: is the article / video of "Unboxing a product" sharing experience about the advantages and excitement for the product to create a real experience for the viewers, to encourage purchases.

Mobile phone and computer companies usually use this tool. It is very powerful, because the videos with comments help viewers experience the product vividly.

Please take notice that the video describing "Unboxing product" is quite compelling: from opening the amazing box, touching the box, holding fresh product, then clicking. This hits the ownership instinct of viewers. It rules the viewer's feelings; torments them and make them long to buy the item at all costs in order to satisfy their burning desire.

You should know that human ownership instinct has a tremendous power. It does not simply stimulate their purchases, but it also pushes them to satisfy their desires at any cost.

Unboxing service: is similar to product unboxing. It is to provide information about a particular service using video on TV, webcast (youtube, vimeo, video zing) to attract viewers and to stimulate the ownership instinct.

Example 1. Language School X collaborates with TV station H to broadcast a special English teaching program for 10-year-old children.

What makes viewers crave for English courses at this school is: the native British teachers explain how to pronounce English using fluent Vietnamese. They speak Vietnamese pretty fluently. This creates a light shock.

Furthermore, children can see and hear the way that "western backpackers" pronounce English in the program, which helps them communicate confidently in English with foreigners in reality.

Example 2. Motivational speakers are those who use the unboxing service most frequently.

They cite, post videos of their exciting speeches on youtube for potential students to search, experience their spirit motivation service. Of course, the better, the more inspirational the video is, the more excited the learners are to buy their service (tapes, books, seminars).

Exhibition: Exhibition has become a tool that "everyone knows", but for further research, we will realize that there are two types of exhibition.

The first type is commercial exhibition which the main purpose is to promote and seek sales opportunities, or contracts.

The second one is to introduce, or to promote products / services of the enterprise to target customer groups, because its primary purpose is to propagandize and to promote corporate reputation.

   – *There are two things that you should keep in mind:*

First, take notice of the look and the aestheticism of your counter versus others, since the exhibition is the ideal place for customers to rank some a company over another.

Second, reporters and journalists always show up at the exhibition. Attract them by using your counter, invite them to ask questions and actively convey your message. But please take notice that, the message must be valuable for them, you should not use the rhetoric words, praising your products relentlessly while in fact no one would care and write about them.

Discussions online: is the discussion on forums, blogs, facebook, or twitter about the prominence of a particular product. How to apply this tool is similar to Forum seeding.

In-dept article: is the articles promoting products / services published in the press (newspapers, online media) to persuade customers buying products, often referred as reason to believe (RTB).

This type of article often integrates evidence, and certification by prestigious institutions guaranteeing the quality and safety of goods. It is similar to Advertorial.

The PR ethics of using this tool is that RTB must be true, and not made up, taking advantage of the negligence or lack of verification from consumers.

But there is an old saying "A wise man speaks halfway, fools that the fool does not know to worry or not", but for the practice of public relations in the 21st century, this has never been allowed, because vague communication only causes suspicion, and it could not create confidence.

Media center: Media center for the press is a group of PR practitioners designated to actively collect, classify and update good stories bringing benefits to enterprises.

It is an effective PR tool in a long run, because good news about enterprises leaked steadily like "long rain causes deep leaking". This means it is better to build and strengthen the feelings towards brands instead of big one time campaigns "It is better to live one day as a lion than a hundred years as sheep".

Fact corner: is to answer about the product / service, commodity… on mainstream newspapers.

Enterprises have to sign a long-term contract funding for a newspaper if they want to place their logos in it.

Online placement: is posting a series of Advertorials on big online newspapers with high rate of access. The purpose of these online placements are to increase the coverage of information and pictures of the brand across the internet.

Hot facebookers: are those whose facebook accounts have thousands of friends.

Enterprises can pay hot facebookers to write articles raising Products cleverly to disseminate the sales message directly to their friends.

Mobile application: is an application running on Windows, iOS or Android that allows users to easily keep track of market, industry, product, price news, etc. This application can be compatible with both smartphones and tablets.

It has a very strong advantage in the near future since people are tightly glued to the screen of their smartphones. Therefore, PR practitioners have 6 suggestions to use mobile application effectively in reality.

Suggestion 1. Milk powder companies can build applications helping them look for the suitable formula, handle common diseases in children and compare milk price in the market today.

Suggestion 2. Travel agencies can make an application introducing tour route, destination images, illustration of exciting experiences and the expenditure for each person.

Suggestion 3. Banks can create an application for smartphones to search transaction places, ATM, POS, as well as to look up interest rates, bank fees, gold, loan conditions, etc.

Suggestion 4. Universities can create applications for smartphones, tablets to check exam result, schedules, class, location and materials, etc.

Suggestion 5. Spice companies can create an application showing housewives methods of cooking healthy and delicious food (eg 10 stewed dishes, 15 soups, 20 fried dishes, 10 deep fried dishes, 8 grilled dishes, 7 desserts, etc). This application also allows them to set alarm, to remind them of shopping for necessary materials. Of course, all the attractive dishes need MSG, seasoning seeds, spices from these companies.

Suggestion 6. Companies producing / trading toys could create an attractive free game, to draw the attention of potential customers and to help them experience the story, the features and characteristics of a toy deeply. This is useful to stimulate purchases.

144

For instance. Manufacturers of RC Airplanes can create a thrilling game like "Space War" to promote their products.

Movie ad-in: is to help the image of the product go into the audience's mind spontaneously since that they are as "vigilant" watching a movie compare an ad.

The mechanism of movie ad-in is quite understandable: The episodes in the movie spread the ways the characters using products to draw the audience's mimicry.

For instance. The way the hero takes a sip of coffee in deep reflection, the way he lights and releases smoke from a full mood, or the way he pours expensive brandy successfully...

These ways will haunt audience's mind. Then, the idols and mimic instinct would make them copy the things their favorite heroes did with the products. They want to do the same to get the same pleasure.

–   *"How to use movie ad-in most effectively?"*

In a movie, to manipulate movie ad-in effectively, PR practitioners should know how to choose a film matching with the product, by evaluating the plot, character's personality, and contexts. Then, enterprises will discuss with the director about the episodes and the forms in which products / services would appear naturally, without any offence to viewers.

Likewise, in a gameshow, PR practitioners must know how to choose a program matching with the products and to manipulate movie ad-in cleverly to help people know and love the products, thus practically support the sales.

My friends, I keep repeating the requirement of subtlety and ingeniousness when applying movie ad-in, because it has been used very ludicrously and poorly in quite a few cases.

Consumer handbook: Consumer Handbook introduces the product to help customers get a better understanding of it and be interested in it.

Moreover, consumer handbook contains two purposes:

- On one hand, it is a product description, manuals, and present quality policy of the producers;

- On the other hand, it is an evidence for the manufacturer to deny any damage caused by the products when they can prove that customers misuse the specifications (or violate the recommendations) that have been officially publicized.

Consumer disc: Consumer disc is the recordings of customers interacting with and experience the service. It is a useful PR tool to bring joy, and excitement to customers.

Customers tend to save, preserve their CD to "show off" to friends, colleagues, thereby promoting corporate services indirectly, naturally and credibly.

For instance, in the field of education - training, enterprises often give students CDs of their presentations, thesis defense and graduation ceremony. Students achieving good results will tend to spread and describe their glory to friends and relatives.

In the milk powder industry, enterprises often give mothers instruction CDs of child caring and child raising.

In the event industry, companies often give their clients CD recording of their meeting, and preparation before the event. The scenes integrated with inspirational songs will impress customers. After that, customers will choose partners that they have sympathy for.

Group three, 11 tools to build trust for a product / service

Table 4.3. 11 tools to build trust for a product / service

Multifunctional communication center	TV expert consulting	TV documentary
Testimonial	Free day	Personal letter
Award	Training person in charge	Authorities contribution record
Offline meeting		
Editorial advertorial		

Multifunctional communication center: is used to educate and widely promote important knowledge and information about a product, or a project undertaken by enterprises.

This center is run constantly by enterprises (units in charge of the project) during the implement of the project.

For instance. Information center of nuclear energy is responsible to widely publicize the knowledge and information about nuclear energy, such as modern technology, high safety and the great value of atomic energy for the independence and development of the country. The Center opens free to the public from Monday to Friday, from 8:00 am to 17:00 pm.

Testimonial: is the comment of celebrities, doctors, professionals or consumers[6] about the product / service. They share positive comments, and support for the value, meaning and role of the product in their daily lives.

For instance. Actress A has decided to choose milk X to supplement calcium for her bones.

Nutrition expert B recommends that mothers should use milk Y for kids who have cow milk allergy, which is the cause of underdevelopment in children.

You have realized that, Testimonial is important to building trust, and appreciation towards a certain product. It creates a reliable social evidence for the product.

What matters here is whether the published positive experience that is real or not. In fact, few consumers are care about that question, because they only listen and trust. That's the advantage of Testimonial.

Award: The award from an independent reliable organization is a convincing testimony to the organization's reputation.

---

[6] Consumers understood as the individuals who are not a celebrity with prominent characteristics. They share characteristics in common with everyone else.

Thus, for PR practitioners, searching, and preparing records and documents to participate in and to achieve the award is very important.

The award is the delicious "food" which is the story about the excellence of the enterprise. On the other hand, it is the guarantee of a third party for that business's reputation.

When applying this tool, PR practitioners should not participate in the awards that are not reliable or those that can be bought with money, because using them to promote company's reputation will ensure a catastrophe.

Offline meeting: is the meeting held for potential customers, and the media.

At an offline meeting, enterprises officially announce the innovation of the product; as well as the use, image and happiness values that it brings consumers.

The Core purpose of offline meeting is to build a deep understanding about the product to important target subjects to establish, and strengthen their confidence towards it.

Editorial advertorial: is the extended form of advertorials promoting the product / service with a neutral and sophisticated writing style.

Often the content is divided into two main parts. The first part emphasizes the need to solve an urgent problem in society. The second one will address directly the values that the product can bring to consumers to solve that problem.

For example:

Milk is an important source of nutrients for the development of children. Milk with high quality and is safe for children is always the top choice for parents for the best early development of their children.

However, there are many poor quality milks in the market causing damage to children such as milk with poor protein causing undernourishment, milk with substandard protein content or fake formula leads to food poisoning, etc. Substandard milk can cause injury to children and it is one of the biggest anxiety of women. They need safe milk for the full development of their kids.

For dairy firm M, milk products must pass 2,000 strict quality checks on quality, composition, content, taste, microorganism… before being shipped off the market. There is no products on the market without passing these quality checks.

The quality and absolute safety of products of M are accepted worldwide for over 100 years, even in countries that have the most rigorous criteria of food safety in the world such as USA, UK, France, Germany, etc.

Through the above example, you may have noticed that editorial advertorial article has a subtle and convincing way to entice purchasing decisions of consumers.

TV expert consulting: is a live consulting session on TV of doctors, healthcare professional or scientists about hot topics of current issues. For example, medical treatment, health care, education for kids, finance, securities, education, vocational orientation, etc.

The contents of consulting sessions revolve around providing scientific knowledge and answering questions of the audience, as well as giving advice, and suggestion about the products.

TV expert consulting is very effective in building trust in products. When deploying this tool, it is important whether or not   doctors, or specialists mention your product in their advice. As far as I'm concerned, it is much better if that they do, if the product / service is really useful and appropriate.

Free day: is the business festival held for a particular group.

For example:

- ⅄ Consulting festival that provides free medical care service for office women.

- ⅄ Study abroad consulting festival for students from 15-20 years old.

- ⅄ Consulting festival on labor export to Japan for youth groups looking for work.

Free day helps enterprises address the needs for sales, and bring benefits to their brand and reputation.

Training person in charge: is funding for training, and improving knowledge and expertise of those in charge of the organizations to enhance their contribution to society.

For instance. Enterprises fund training and knowledge learning for English teachers in high schools, colleges and universities; or improve childcare skills of nurses in kindergartens; or sponsoring advanced training for midwives at hospitals across the country, etc.

This is a valuable tool contributing a lot to society and it is highly appreciated by the community. Enterprises applying this tool have not only social responsibility, but also great reputation in the community.

TV documentary: is a report broadcasting on golden hours on television stations, which is to share information about business history, philosophy, as well as modern technologies to provide customers with useful products.

The purpose of TV documentary is to provide really vivid evidences to help customers have a better understand on how products are created and to persuade them to believe in the products' quality.

Personal letter: is a letter written by friendly CEOs to tell good stories, or new events that are related to you and their business. The letter says exactly what you are and will be concerned about their product / service.

I appreciate this tool, because its sincerity can shorten the distance between sellers and buyers. Who does not appreciate a handwritten letter of an awfully busy and dedicated friend.

You only need to consider the most important customer group (rather than all of them) to examine and understand their feelings, to send them letters worth reading.

In fact, with a list of 10,000 important customers, developing personal letters requires a tremendous effort. Thus, PR practitioners should consult CEOs an effective way to approach this.

Take notice that using sample letter, scanned signatures on file, making a series of copies sending to clients is exactly a wasted, and useless solution. It is the evidence of apathy, cursoriness, and emotionless. Just like giving leaflets at markets. If you really like personal letter and want to implement it, just email me.

Authorities contribution record: is the certificates of achievement, social contribution, product quality, merit, awards… granted by prestigious organizations.

This is a very effective evidence which by itself, it can say what needed to be said to those who want to hear. Upload them on the mass media. Hang them at all headquarters, and branch offices of enterprises across the country. This will help increase customer's confidence and sympathy towards products / services.

Group four, 5 defense tools

Table 4.4. 5 defense tools

Monitoring & tracking	Crisis management plan
Hotline 24/7	Shareholder analyzing
Contact list	

Monitoring & tracking: is monitoring, updating, filing daily news, articles, speeches, reviews of state agencies, the media, and the competitors on the mass media.

The purpose of monitoring & tracking is to provide news resources for brand management activities, as well as to promptly detect and prevent potential risks that likely lead to a crisis. In addition, this also helps reflect the way enterprises are recognized in the market.

Hotline 24/7[7]: is the hot number of enterprises ready to receive questions and to provide the necessary advice to customers.

When customers feel discomfort enough to call the hotline to complain, then they expect a response, and expect to know what is happening. Therefore receiving

---

[7] 24/7 means 24 hours in 7 days without a break.

comments and explaining promptly will help subside somewhat the resistant emotion and get back their trust (see Box 4.3).

Hotline 24/7 is classified into defense group because it is to reduce the discomfort of customers due to misunderstandings or errors caused by the Product / service. It also plays a very important role in crisis management that I will present in detail in Chapter 7 - *The art of risk and crisis management.*

Box 4.3:

Look at customer's complaint as a gift[8]

Why is it really a gift?

➤ Because when they are angry and share us their emotions, that means they tell us what they want.

➤ Because when they are angry and let us know, this means they still want to cooperate.

➤ Because when they get angry, and let us know why they are unhappy, that means they also give us a chance to respond, and to fix it.

If we can explain the misunderstanding, or solve situations well, we win their heart. At that moment, we have touched and changed their attitude towards us - from negative to positive.

They will not leave us, they will continue to go with us, because we "understand" them.

And now, you have realized that, their "complaint" is really a gift.

Contact list: is contact information of those who have the ability to help enterprises in crisis, including the press, consumer associations, industry associations, government agencies, experts, quality measurement agencies, key investors and victims of the incident.

---

[8] Copyright by Le Tran Bao Phuong.

Contact list is based on the relationships previously established between them and PR practitioners (or CEO). Contact list is used when crisis occurs. Take notice of how to work with them, which will be introduced in Chapter 7.

Crisis management plan: is to minimize the damage, to save and to restore the reputation of enterprises in unfavorable conditions.

This plan contains detailed instructions on how to react, to solve, and to take advantage of relationships, or to make other strategic steps.

Crisis management plan is the most comprehensive defense tool that enterprises should consider setting up early. I will present this in details in Chapter 7.

Shareholder analyzing: is the analysis of the condition of the existing and potential shareholders to know who own the majority of shares and assess whether or not the organization is facing the risk of acquisition.

There are 5 basic questions that need to be answered adequately in Shareholder Analyzing:

- Who are the largest shareholders of the company?
- Is there any significant change in the largest shareholders? If so, what is it? Why?
- Is there any sign showing that the company is a target of the acquisition?
- Has the company received any proposal?
- What is the company's view on this issue?

From the analysis, PR practitioners will advise the board and company leadership on how to protect founders' interest and prevent acquisitions or hidden evil intrigues.

Group five, 13 tools to protect enterprises' reputation during crisis

- *"What is crisis? Is it dangerous?"*
- *"How do you know when it is going to happen to prevent?"*

– "How PR can protect enterprises from an crisis? How?"

My friend, we will completely discuss these three questions above in Chapter 7. For the time being, I will answer the question "how?"

When a crisis occurs, poor management will turn common diseases into chronic complications, ruining all the efforts and achievements of the emotional brand that have been built so far. The weakness couple with crisis can break down even a long - standing brand.

Therefore, active interpreting, and updating information for the public to know and understand about the incident, damage and danger rate, as well as how they overcome it is the most important thing for enterprises to do. Therefore, the study of 13 tools to protect corporate reputation in crisis is essential.

Table 4.5. 13 tools to protect enterprises' reputation during crisis

Complaint record	Issue photo	Urgent meeting
Filming	Issue tape	Lawyer
Fact sheet	Letter to Editor	Media roundtable meeting
Calendar listing	Letter to Consumer Association	Integrated tools
Press release		

Complaint record: is the summary of all the complaints of consumers, clients and the media about incidents caused by products / services, through the statistics of Hotline 24/7, letters, and emails from consumers.

The purpose of the complaint record is to fully and timely update questions, and complaints of customers for enterprise to repair accordingly.

Additionally, verifiable information from complaint record is also very beneficial for PR practitioners considering the real possibility of errors of the products.

For instance. If only one customer calls and accuse product A to be erroneous, PR practitioners can deduce that the product possibly get damaged during the transportation; but if there are hundreds of customers across the country complain about the poor quality of product A, he can blame it on the production process.

Filming: is the recording of all the events taking place within the process of investigating the cause of the crisis. Such as random check of sample shipments, waste at sewage holes... with the witness of concerned parties (representatives of state authorities, representatives of enterprises, lawyers, representatives of residents around the plant, the press, or television stations).

Filming not only helps record the real movements, but also collects materials for the campaign to restore the brand reputation after crisis.

Fact sheet: is the detailed description of all moments, movements, losses and speeches of people involved in the accusation of the short comings of a product.

Businesses often actively prepare fact sheet for the media, and the authorities to officially announce the facts of the incident, avoiding distorted truth which could bring disadvantage to businesses.

Calendar listing: is to announce the schedule for repairing activities (such as recalling detective product, new products exchange), as well as to update the results obtained from fixing the incidents.

The announcement will be posted on the official website of enterprises to demonstrate the commitment, accountability and devotion of the organizations to overcome the incident.

Press release: Press release is the indispensable communication tool in crisis management. Press Release is often quickly prepared by PR practitioners to send to press agencies in time.

It is to provide, and to update official information to the press about what is happening such as events, causes, sphere of influence, damages, as well as acts of prevention, and repairing activities that are being carried out.

Choosing an appropriate sending time is an art that need to be learnt. For example:

- PR practitioners don't have to send a press release if it is just a small and isolated incident that is to be fixed;

⁂ PR practitioners should be careful considering the issue of the press release, because of the possibility of creating market unrest due to inaccurate data sources.

Besides, PR practitioners should be discreet when using words in the crisis message. It must be short, accurate, univocal, easy to understand, and could not be misinterpreted. This will help to prevent bad guys, and those who oppose enterprises to quote out of context.

Issue photo: is a series of images illustrating the effort of business to overcome, and to improve the incident situation.

In big incidents, issue photo is recommended with press release, and letter to editor / consumer association to restore the community's feelings of enterprises.

Issue tape: is the recording of corporate leaders' speeches presenting their views on a crisis. It often follows closely the contents of the press release.

Issue tape can be sent to public through radio, and websites with a large number of visitors.

Letter to Editor: the official letter of an enterprise sent to the chief editor of a newspaper (print, or online media) aiming to stop using misleading articles detrimental to business and require immediate correction..

Letter to Editor is based on the untruthfulness of the article. When the cause of the incident is still in the investigation process, then article has created misconceptions about it, in some cases, there are even indications that the opposing forces of the business are behind after those articles.

The boundary between black and white in this case is easy to recognize based on the attitude of the newspaper when enterprises require them to correct the articles and arguments, or cooperative attitude of the newspaper on article correction.

Letter to Consumer Association: is the official dispatch sent to consumer protection association to explain about product errors to the association and to consumers.

Its contents will be based on the core of a press release that is already sent to the media to create consistent responses regarding the incident.

Urgent meeting: between enterprises and those who directly reported about the quality of products / services.

The goal is to learn, to record comments, to share views, to make reports of received sample, and to set appointment to give out answers after analyzing the results and, finding out the reason.

As for enterprises, urgent meeting not only helps them take responsibility for the products, but also restricts bad news being spread to the market before finding the real cause.

Also for those who complaint, it is to give them an official deadline to receive a satisfactory answer from enterprises about the defective, or substandard products.

Well, you have realized that, urgent meeting is a valuable PR tool for both parties.

Lawyer: is the use of lawyers to retaliate against cheap shots of competitors by showing the evidence proving the innocence of the enterprise against ridiculous allegations.

Lawyers' fact is a worthwhile source for PR practitioners to establish and to transmit beneficial messages to the community.

Lawyer is considered as a powerful tool for communication crisis management. It shows the determination of enterprises in the pursuit of the truth to the last breath.

Media roundtable meeting: is the meeting between business representatives and those from press agencies.

It is more intimate than press conference, but it is not different from a press conference, in which business representatives have the opportunity to justify, to present evidence and to send messages about the incident, as well as to answer questions from the media about the case officially.

Integrated tools: is a crisis management tool that integrate many other media tools such as press release, editorial, letter to employee / supplier / investor / editor, press conference, TV interview, Expert voice, etc.

The use of integrated tools is to convey powerfully, and deeply a message with compelling evidence to consumers, in every corner of the market, allowing the case to be understood properly, dislodging the doubts, and fear of choosing products, hence recovering the business.

Group six, 5 supreme PR tools

- *"What are the 5 supreme PR tools?" Is it different from 100 tools above? "*

- *"Do they contain a much more aggressive power?"*

Yes!

They are the top powerful PR tools that could profoundly change the perception, attitude and behavior of many people, or generations by shaping the existing beliefs, stimulating millions of people to think and to do things differently, voluntarily, or even consciously.

I would like to talk about a book, a movie, a song, a lecture or a word of mouth with an extensive spread.

Table 4.6. 5 supreme PR tools

Books	Giving a lecture (GAL)
Movies	Word of mouth (WoM)
Music	

- *"Why is a book a supreme PR tool?"*

A Book: Books are the source of knowledge containing infinite benefits for readers. Readers can travel different worlds to get different experiences and to learn knowledge of different fields. Books enlighten people's mind, provide insight to help people get a new and deeper view of life. Books could not be exhausted during consumption. It exists for generations.

Books have great importance in changing the perception, attitude and the fate of mankind since "A drop of ink may make a million think; a good book can change many people's fate." (Lord Byron, 1788-1824)[9]

⅄ In the business field, we have realized that the companies producing Swiss watches have known how to use this supreme PR tool for a long time.

They always put in the boxes of those expensive watch little books about the watch's origin history, and about how to manufacture manually over 1,000 detailed components to create a classy watch.

The information in this book has multiplied the intangible value of the watch many times. This information boost the ego of those who own the watch into ecstasy. You see, books are truly a supreme PR tool.

⅄ In the field of business, we have found that formula Milk Powder manufacturers have known how to use this supreme PR tool for a long time.

They collaborate with nutrition experts and publishers to release books instructing parents how to choose an appropriate source of nutrition for their children.

Aside from providing guidelines to create a favorable living environment conditions for children to develop their intelligence, analytical skills, and communication skills, the book also give instructions for getting the optimal nutrition for the growth of children's brain. Of course, the products of that milk powder company diet is indispensable to this optimal diet. As the result, they can either sell books or buy the trust of mothers. This company is too wise.

Illustration. The following is the preface of a book similar to one mentioned before from milk company F.

> "Company F would like to give those who were, are or will become parents a meaningful gift. We are always your fellow in the development of your babies. Yours faithfully!"

---

[9] Lord Byron (1788-1824) was an English poet, and was one of the world's big poets in the 19th century.

My friend, personally, I don't advocate company F in this case, because it more or less affects the rights of children, but I could not deny their books is a supreme PR tool that is manipulated quite thoroughly.

- *"Why is a movie a supreme PR tool?"*

A Movie: A movie is a supreme PR tool because:

- First, it is capable of making the messages much more perceivable even to those that are illiterates.

- Second, movies easily affect world view and emotions of viewers to push them perform a certain behavior.

- Third, movies have the ability to make viewers behave the same way in real life like their favorite characters in movies.

According to the "theory of priming effects" by Jo & Berkowitz (1994), the events that a person experiences through the mass media (like movies) will trigger ideas , thoughts, emotions and orientation for action in his mind. In other words, he feels and rehearses in his mind, then acting so in reality.

- *"Is there any enterprise has used this supreme PR tool yet?"*

My friend, Nokia is the one that has been using this Movie tool regularly.

They have created and released globally movies that have the great ability to inspire such as Cellular - the phone saving people (2004) - a film about the rescue kidnap victims through Nokia 6600 smartphone; or the promotion of Lumia 900 handset Batman Edition using The Dark Knight Rises movie; or Nokia X7 groundbreaking design style and entertainment capabilities for young people with Transformer 3..

In short, with the impact on a large and comprehensive scale, movies are able to inspire and push the crowd action according to the intention of manufacturers. With such power, Movies are also manipulated in the field of propaganda. (see Case study 4.1).

> **Case study 4.1:**
>
> ### Movies used in the race for the White House
>
> According to Tuong Pham (2013)[10],the documentary movie about president Barack Obama titled "The Road We've Traveled" lasting 7 minutes was used to "rally" Mr Barack Obama in the incoming race for the White House.
>
> The movie highlights the achievements of President Barack Obama in his last term, such as the growth of the economy, the end of Iraq war, killing Osama Bin Laden, expansion of student loan repayment program, reformation of Wall Street, etc.
>
> The movie was directed by Davis Guggenheim, the former Oscar-winner and it was narrated by Hollywood actor Tom Hanks.

2012 - 2016 Presidential Election Results: Barack Obama was re-elected as US president with 303 votes while the candidate Mitt Romney received 206 votes[11].

- *"Why is music a supreme PR tool?"*

A Music: Music is a form of emotional sound. Thus, it has a very strong impact on the emotions of human beings. Music creates in our heart different emotions, leading to different reactions.

When listening to music, we have a melancholic feeling. When listening to music, then we can be cheerful, inspired. Music adjusts our feelings. This is its great power.

According to Oriental interpretation, human body is encompassed by a lot of substances. These substances formed by very light, sound, invisible atoms. Music itself has the same vibration as the vibration of the substances, thus causing a huge influence on people. Music creates a trace on the human body that directly affects

---

[10] Tuong Pham. (2013). *Does Hollywood help Obama be re-elected?* At http://cstc.cand.com.vn/vi-VN/hoso/hosointepol/2012/4/183162.cand [Date of Access: May 22th, 2013]

[11]Vneconomy. (2013). Obama has won re-election. At
http://vneconomy.vn/20121106054121424P0C99/obama-tai-dac-cu-voi-chien-thang-vuot-troi.htm
[Date of Access: November 25th, 2013]

their characters, and actions. Music is stronger than dogmas because it directly affects the invisible substances[12].

According to Baddish Priest Thich Quang Hue (2011)[13]:"500 BC, Confucius grasped the nature and the effect of music. He said that music could change the moral and social practices. Confucius concluded that one knows the secret of the music knows the secrets to shake people's hearts, this means he knows how to lead people. Who knows the secret to lead people knows the secret to rule them".

According to modern neurology, the power of music is related to human brain waves.

Simply put, the source of all thoughts, emotions and behavior of human beings is the communication between nerve cells in the brain; and basic brain wave is the electric impulses created when nerve cells communicate with each other.

And by EEG, scientists have found 4 types of brain wave Beta, Alpha, Theta and Delta.

Specifically, beta wave (13-60 Hz/ sec) could make people enhance the sense of vigilance, or make people become agitated, nervous, scared. Alpha wave (7-13 Hz / sec) makes people relax both physically and mentally. Theta wave (4-7 Hz / sec) can cause drowsiness and decrease consciousness. Delta wave (0.1 to 4 Hz / sec) can cause unconsciousness, deep sleep or numbness.

– *"Are these information useful for us?"*

In fact, the power of music is applied quite universally in the field of communication (education, business, religion and politics) for either good or evil purposes.

Many organizations has the intention to use music to inspire, to create an optimistic and positive attitude,; or to increase hope of a group of people so that they will naturally react with responses beneficial to the organization. You may notice that the epics written specifically for the organizations are always towards these goals.

---

[12] Blair T.Spalding. (2011). Life and Teaching of the Masters of the Far East (pg. 133-134). Publish house: Hong Duc

[13] Thich Quang Hue. (2013). The role of music in modern life. At http://chuahieuquang.com/Modules/News/NewDetail.aspx?page=35&moduleId=48&news=431[Date of Access: July 17th, 2013]

Besides, the power of music can also be used to influence the reputation and share value of an organization with the support of social media (see case study 4.2).

Case study 4.2:

The power of music

According to Thanh Hai (2013)[14] United Airlines might never have guessed that the sweet sound from a guitar could lose 10% of its stock value, approximately 180 million USD.

This stems from the story that a porter of United broke Dave Carroll's guitar. United refused paying compensation after over 9 months.

Before this sluggish response, Carroll composed the song United Breaks Guitars and uploaded to YouTube. His song drew 14.5 million views and more than 1 million comments.

Notably, its stock price fell 10%, equivalent to $ 180 million. The BOD hastily apologized Carroll and paid for repairs of his guitar. The company also got him a bunch of free airfares.

Discussion Question:

1) Music, in this situation, was used for what purpose?
2) How did Music influence United Airlines share prices?

– *"Why is giving a lecture (GAL) a supreme PR tool?"*

GAL (Giving a lecture): GAL is the art of public speaking to educate, to persuade, to change attitudes, as well as behavior of the masses and gain their support for a particular issue.

It has been developed from ancient Greek. This art was known through ancient writings. The first textbook on this subject was written over 2,400 years ago.

---

[14] Thanh Hai. (2013). *The bitter lessons about brands in the digital era.* At:http://doanhnhan.vneconomy.vn/20130626071232683P0C5/nhung-bai-hoc-thuong-hieu-chua-xot-trong-ky-nguyen-so.htm [Date of access 27th June, 2013].

Greek orators gave a lecture as individuals rather than behalves of clients or the public, so anyone who wants to succeed in court, in politics or in social life must learn the technique of public speaking (see Figure 4.2).

Picture 4.2. The frescoes of Cesare Maccari (1840-1919): Cicero rejected Catiline (source: Wikipedia).

According to Edward Bernays, during Roman and post Egypt era, giving a lecture had proven itself as a supreme tool capable of influencing personal and public opinion.

According to him, GAL is "a powerful tool that it is still valuable so far. Politicians, religious leaders are still giving lectures from the podium, outdoor, on TV and Radio "[15] to persuade, or to gain the support of the masses.

My friends, there are many courses of giving lectures, so I just want to emphasize that GAL is not to present the great things in a great way, but it is talking about the great things in the most simple and understandable way.

Speak clearly and coherently, avoid flamboyant style, because the greatness is right in the presented information; and if the information is not then trying to be melodramatic, will mean that there are be pompous words, and clichés which in turn

---

[15]Edward L. Bernays. 1923. *Crystallizing Public Opinion* (tr. ix). Liveright Publishing Corporation.

would be counterproductive We naturally dislike the pompousness. We love the rustiness, and sincerity.

In the business sector, GAL is an indispensable PR tool. Therefore, organizations must truly concern about the ability to giving speeches of the leaders. If their public speaking skill is poor, the consequences will be extremely bad. The consequences will result undamaged admiration of the leader, in submission from the entire staff, but also in shaken belief of the community toward organizations

- *"Why is Word of mouth a supreme PR tool?"*

WoM (word of mouth)**:** Word of mouth is known as the spread of information (in term of text, picture, video) from one person to another about a particular issue.

The nature of WoM is "exaggerating" an issue to draw public attention and concern.

Word of mouth is divided into 3 main types: oral tradition, oral history and storytelling.

- Oral tradition is passing the information from generation to generation orally.

- Oral history is recording, preserving and interpreting historical information based on personal experience and opinion of the speakers.

- Storytelling is a form that one person narrates to the others about an event, phenomenon or experience that he has been through. Storytelling is the oldest WoM.

There are some ideas for PR practitioners to apply WoM as follows:

- Leak information "unintentionally" about a new product promising to have many unique features; or disclose a sales campaign with 0 USD budget to stimulate consumer to buzz, gossip, whisper;

- Enterprise deploy unique customer services. For example, infinite warranty, 100% refund, samples delivery at home, delivery within 30 minutes across the country;

- Established supporter clubs to spread, to attract, and to admit many new members;

- Borrow quotes of a famous person that has many fans, or of an influential person to speak positively about the product;

- Allow employees to share with friends on facebook, or google plus on how company's products have helped their lives, and those of their children and their families to be happier, and better.

Transition

My friend, you have completed Chapter 4 and you might have learned more than 100 PR tools capable of strongly disseminating your inspirational message.

Maybe you're confused about choosing an optimal way, because there are too many options. Don't worry, we will have a Chapter 6. *The art of building a comprehensive PR strategy* to solve that concern.

You might be thinking that you're ready to design a comprehensive PR campaign, because you have had a convincing message and over 100 PR tools to spread it out.

- *No! There are 3 sections; 2 is not enough ".*

Part 3 is also Chapter 5. *The art of adjusting human behavior.*

Therefore, you should definitely study the Chapter 5, because it will help you achieve the profundity in setting up a comprehensive PR strategy.

- *"Ready to begin?"*

5

The art of adjusting human behaviors

GENERAL CONTENT

The third supreme art is the art of adjusting human behaviors. This art is developed from the third ancient ruling wisdom: "Hit the vulnerable spots of human behaviors to create an unanimous response from the crowd."

These 3 vulnerable spots of human behaviors are *natural instincts, childhood beliefs and self-determination.*

Natural instinct is the natural reaction of human beings to an exterior stimulus without any rational consideration. Meanwhile, childhood belief is a factor leading to decisions with little judgment, because it conforms the prejudices, beliefs and personal experience. Self-determination is self-selection through rational thinking, analysis, evaluation, comparison, consideration and selection.

– *"Imagine this: how are you going to use this art to influence the crowd's behavior?"*

Chapter 5 will provide you with many valuable suggestions that you could not find anywhere else.

– *"Come on! Let's get it started!"*

The amount of new information, knowledge is more and more abundant. It is many times greater than our consumption. It grows too fast. It causes dyspepsia.

The amount of new information and knowledge goes viral too fast thanks to the internet. Information surrounds us for the whole day, from waking up in the morning to hitting the sack at night.

The amount of new information and knowledge is too multidimensional. It easily shakes our points. They make it impossible to discern what is true and what is false. And in the absence of wisdom, truth and false are the same.

Therefore, we tend to be less confident about something right from the start. We always need to check google about everything from work, study, relationships, health to daily issues.

However, we do not have enough time to learn everything thoroughly. Therefore, in a state of fatigue, we often allow our actions to be guided by natural instincts, ego and self-compromising thoughts.

Just imagine that in one day, a generous guy stops by a fashion store looking for a nice bargain, because he sees the offer of 30% to 50% discount for all items in that today.

He gets in store, but did not find any discounted good worth buying. Patiently, he thinks he should browse for some other items.

A cute enthusiastic sales girl suggests him a highly sought after pair of shoes that they have only one left in stock. She believes that it fits his chivalrous walk and he seems to miss it.

He is excited to be the owner of the new pair of shoes, and forgets his initial purpose to find a good bargain. Finally he buys a new pair of shoes. And to rationalize the purchase, he explains to himself that his shoes are too old and they are needed to be replaced soon.

This is just a hypothetical situation, but it helps you experience the loss of money due to the fear of scarcity. Furthermore, you have also realized that he suffered the loss because of his self-deception. A self-deceiving person would never be wise. Thus, apart from losing money, he also lost his reason.

When interviewed about unconscious actions leading to mistakes, the majority of PR practitioners claimed that they are independent, and wise people that have knowledge, political views, full awareness, intellect and restraint about what should do, and what should not do.

Everyone claims that they have a clear stance and want to make decisions about anything related to their life. They claim that they could not be deluded, or deceived, unless they compromised, because they simply could not be wrong for their 5 senses works very well.

- *"Is that true?"*

- *"Yes, but it is not what you think!"*

They think they are right because they do not know that despite their 5 well functioned senses, all the mistakes will arise immediately when their choices are influenced by the will of others, and are suppressed by new doubts in them, when their choices attach to their emotions, ego, when their actions are influenced with their fear, and especially when their beliefs are oppressed by many contradictory proofs.

Actually, there are many deeper layers of consciousness such as sub-consciousness, unconsciousness and super-consciousness. They are beyond our mind, silently affecting our senses to adjust our actions.

- *"Just ask yourself, have you ever made decisions depending on the will of others?"*

We often depend on the opinions and expectations of others. For example, when I am happy, someone tells me that "Your eyes look sad, maybe you have many troubles. Your clothes speak for themselves also, as black as pitch! " So should I be happy or sad? I am confused because it might be right.

I reconsider and learn that I do have many troubles. But in "the sea of misery", everyone has his own issues. At this point, you were obviously affected by other people's opinion that changed your current emotion, from "cheerful" to "worried" appropriate to the belief that you have just set yourself.

Through this example, we realize that we often see ourselves through the eyes of other people, hence we entrust our fate in their hands. Bitterly, everyone wants to shape the attitudes, opinions and decisions of others, because he wants others to follow his belief in order to protect what he believes, and everyone wants to make out his case to protect his vulnerable ego.

- *"Have you ever suspected the preciseness of something?"*

You suspect something because you do not have enough information to confirm it, or you cannot trust those who tell it, or you do not know whether the source is reliable or not. You simply suspect because you cannot believe it. For whatever reason, your doubt has emerged.

My friends, please understand that doubt is a form of strange power that could adjust behaviors. Your doubt easily subdues your determination. You cannot take action even though deep down inside you are eager to do it, just because you have doubt about that.

- *"Have you ever regretted what you have done?"*

Definitely yes, because the underneath of your actions is profound reasons that you yourself could not understand. Maybe you were obsessed by events in your childhood, or urged by strong emotions. Maybe you were affected by circumstances and lessons from the past.

You do not dare to do something differently from what you have known because the unknowns are much scary. They are more dangerous. You would rather choose the same old things because you can control them, but subsequently you will regret for not daring to do something new. You feel regretful.

- *"Have you understood all of your behaviors yet?"*

Certainly not, because behind the arguments used to justify your behaviors, there are secret reasons that you do not dare to admit to anyone, not even to yourself, or maybe you are either suffering from an inescapable compulsion, or deceiving yourself to escape from inner conflicts, or playing a role in a play. They got you confused about your behavior.

People are less likely to understand their behaviors because the most of people life is unconscious. Osho said that, people are rarely present before themselves to consider, or to evaluate their actions and reactions that are taking place. They are walking, eating, laughing and working under the guidance of the routine. At the moment, they often do not recognize who they are. They do not understand their behavior. They are constantly led by the unconsciousness.[1]

Also, human behaviors and attitudes are also often influenced by their emotions and ego. We should know that, at anywhere and anytime, our emotions and ego are always able to appear before us to blur our clarity and objectivity, adjusting our decisions. We often pilot our decisions from rational objectivity to emotional subjectivity.

All in all, people rarely understand their behaviors, because they are often manipulated by their unconsciousness, emotion, ego and unclear reasons.

From this comprehension and the application of the third ancient ruling wisdom in the field of modern PR, we can summarize that: to influence the crowd's behavior, a persuader can push the three vulnerable spots of human behavior to take advantage of un-consciousness, waking up their subjective feeling, praising their ego and convincing their sleepy reason.

Three vulnerable spots of human behavior are *natural instincts, childhood beliefs and self-determination.*

- *"What would happen if I stimulate these three three vulnerable spots?"*
- *Good question! Let's discover these interesting things."*

5.1. Stimulate natural instincts

---

[1] Osho (1931-1990) was a famous Indian theoretician.

Natural instinct is the natural reaction of human beings to an exterior stimulus without any rational consideration.

There is a tremendous amount of knowledge in this field, but in this book, I present 18 kinds of instincts that have been and will be applied effectively in the field of modern PR.

Table 5.1. Stimulate 18 types of human natural instincts

1. Stimulate the fear	10. Stimulate primitive virtues
2. Stimulate the instinct of avoid disgusting things	11. Stimulate penitent instinct
3. Stimulate fighting instinct	12. Stimulate the belief in established prestige
4. Stimulate sexual instinct	13. Stimulate responsive instinct
5. Stimulate self-reverence	14. Stimulate the consistency in word and action
6. Stimulate the curiosity	15. Stimulate flattery instinct
7. Stimulating loving instinct	16. Stimulate the herd mentality
8. Stimulating snobbish instinct	17. Stimulate human intuitions
9. Stimulate imitative instinct	18. Stimulate survival instinct

The fear?

1. Stimulate the fear

Fear is the most powerful emotion. It warns us that we are in danger. It causes discomfort, fatigue, and confusion. It motivates people acting immediately to remove the fear and return to their safety.

Everyone has their own fears. Different people have different fears, but they are all weaknesses in their mind. Therefore, there are many dark PR practitioners have deliberately created fears, and anxieties among the masses. As people are at peace, they would careless about any problem, but when they are anxious or frightened, their assumption and inference will appear immediately, although they are very powerful, they aren't the cleverest choices; and that is the golden time to "put" information in their heads, inducing them to act immediately to eliminate their pain or discomfort.

You should also know that the greatest enemy of any communication effort to change human habits is *the psychological inertia* of human beings. This nature makes people reject easily the change, even though it can better their lives.

This psychological inertia can only be defeated if people raise their fear about it and their attitudes toward it become urgent. The urgency can only be created with two conditions:

- The terrible fear, or anticipation of a bad outcome to listeners,

- Disclose that they still have time, to solve it and they can save it.

In the field of business, to defeat the psychological inertia and successfully stimulate the fear of the crowd, PR practitioner needs the following necessary conditions:

(1) Reliable sources,

(2) The hidden threat and solution,

(3) Human perception about the need to act immediately.

For instance:

The World Health Organization (WHO) has just warned that dengue fever is spreading widely in Asia. The Number of hospitalizations and severe cases is increasing rapidly. According to WHO, the number of dengue cases in Asia increases due to high temperatures, rainy season, high population and people traveling between big countries.

Early detection and timely treatment can help reduce the risk of death significantly. WHO recommends families to use preventive measures such as keeping home clean, no stagnant water around living areas, sleeping inside curtain and putting on anti-insect clothing.

We found that the example above contains 3 necessary conditions to defeat the psychological inertia and stimulate the fear of the crowd to call for their actions:

- Reliable sources: World Health Organization (WHO),

- The threat: death (due to dengue fever),

- The perception of people about the need to act: avoiding death.

- Defeat the psychological inertia:

  o Warning the negative outcome: Dengue Death.

  o Solution: simple, keeping home clean, no stagnant water around living areas, sleeping inside curtain, and putting on anti-insect clothing.

  o Possibility: simple.

This is a good example of stimulating human fear with positive purpose.

Box 5.3: Warning 1

You should not manipulate fear to make things too scary. It could lead to disaster for enterprise's reputation. Because it can make the whole community hate those who have launched the cruel information. Public perception of enterprises will just as bad as the unfortunate messages that they have sent out.

---

2. Stimulate the instinct of avoid disgusting things

The most basic thing that differs human beings from machine is that they can assign to a thing, or an event a certain meaning or feeling appropriate to their experience and their understanding of it.

In other words, human beings figure out something according to their own beliefs and prejudices, just like "doctors see germs everywhere".

However, there is a feeling people share the same awareness, which is the condemnation and avoidance of evil and disgusting things.

Therefore, in PR, by assigning to something an evil nature or a disgusting feeling using words or terms, practitioner can deliberately isolate it from the crowd.

For instance. In late 2010, a number of churches in Vietnam conducted the campaign calling for the community to join hands in opposing abortion among families that want sons and among adolescents.

On the one hand, the churches taught about morality, and human rights. On the other hand, they stuck many real pictures of little bodies had not formed yet were cut up into small pieces (head, legs and arms) to meet the needs of their parents and spoiled girls.

By encouraging people to stay away from that abomination, the campaign helped the community understand better about this sin. This firm grasp has immediately changed human mind and behavior comprehensively. This reminds them to stay away from the abomination.

3. Stimulate fighting instinct

Stimulating fighting instinct is a technique to provoke public opinion to enlist the support of the crowd, for the benefit of the persuader (himself).

In fact, the persuader can use this technique to generate opposition from the crowd in order to suppress an opinion, a belief that is somehow detrimental to him.

– *"How?"*

He speaks on the issue of competitors in a way that the crowd would protest and resist. Because he knows that fighting for justice has always been accepted and praised by the society.

Experience has shown, there were many times someone like him (the persuader) had used the technique to stimulate fighting instinct to create anger in the community towards a case of injustice, thus creating a collective behavior beneficial to him. He drafted out all of the events could happen so that they could consecutively generate waves of fights for justice drawing the crowds' action.

For instance. To cheer for the anti-smoking strategy, he will talk about a deadly number of people are dying to lung cancer at an alarming rate (for example, every 1 minute, 100 people died to tobacco) and the prosperity of tobacco manufacturers is in direct proportion to the mortality due to smoking.

By stimulating fighting instinct, he successfully called for the smoking cessation of guys. They quit smoking not because they were scared of the death. They did because they wanted to fight against the prosperity of tobacco companies that had "killed" a lot of people like them.

Dear friends, this is the technique to stimulate fighting instinct type 1. And the second one is technique to create fierce debates on forums.

Imagine what would happen if a lover of Apple iPhone 7 praises his sanity for not purchasing Samsung Galaxy S6 on a technology forum. A fierce debate between technology believers will inevitably break out. It cannot be helped

You may have noticed, in a debate, people often feel insulted when their choices and beliefs are denied. Therefore, they will fight to the end for theirs. They will create and maintain a permanent debate on the board until their choice and faith are recognized better.

And you should realize that a prolonged debate that would attract the attention of the crowd much more than a half-day seminar. It is free for the initiator. It just takes time and effort of the "typing heroes". It brings many benefits to him.

–   *"What did he get?"*

He has drawn the attention of the crowd on a message that he wanted them to recognize, to understand and to bear in mind.

4. Stimulate sexual instinct

Sexual instinct has a tremendous power pushing people to overcome the barriers of reason. It is not natural that technology items or expensive cars are always surrounded by young girls and sexy models. The sexiness and attraction are intentionally created to catch the glances and to shorten the distance between the items and gentlemen.

In fact, many companies have tried to take advantage of this instinct in the ads of cars, technology events with sexy long legs.

However, you should note that, in media activities, if this kind of instinct is excessively manipulated, it would be counterproductive, because the stronger sexual appeal is, the easier it is for people to neglect the information about the characteristics, and the advantages of new products.

Stimulating sexual instinct often works well in promotion campaigns of specific products such as perfume, fashion, condom, lingerie, and expensive jewelry as well as social campaigns like HIV prevention, against abortion or praising fidelity.

5. Stimulate self-reverence

Self-reverence is a form of primitive human instinct. It motivates people trying to prove that they themselves are important, and they are the center of everything.

Successful people demonstrate their wealth by colossal asset while the poor prove their strength by all the bitterness and misery they have experienced through... Self-reverence turns everything they have done into greatness. Really they are all great things from their perspective towards themselves.

In the field of PR, stimulating the self-reverence instinct has a very strong impact on human behaviors. Its power is equivalent to the overwhelming power of fear and sexual instinct. From business perspective, PR practitioner can manipulate this powerful instinct to put pressure on human buying behavior.

- *"Is there any valuable suggestion for me?"*

- *Yes, of course! There are two valuable hints for you. But applying them either positively or negatively is just your choice.*

Suggestion 1. Enterprises launch an expensive product with only limited quantity for very rich people, then positioning those who own it as classy, successful and happy people.

Suggestion 2. Enterprises position high-profile personalities and images of consumers as they own their products and services.

Such as special cosmetics for famous models; high-end perfume for bosses; mysterious black suits for gentlemen; expensive jewelry for charming women...

It is to assign the product / service a necessary spiritual value to boost the sales. People do not buy products, they buy these spiritual values. The spiritual values boost their egos, thus bribing their buying behavior.

My friend, in developed countries, where these kinds of artificially spiritual values like this were no longer appreciated, people tend to demonstrate their special selves by products made by themselves, then these two techniques are less effective.

But in the developing countries, where people are still passionate about the fake illusion brought by branded items to prove their identity, the two techniques to influence buying behavior still work very effectively.

6. Stimulate the curiosity

Curiosity is a natural human instinct. According to Edward Bernays (1928), human mind is fundamentally proportional and steady. Therefore, if a thing or fact whose characteristics or natures may disturb the order of the old perception, it is likely to attract their attention. They learn new things in order to please their curiosity, restoring the balance in their mindset.

Curiosity has been thoroughly manipulated in the field of PR. Apple is a good example. They kept being ambiguous, leaking information about the new iPhone around the world before launching it in order to attract public attention.

7. Stimulating loving instinct

Human inborn characteristics are enjoying doing good things, as well as taking and giving sincere affection.

Love has countless ways to describe. It is love for children, love between man and woman, love for family, love for fatherland, homesickness, compassion, empathy...

If human life cannot lack love, the art of stimulating human instincts cannot lack the technique to stimulate loving instinct. To use this technique, I have two suggestions as follows:

Suggestion 1. By using an image of an innocent, playful child, and / or a warm family reunion, PR practitioners can make a more retentive message of happiness that

178

they want to transmit to consumers encouraging them purchase more products. They buy the value of the product and the warmth it brings.

Suggestion 2. Implement humanitarian programs to raise funds for unfortunate people, highlighting enterprises' humanity.

Box 5.2: Warning 2 (for suggestion 2)

You should remember that taking advantage of images, personal stories of unfortunate people to gain benefits for organizations can be panned by the masses.

You can see that in front of the screen, unfortunate people are bursting into tears. This is not only for the joy of getting a new house engraved with names of the sponsors, but also for their humiliation and the misfortune of their children.

They cry because they themselves may not want to share their misery and misfortune. They cry because they do not want to confess to everyone of their deepest suffering.

Well, you should pay attention to this warning most seriously.

---

8. Stimulating snobbish instinct

Snobbishness is a natural human instinct. It urges people to own the better, more beautiful, prominent things than the current one.

Snobbishness formed when the thing we have already owned is outdated or worse than what we long for. The more money we have, the more snobbish we would be. It stimulates our action to level up the difference between the present and the ideal. It stimulates us to buy.

In fact, high-tech companies (smartphone, tablet) are genius in stimulating the snobbish instinct. They encourage consumers to spend money based on the scenario that has been planned very wisely.

> For instance. A phone company knows very well how a perfect phone should be according to the demand of consumers, but they are not stupid to launch it. They split their innovation into steps through several versions.

Given, the latest Phone 7 with bigger, thinner and stronger screen has a huge impact on technology addicts using an outdated version of Phone 6. They are in an urge to purchase the new one and they definitely have purchased it. A year later, a Phone 8 with 3D display continues tormenting the desire of these snobbish victims. They could not endure and they continue to buy it. And so, again and again, they continue paying.

The purchase caused by snobbishness is neither bad nor good. It depends on the financial condition of each person. For the snobbish poor, this is a shameful and blind self-indulgence. For the rich, this is known as enjoying a good life and not being a slave for money. Who are you?

9. Stimulate imitative instinct

Stimulating imitative instinct is the technique of using movies, celebrities, politicians, monks, priests or key influencers to mobilize the crowds performing some desired behaviors.

"I choose this hairstyle to look like Tom Cruise" is a form of the results of this technique. The principle of this technique is to exploit human hidden desires, that they always eager to become the person they admire. Those people are the embodiments of success, knowledge, skills, wisdom or have certain some qualities that they do not have.

Movie (presented in Chapter 4) is a very powerful tool. It can be used to stimulate the imitative instinct. Did you notice that, movies can create an imitation among the crowd, from humanistic acts to cases of running away from home just like characters in movies (see case study 5.1).

Case study 5.1:

Movies guide human behaviors

Being impressed by The Wanderings of Sanmao (a Chinese drama), NA (born in 1989), a 9th grade student at Hanoi ran away from home to resemble Sanmao's life.

Before leaving, she had written a letter said: "... I want to try something like Sanmao's life..."[2]

NA got a haircut to make her look like a boy. Then, she went to Hanoi catching a train to Thanh Hoa, Sam Son, even Quang Tien (Vietnam) fishing village and got into residences asking for tending horses like Sanmao, unfortunately there are no horse in a fishing village.

Then, turning to the fishermen, she asked them to allow her to join their squid fishing. Fishermen were in doubt and told authorities to take her home.

Discussion question:

1) How have movies influenced NA?
2) According to you, what made her imitate Sanmao?

10. Stimulate primitive virtues

Primitive virtue is the moral values deep down inside human spirit that is accepted and respected by the crowd. Primitive virtue has a great power that can defeat any suspicion and conservativeness, because most people believe that virtue is very important, and life cannot go well without it.

Primitive virtue includes 9 true values existing over time. Those who use them subtly can have great influence on the behavior of the crowd miraculously.

- *What are they?*

- *"They are: religious belief, fairness, compassion, loyalty, courage, progressive desire, wise behavior, self-esteem and submission to the majority".*

- ⋏ *Religious belief:*

---

[2] Y.A. Watching movies made a student leave home to roam the world. (2004). At: http://nld.com.vn/phap-luat/xem-phim-khien-mot-hoc-sinh-bo-nha-phieu-bat-91751.htm [Date of Access: Oct 5th, 2012]

When people put their faith in a religion, a savior or a saint, they rarely dare to make any detrimental judgment to the supreme beings. They would never dare doubt the preciseness of the commandments. They worship fervently, and believe resignedly.

Hence, since ancient time, people have taken advantage of religious beliefs to encourage the martyrdom of faithful followers, serving for personal hidden benefits under the implementation of a sacred belief.

Nowadays, invisible rulers[3] know how to manipulate the religious spirit subtly in business.

He knows that human beings are often too dependent on their assumption and inference in everything. They often ponder about the past and worry about the future seemingly unstable. Hence, everyone prefers all things that can better prepare them for the future.

Therefore, everyone is convinced that "persistently brushing in the morning and before going to bed with toothpaste X is no longer an usual act, but a necessary ritual to protect their health and happiness, just like burning incense daily to be at peace in a life full of risks and uncertainties". It's a real example illustrated the application of religious beliefs in the field of business.

> ⊀ *Fairness* praises honesty, human rights and the demand of clear distinction between right and wrong.

Fairness stimulates anger, and fighting spirit against injustice. An Invisible ruler can create a story contains injustice and call for action against it. The action of the masses indirectly generates benefits for him.

My friend, a classic illustration praising "fairness" is the "Torch of Freedom" (1929) calling for gender equality which has helped increase the sales of tobacco firms. Women smoking were concerned to be a symbol of women emancipation and equality with men.

---

[3] Review Chapter 1 "Invisible rulers, who are you?"

⅄ *Compassion* is synonymous with wisdom. Compassion promotes love and tolerance.

The message calling for blood donation is often "blood is thicker than water". You have noticed that, this message promotes humanity in sharing precious drops of blood to save the lives of unfortunate people. The message is brief, concise, and easy to understand. It appeals to human compassion. It is about love.

⅄ *Loyalty* always goes hand in hand with faithfulness and a deep admiration for the origin. PR practitioners often use this virtue to call for purchase and consumption of local products of local enterprises.

⅄ *Courage* praises the recklessness and courage.

⅄ *Progressive desire* praises the efforts to promote social development, making the world a better place, and elevating the quality of people's lives. It motivates people to always keep striving and growing.

⅄ *Wise behavior* praises the judiciousness, moderation, restraint and prudence, such as calling for "smart consumption".

⅄ *Self-esteem* criticizes bad habits of keeping up with vainglory, frivolity, egotism and distorting the truth. Dignity cheers for modesty.

⅄ *Submission to the majority* is the submission of an individual under the will of the crowd. It makes one feel more comfortable agreeing with the opinion of the majority, rather than their own choice.

11. Stimulate penitent instinct

Penitent instinct triggers human penitence afterward mistakes. It makes people feel guilty and deeply painful that they always want to be free from it to get a peace of mind.

It creates negative feelings in contrast to the original virtue. PR practitioners can stimulate this instinct to create an uncomfortable feeling, and depression to motivate penitence-modification in humans.

To understand the application of this kind of instinct, let's analyze the following message: "We must be grateful to the soldiers, because the peace which we are enjoying is the result of their noble sacrifice. We must support them with all of our sincerity and all our efforts, even it is just a few cents. "

This is a message mobilizing people to contribute to the preparation of a war. You have realized that the message was created for us (those who enjoy a peaceful life) to feel sorry for the soldiers who are disadvantaged in all aspects. The message hints us to donate money for the army, as this can make us gather some compassion for them. I completely support it.

You see, the penitent instinct has big impact on human behavior according to the main purpose of the creator.

12. Stimulating belief in established prestige

Established prestige is one type of supreme power dominates our reasons. It has the power to paralyze all of the attack. It likely prevents us from resistance from within. Its power is so tremendous that it is capable of preventing us to see things as their natures. Unreliable things supported by prestige will not be suspected.

In fact, trust which is earned by established prestige can strongly suppress any of our reasoning. So when faced with this kind of belief, our reasoning will be destroyed easily. Therefore, using the prestige of an individual, or an organization to create belief and to mobilize the support of the crowd is one of the most important principles of PR secret.

13. Stimulate tit for tat instinct

Naturally, we human should appreciate someone for doing us a favor. In given chances, we willingly repay them with something equivalent or more valuable than what they gave us. However, we would like to return greater pain than what the enemy has done to us.

- *"How come?"*

Most people are always influenced by their natural instincts to response according to the law of balanced emotion. If received benevolence, they will reciprocate, or when they are attacked, they will revenge. They want to balance the fluctuating emotions.

So if enterprises want to be owned by clients, or to gain the support of the society, they should actively disseminate what they want to reap. How?

Create favors unconditionally to gain sympathy, reciprocation, and long-term support of consumers.

For instance. Enterprises supply their products for victims of natural disasters; offer emergency medical care for victims of accident; or provide free vaccines and medicines for poor patients.

Their unconditional kindness would lead to a positive return from the community. They will naturally tend to say good things about enterprises, to buy, to use or to consume the products that are "useful to the community ".

For instance. When building houses, I will buy steel from companies that are serious about building dream houses for unfortunate people who always strive to pursue a better life. I will buy boxes of instant noodle of the companies that volunteer to supply food for starving victims of natural disasters, floods and epidemics. I will buy the drug from pharmacies giving free medications for poor children... because I love to do it. Buying these products make me feel comfortable and happy.

Note:

When stimulating tit for tat instinct, PR practitioners should pay attention to creating a reasonable level of gratefulness, because too big ones could make people feel ashamed, evade or overreact.

---

14. Stimulate consistency in word and action

Take a look at the below example before starting to study this type of stimulation.

Siuation.

On Sunday morning, a twenty year old girl next door in a tight red
T-shirt, white short skirt and sexy black stockings approached the

guy's house. She asked if her relatives could park 2 motorcycles in his large yard. She said that his home was not only broad but also safe.

This seemed too easy to a generous man. He agreed... Half an hour later, she shyly asked to add 4 other ones. The young man hesitated a bit but he could not refuse since he was generous. He agreed.

Then he had to keep eyes on the 6 moto-bikes to ensure they were not stolen. Time flied, 1 hour then 2 hours, 3 hours, he looked forward to her to taking back those inanimate engines.

Crazy! He did not want to sit there and wait. But there was something compelling him to act that way. What is that?

Through this case, we can identify some deep causes have influenced his action.

He agreed to lend his large yard for parking because the sexual instinct of a man wanted to maintain an amicable relationship with the beautiful neighbor. He was willing to sacrifice his comfort to impress her.

Then he agreed to add four more moto-bikes to protect the consistency of his generosity. Watching the moto-bikes, and being afraid that they were stolen are from his desire to protect the belief the girl has attributed to his home - safety. Also, if those bikes were stolen, his ego would severely get hurt, so he had to take care of them.

You can see that by just a simple suggestion of the girl was able to compulsively put an array of mysterious pressure on the behavior of a guy. Thus, the consistency in word and action has been inspired by people's commitment with their initial affirmation. It presses their following actions to be consistent with their words, and actions that they do not want to do earlier.

- *"How much can we manipulate this power in business?"*
- *"Much more than you think!"*

And you just need to grab a key philosophy: "Create the opportunity to make target public groups to have to pledge to us by promises or by handwritings. Consistency in the promise and the text will coercive them, forcing them to comply with the commitment".

Suggestion 1. Practitioners can filter the list of clients with high turnover, inviting them to a party dedicated to loyal clients, then asking them to sign on an honor roll (for evidence).

This evidence cannot be reversed and everyone can see it. It affects the behavior of customers, strengthens their beliefs and actions, simply because they cannot deny that they have committed and that other people have seen them doing so. Their ego will make it difficult for themselves.

Suggestion 2. Enterprises hold a contest of writing comment on new products with the main prize is these products itself.

Sounds simple but this strategy is rather crafty. It makes contestants rack their brain to compile very nice comments on the new product.

This even makes them believe that the new product is perfect. At large, this technique has drawn a lot of participants because of the greediness. It makes a lot of people spend great efforts praising the new product and seduce the whole community the products' new features.

How is the result? Only a few individuals get rewards, many of the rest become foolish ephemera.

Suggestion 3. Practitioners treat journalists as loyal friends.

To appreciate the favor of PR practitioner, journalists often respond with an adequate kindness. They will promise to help businesses in professional journalism. The promise is just that small, neither detrimental nor helpful to anyone, but it is a pledge. It will be the first important step for practitioner to move on his more daring requirements.

15. Stimulate flattery instinct

- *"Do you like being flattered?"*

- *"Oh, of course not! I do not enjoy the deceit".*

- *"Oh come on, you would love to be flattered whether you're trying to deny it. Even when hidden under many layers of your reasons, your ego always make you crave to be important, cherished and admired by everyone ".*

Flattery always has a great impact on human behaviors. By reasoning we know that these guys are trying to seek a certain benefit from us, but we still like to believe in their praises, because our ego is always longing to be caressed.

In fact, every 40 year old woman is happy when a man praises them for their youth. Despite knowing that it is just a blandishment, but they would find all the arguments to convince themselves that, "he is reasonable." They cannot go against what they want to believe.

And all men would love to be praised for his bravery against all adversities by a beautiful girl. Receiving sweet praise, he will rummage his old memories to look for convincing evidences, then nodding repeatedly out of satisfaction for quite a correct remark of the beautiful girl. She is definitely right!

She is not right about him, but right in stimulating his flattery instinct.

My friend, although someone uses this flattery technique sophisticatedly, cordial blandishments always bring the best performance, because it satisfies one's desire to be great.

We ourselves must be someone great (politician, businessperson, scholar, doctor, engineer, celebrity ...) and the desire to be someone great is a pain in the spirit of each person always.

Therefore, it is not natural that we often have feelings and a desire to satisfy the aspirations of those who praise us regarding the models that we want to become. I mean, blandishment is really powerful in guiding us into the trap of promise.

- *How do PR practitioners use this technique?*

In a subtle way, PR practitioner should flatter his customers to gain their support and respect.

– *"How?"*

Just praise their children. We will praise their intelligence, talent; we will take care of their children as of our children. If we also love people that they love the most (even more than themselves), they will reciprocate our love.

Therefore, there are some interesting ideas for PR practitioners in expressing their praise for clients' kids as follows:

Suggestion 1. Organize a feast day for children of big customers on the International Children's Day (June 1st) to maintain a close relationship with them.

Suggestion 2. Give scholarships, books for children of employees on the occasion of year end summary.

Suggestion 3. Donate toys that stimulate intelligence and creativity to the children of employees, because these significant toys are always attractive to parents. They will be thankful for their companies. They will keep it in their mind and strive to work harder.

16. Stimulate herd mentality

– *"What is herd mentality?"*

Herd mentality is a special psychological state when a crowd had the same hunch about something (positive or negative) that is about to happen. Once there is a sign that it begins to happen, the first reaction will entail mass imitation of others and it keeps going viral in the whole society.

Nowadays, the power of the internet even strongly supports the technique of stimulating the herd mentality. It spreads false information freely. It disseminates the fear easily. It has people in a constant state of insecurity. It warns them to get ready for action. They act to get for a certain bargain or to avoid a threat that could be detrimental if they react slowly. They all have no idea about an unidentified source of information that is inducing them. They are all unconscious.

Illustration.

Enterprises will offer special sale program with a desirable price of a new product that has many advantages.

All people who viral this program on their facebook wall will have change to win this product. So, they'll try to spread this exciting news to create a pandemic, enticing those who enjoy cheap price coming in flocks.

Their participation will be a tool cheering for the emerging trend of this new product. Their enthusiasm for rare bargains will be used as an evidence to create the illusion for the rest of world about the favorite of a new product.

The herb mentality instinct will make itself complete, people will imitate each other to buy. They may tell you that "they are about to buy that product because it is unique. My friend just bought it yesterday, no one has the same."

17. Stimulate human intuitions

Intuition is the hunch, or inner feelings guiding our decisions and actions. Intuition can directly create people's behaviors that do not need to be processed by their logic thinking.

There are two types of intuitions: specialist and strategic intuitions.

Specialist intuition was formed early because children's brains know how to analyze good and bad information ... and to store them as a source of reference data.

In other words, it is based on the experience and information gathered from the past in order to have immediate reactions and decisions when dealing with similar problems / situations.

Strategic intuition was formed from discrete data from many situations, and sources that people have gathered and connected into a meaningful initiative.

Intuition appears in human mind all of a sudden to create a complete picture. The picture contains an innovative solution and a firm belief in success.

18. Stimulate survival instinct

In critical situations, survival instincts will awake the hidden potential within that normally people often does not recognize it. Survival instinct helps us defend ourselves against dangers to protect our lives.

Survival instinct is a kind of the earliest instinct of human beings, since deep down inside our consciousness; we understand that death is the end. If the death occurs, it will be game over. We don't want it that way.

My friends, the power of survival instinct is extraordinarily huge. To protect the life of the subject, the survival instinct beats everything blocking its path. It easily get rid of the ego, pride, face and morality. Also because of the domination of the powerful survival instinct, stimulating it in order to benefit the business is extremely attractive (see case study 5.2).

Case study 5.2:

The safest car in the world

The New V40 model of Volvo auto has just been certified as the world's safest cars in Euro NCAP[4].

---

[4] My Lan. (2012). *Volvo 40 - The safest car in the world*. At: http://www.tinmoi.vn/volvo-v40-xe-an-toan-nhat-the-gioi-011028116.html [Date of Access: Jan 18th, 2013]

> The new V40 was rated in four aspects (interior safety, children's safety, pedestrian's safety and safe assistance). Its safety has been rated up to 98% for adults, 75% for children and 100% for supporting standards.

In the story of V40, the safety was praised and human life was given particular prominence.

- *"Do you have any sympathy for V40?"*

- *...*

For those who do not care about safety, just go to the orthopedic hospital to see the victims of traffic accidents. Visit there to understand thatwell beings and safety of life are so precious. I especially like the V40. I am into safety.

Box 5.3: Warning 3

I cannot wait to share with you my serious note about ethical issues when using natural instincts to adjust human behaviors.

No matter what purpose (competition in business, politics or religion) it is, before doing anything, you should ask yourself the 3 following questions:

- Accordingly, does influencing human behavior by stimulating their natural instincts violate ethical code?

- Can we convince customers in other ways?

- Is it fair for those who are affected?

The three questions above will guide you before using 18 techniques to stimulate human instincts. As for those who see morality as something flexible, the law and the karma would be the judge of his dark actions.

5.2. Adjusting childhood belief

- *"What is childhood belief?"*

- *"Which elements generate childhood belief of a person?"*

- *"How do we manipulate that childhood belief?"*

192

Childhood belief is the experience accumulating in people's mind from childhood about what should be and should not be done, as well as good and bad things.

Childhood beliefs are so profound that they become people's immutable preconception later in life. It is a factor leading to the selection with very little judgment, because it is so clear and easy to understand that people will immediately make decisions according to their personal experience.

Once finding out the early childhood belief of a person, PR practitioners can easily take advantage of it to persuade him to trust and act upon their guidance.

As far as I am concerned, there are 3 key components forming childhood belief which are are *childhood upbringing, parents and faith.*

- *Childhood upbringing* writes on immature souls direct feelings about life, as well as survival experience of the world around them.

It includes culture, living environment, growing condition, education, family condition and events that have happened along the way. They engrave on children's brain with values and beliefs that are not easily denied later in adult life.

They mold the child's perspective toward life ever since. They become a special len through that the child would look at their life consistently. They shape the social behavior of the child later on.

So to speak, a child's upbringing lefts memories and obsession that can affect strongly the his mind, thus influencing his behavior down the line .

> "Some childhood wounds would never heal, they're just forgotten
> for some time for us to grow up, then coming back formidably."
> (Marc Levy – a French writer)

Those old memories are likely detrimental to the child's consumption subsequently. For example, if in his childhood, the child has witnessed the misery of his family for lacking wealth, he would probably tend to find ways to make more money afterwards because for which his family was shattered.

With such mentality, he rarely wants to keep money, or wants to save it and to invest. He is suffering from a certain psychological disease. He hates money although money itself is only a medium of exchange.

- *His parents* have a strong influence on his perception, psychology, attitudes, thinking, and reaction towards life.

In his mind, he thinks he owns his parents so much that he just does things according to their wish to pay off the debt of giving his birth and raising him. Growing up obediently, he would look at life with the attitude and behavior framed by his parents.

Actually, parents cram into children prejudices, stereotypes of attitudes and behaviors as well as reaction to a particular incident. Thus, children learn about life mostly from their parents.

For example, the child will forgive those who show repentance if his parents are generous; or he tends to be vengeful to satisfy his anger if his parents are ruthless.

With these beliefs and views, parents have imposed upon their children a certain personality that even they themselves did not recognize.

- *Faith* is what people create and attribute to children's soul in an early age which will become their belief.

The child will become an honest man if his parents and people around him assert so; or he will be wicked if everyone believes that his nature is very bad and cannot be different.

Ultimately, we have known that childhood belief was formed from three key factors are *childhood upbringing, parents and faith.*

Please return to the main question:

- *"How do we manipulate childhood beliefs in the field of PR?"*

Good question, but to make it clearer we can ask: Since adult's upbringing, parents and faith are very hard to change, then how can PR create in children a good faith about the product?

This is either a million-dollar question or a too dangerous one about "PR to children". It is dangerous because the answer is the philosophy of dark PR.

That philosophy is:

To build trust for the young potential customer group, dark PR practitioners will create favorable conditions for the children to be constantly exposed to their brand through toys, amusement parks, impressive events, or cute cartoon characters along with magical fairy tales - things that closely link to the name, color and logo of the product, are repeated again and again to engrave in the children's mind.

– *"For what?"*

When they grow up, those sweet memories will turn them into a force of powerful consumers willing to support the products that have had a soft spot in their heart since childhood when they did not have enough awareness to choose them[5].

– *"You have understood the philosophy, haven't you?"*
– *Do you support this approach?*

The answer depends on your perspective.

5.2. Influence the self-determination

– *"What is self-purchasing decision?"*

– *"What factors influence our decision?"*

– *"How can PR help in guiding consumers to buy the products?"*

Self-purchasing -decision is the analysis and evaluation (based on habits, knowledge, prejudices, beliefs, and experience) of a consumer to make a decision whether to buy a certain good or not.

---

[5] The idea is presented only to warn the community about dark PR techniques that should be strictly controlled.

In order to influence the self-purchasing decision of the crowd, the power of PR can influence *the awareness* of shoppers by two techniques:

» Offer them knowledge about the value and benefits of the products to promote their consumption needs,

» Attribute the product to images of being fashionable or trendy, youthful or dynamic, elegant or luxury, aristocratic or classy, durability or quality... to provide customers with an invisible value that they are craving.

To understand these two techniques, we will analyze the role of PR in 6 stages of self-determination as follows:

1. Aware of demand

The demand for a certain type of goods arises from human's desire to a convenient daily life or because they have just discovered a practical and beneficial feature of products that trigger the demand.

In this (1) stage, PR practitioners have an important role in triggering or creating an urgent need, meanwhile attracting public attention and concern about a product that is able to meet their needs.

2. Seek information

When people have known that they need a product / service to satisfy their demand, or to solve a problem in life, they will take the initiative to seek information about the products / services from many providers, many different companies. They want to buy good products at a right price and with a good after sales service. They want to compare options.

In stage (2), PR practitioners start to persuade customers by giving them chances to experience the products and to disseminate good stories about the social value of products / services on the media channels that target customers can easily access to.

3. Compare and Consider

Consumers will compare, and consider buying products according to their criteria. Some are serious about the quality, or brand name, some might go for price. That is in theory.

According to real experience, consumers will compare the products according to the following factors: the prestige of manufacturers, price, features, performance, advantages and disadvantages, warranty policy, promotion policy / discount, or shipping.

In this (3) stage, the quality of the product, distinctive features, pricing policy, and direct consulting services are core elements to convince consumers to purchase.

4. Purchase

Customers will only buy when they realize that the money they spend is adequate to or below the usage value and image value that the product gives them.

– *"What is the role of PR practitioner in stage (4)?"*
– *"Practitioner should review the effect of previous stages (1, 2, 3)"*

5. Use, experience and evaluate

During this period, it is neither PR messages, fine ads, the promise nor prestige of hundreds of years of the manufacturers that affect the customers, but the real feelings of consumers about products that will persuade them to trust in the enterprise and their products.

During stage (5), the role of PR practitioners is to carry on sending customers documents, video manuals and how to repair minor faults of products, while recording their feedback and comments (via email).

6. Continue shopping, or abandon the product / service

With their experience about the products / services, customers will decide to continue or to abandon the product / service, even to boycott. They may also criticize or convince others to stay away from the products. They ruin the reputation of the enterprise.

During stage (6), if the final feeling of clients is negative, PR practitioners should become an ambassador of peace. They have to learn the honest feedback from customers, then retransmitting it to responsible departments of the company to find solutions. If their feeling is positive, PR practitioners continue their mission which is customer care and referring them to other product lines.

Transition

Dear friends, through Chapter 5, I hope that you have gained many useful insights, especially when we have traveled together for such a long way.

If you have also completed Chapter 2, 3, 4, then you are ready to take it to a higher level of strategic thinking and applying effectively the power of PR in business.

– *"But what would help lift us up?"*

– *"It is a good question!"*

It is the art of building a comprehensive PR strategy with

- Strategy of sales promotion,
- Strategy of managing the mutual relationship between an enterprise and its target public groups,
- Strategy of Retaliation in unfavorable situations.

In addition to meticulously describe how to build these 3 strategies, the book will provide you with practical case studies to help you truly understand them.

– *"Ready to begin?"*

6

The art of building a comprehensive PR strategy

GENERAL CONTENT

The fourth supreme art is *the art of building a comprehensive PR strategy*.

When applying this ruling wisdom in the field of modern PR, the word "comprehensive" is very satisfactory, because it describes the three overarching PR strategies that support efficiently the survival and the development of any commercial organization, which are to push up the consumption of goods; to gain the support of the crowd; and to fight off negative effects of external forces from the market.

Named exuberantly in terms of modern PR, those 3 PR strategies are:

1. Strategy of sales promotion,
2. Strategy of managing the mutual relationship between an enterprise and its target public groups,
3. Strategy of Retaliation in unfavorable situations.

These three strategies are guided by the fourth ancient ruling wisdom: "To be able to change the behavior of the crowd, we should be able to change their attitude first".

Each strategy has different roles and purposes, and all of them have a tremendous power influencing the crowd's behavior. What will you be able to achieve if you apply all 3 types of power skillfully?

W elcome to Chapter 6 after you have gained necessary knowledge about the art of creating, spreading messages, and adjusting human behavior to influence the crowd's behavior .

Therefore, this is the golden time for us to discuss the art of building a comprehensive PR strategy to combine all these arts into an extreme power.

Before talking about it on a deeper level, we should understand the following two basic things:

- *"What is a PR strategy?"*
- *"Is it necessary to me?"*

On the basic level, PR is often detained in elementary functions such as issuing press releases and drafting speeches for the board of executives.

And on this level, PR practitioners are more into flashy propagandas than in-depth PR strategies.

Hence, the work of PR practitioners is merely operational: sending journalists press releases telling good things about an enterprise in hope that its names will be mentioned in published articles. This is not a strategy. It is more like a tactic, and "PR strategy" is just an ambiguous and beautiful word.

On a higher level, the role of PR is very different. Whenever we mention PR, we must mention "PR strategy". Enterprises need PR strategy to constantly educate and to enlighten the society about long-term business goals of enterprises. Enterprises need PR strategy to protect their reputation, or at least to put in, and to improve customer's trust over their incident in the past.

In fact, a lot of negative information and articles about enterprises are still stored on the internet for a long term, such as catastrophes, violation of consumers' right, or breach of business ethic.

These bad news can always be dug up, and recalled anytime by anyone that wants to learn about enterprises. This means people can "pull out" the past of enterprises to evaluate, to comment, or to give attribute whenever they want, hence allowing bad preconceptions about the enterprises to be generated anytime.

With this vision, PR is obviously not beautiful when someone claims that he is working in an upscale field with the relationship with media, but PR is a smokeless industry that really needs people who are wise, mature, thoughtful and adept.

Understanding the art of building a comprehensive PR strategy is very useful for those who do not want to be influenced by bad people in term of attitudes, opinions and behaviors. Also this is very useful for those who want to design effective PR strategies.

In chapter 6, I will show you how to build the 3 most important types of PR strategy :

- ✿ Section 6.1. Strategy of sales promotion,
- ✿ Section 6.2. Strategy of managing the mutual relationship between an enterprise and its target public groups,
- ✿ Section 6.3. Strategy of Retaliation in unfavorable situations.

6.1. Strategy of sales promotion

⊾ *What is an effective sales promotion strategy?*

It should be able to bring enterprises maximum benefits in:

- Sales volume: increasing sales in distribution channels,

- Brand name: is well known, recognized as high-quality products, supported by customers, and linked to positive properties (like convenient, safe, classy and trust-worthy),

- Customers: get new customers or retain old ones.

To achieve this, as for PR strategy, we should clarify the needs hidden deep down inside consumers' minds to entice their actions.

In addition, the PR tools have to target to right audiences, thereby generating compelling message at the right time to induce their purchase.

⋏ *Three approaches of PR strategy for an effective sales promotion*

Dear friends, the trust of customers of the product / service is the key factor determining the success of brand.

If customers have no belief in the product / service, they will doubt and deny them. We human are learning how to suspect and suspicion always has a strange power, it easily change our intention to purchase at first.

- *"But what is the belief of customers?"*
- *"What creates it?"*

The belief of customers of the product / service is their understandings and positive attitude toward the item at the highest level, through information about the product / service and through direct experience they get from the consumption of it.

Therefore, there are two things that are needed to be done to promote sales revenue, which are:

- ✿ Strengthening the crowd's interest in product / service. Making them interested in or longing for the item.
- ✿ Developing a PR strategy generating buying pressure on the crowd for a particular item. This strategy could persuade, threaten, or promise to definitively settle anxiety, and sorrow; or commit to bringing satisfaction to buyers.

To strengthen the attention and to create a pressure in the crowd, there are 3 approaches in strategy of sales promotion:

1. Positive approach
2. Negative approach
3. Story-based approach

PR STRATEGY FOR SALES PROMOTION IN THE POSITIVE APPROACH

PR strategy for sales promotion in a positive approach (aka positive PR strategy) focuses on the promises of satisfying the desire originated from a certain insecurity of the target customer groups, forcing their aspiration for purchase.

For instance. Dairy companies understand the psychology of moms that always want their little children to be healthy and smart. But in fact, children become pale, sick and are very vulnerable to infection. Therefore, the positive PR strategy will make a commitment with moms that their products will help children stay healthy and smart.

Illustration article:

> Soon after birth, children are faced with a series of potential hazards while their immune system is still weak. Therefore, they are susceptible to respiratory diseases, inflammatory diseases, diarrhea...
>
> In this situation, the maternal colostrum is an invaluable source of nutrition to help improve quickly the immune system protecting the baby's health. Colostrum can be seen as a natural vaccine which is absolutely safe because it contains a large amount of globulin (IgG) that helps children avoid intestinal infection.
>
> Through researches, experts have identified cow's colostrum containing IgG and components similar to maternal colostrum. Interestingly, cow milk has even a bigger content of IgG then maternal colostrum...
>
> "Milk X" with precious colostrum is the latest product of SBT specializing in colostrum and infant formula from New Zealand. For many years, milk X has been widely used in many countries around the world to help improve and complete babies' immune system, keeping infectious diseases at bay.

You have realized that, the positive message of SBT company is "Milk X contains valuable colostrum, and is widely used in many countries around the world to help improve and complete the immune system of babies, keeping infectious diseases at bay."

- *"Will Moms of frequently sick kids be interested in milk X?"*

- *"Yes!"*

Case study 6.1:

PR strategy for sales promotion in a positive approach

Context:

University C specializes in training technical staff and workers. Every year, this university trains about 30,000 students.

It will be the University's 50th year of operation in 2015 and it will have the honor of receiving the 2nd class Labor Order from the government. Through this event, University C wants to implement a PR strategy to:

» Enhance public awareness of University C,

» Highlight the university achievements on training which will be beneficial for the following year's enrollment.

Target audiences:

» Customers: Students (grade 10, 11, 12) of high schools across the country;

» National Training and Education Division.

Positive PR strategy:

Phase 1: Enhance public awareness of "University C" with the award ceremony

   Before the event:

1) Editorial: to tell a moving story about the school's arduous journey of 50 years telling its formation and development and to announce the ceremony granting them the second class Labor Order Medal, then to publish it in 20 official newspapers, 15 large websites (aimed at parents, pupils and students).

---

2) TV documentary: to make report on the 50-year journey of education by interviewing the principal, teachers and students, then broadcast in primetime on a national television station, which in turn will be broadcast in 9 major cities across the country.

3) Yearbook: to build records of essential facts during 50 years, and there would be 2,000 copies for state agencies, universities, faculty members and students.

4) Career expo: to organize career expos for senior students by inviting 50 enterprises (whose production activities are equivalent to subjects that they have been training such as business management, tourism, banking, insurance, IT, Chemical and Food Technology ...) for exhibiting, and branding 2-3 days before the event.

In the event: the medal ceremony was broadcasted live nationwide with the participation of 2,000 people, including government officers, the press as well as typical lecturers and students of the university.

Phase 2: Highlight the university achievements on training which are beneficial for the following year's enrollment

After event:

1) News release: 50 newspapers, 10 television stations, and 5 radio stations that simultaneously talk about University C thanks to the quality of its training over the last 50 years and their honor to receive the Medal from The president.

2) Editorial: to publish the Praise and Congratulations Letter of the President, together with the images of the medal in over 40 newspapers, and 20 largest online newspapers in the country.

3) Old student testimonial: to publish numerous articles on the education quality of University C and on current successful alumni holding high positions in their career.

4) Business testimonials: to publish many good reviews of big enterprises about the quality of graduates of University C.

5) Government testimonials: to post positive remarks of the Ministry of Education about the contribution of University C in the development of high quality human resources for the country.

6) Forum seeding: for students to express their pride of being part of the university C.

7) Contest: to hold learning contests on the achievements of University C over the past 50 years with attractive prizes. Contestants are all high school students nationwide. The contest will take place on the internet.

8) Website and Facebook of University C: are used as an official information portal to of pictures, articles and reports during the campaign.

Project timeline: phase 1 (one month) and phase 2 (two months), with the interference between two stages.

Budget: 100.000 USD

* Note: To protect the privacy of clients mentioned in the case study, I have changed their names and revised other details.

Discussion question:

1) What are the evidences making you realize that this is a PR strategy?

2) Did the PR strategy above convince students (grade 10, 11, 12) to enroll in this university? How?

PR STRATEGY FOR SALES PROMOTION IN THE NEGATIVE APPROACH

If the positive approach is to to give solutions to the festering problems, the PR negative approach advocates strongly to raise the awareness of a potential danger/loss that the target public groups do not realize, or pay little attention to it.

In other words, negative PR strategy proactively creates in public opinion a disturbing incident or a dire threat that attracts the attention of everyone. It evokes a dark yet guided premonition. It creates a necessary sense of fear in the community with a hopeful solution that forces them to act quickly to address their uneasiness.

For instance. Companies specializing in international education understands the common desire of parents is the full development of their children, expansion of their visions , and a good career, successful and happy life in the future. The negative PR strategy usually includes two steps:

First, (1) they evoke an enormous fear of damage on students' future resulted from wrong decisions of studying abroad, then (2) they paint a perfect picture titled "outstanding success" when people choose their service.

Illustration

"The desire of children studying in developed countries with advanced education (for children's comprehensive development in either extensive expertise or useful living skills, thus helping themselves get more advantage in career, income and promotion) has become the top concern and trendy option among parents currently.

Based on the experience of parents who have children studying abroad that get a degree from a prestigious university in the world, they also achieve other "degrees" on different aspects such as real life experience, international cultures, foreign languages ... This is why they have many outstanding advantages concerning income and career promotion..

Study abroad brings great benefits. But the issue being discussed here is how to avoid "loosing both money and future", or how to ensure the best result of studying abroad.

Before thousands of offers at present, making the right decision on which country and which school to study has always been the perennial challenge for parents. They get stuck due to many options.

Before this issue, Mrs. N, Director of International Education Group APA shared: "For Vietnamese students, New Zealand is currently a particularly attractive destination. During the recession period, studying in New Zealand has brought many benefits.

In particular, getting a visa to study in New Zealand is simple with quick processing time, GES visa ratio is 100% up to now. The cost to study in New Zealand is equivalent to the cost to study in an

Asian country (Singapore) and is only a half of the cost in the US. Aside from high quality education, studying in this country has many advantages in cost saving.

TCA school located near downtown Auckland is currently rated as the most brilliant option in New Zealand.

With professional learning environment, along with the dedicated guidance of lecturers, students can develop their personal potential to the highest degree and can achieve excellent results in their studies. After completing courses at TCA, students are more likely to be admitted to prestigious universities in New Zealand such as University of Auckland, AUT University, Massey University. "

You may have realized that by cleverly integrating the answer to the question "where to study abroad", it is the sales message of International Education Group APA. They suggest that "study in New Zealand to avoid "loosing both money and future" and TCA is the best option."

If you wish to study abroad, you will be interested in New Zealand and TCA school.

Case study 6.2:

PR strategy for sales promotion in a negative approach

Context:

The anti-motion sickness drug N (pills) of the AS pharmaceutical firm has led the market for years with approximately 50% of the market share.

However, it is facing a fierce competition from substitute products (in the form of patches) and many kinds of fake products with a lower price.

AS company has suffered from this situation. Loss of customers, sharp decline of revenue, along with disaster for the brands of AS because of the risk of consumers being hurt by the use of counterfeit drugs N is very large.

Goals:

>> Customers can distinguish between genuine products N versus counterfeit products;

>> Customers re-use drug N (pills).

Target audiences:

>> People over 18 years old;

>> In 6 big cities.

Negative PR strategy:

>> Create a collective awareness about a disturbing threat to human health when using the motion sickness patch, because this type of product contains scopolamine[1].

>> Spread negative information about the danger of scopolamine across the multiple information fronts from mass media to new media.

>> Create a collective demand for a good, safe, reliable and convenient product: "The N pill" with new wrapping.

Implement[2]

Phase 1: Use the voice of doctors and healthcare professionals to educate people about the dangers of scopolamine

Tools:

1) Expert editorial: Professional articles discuss about scopolamine, published in 20 mainstream newspapers, 15 popular websites and 10 homepages of large hospitals.

2) TV documentary: to report about victims of scopolamine.

3) Expert advice corner: to open healthcare consulting corner advising how to prevent motion sickness, published in 10 major newspapers.

---

[1] Scopolamine (aka Devil's Breath) is a drug that is used by criminals to wipe the victims' the memory and make them loose temporary consciousness. It is derived from Borrachero, a wild plant popular in Bogota, Colombia.

Source: Kenh14. (2013). *Hypnotic drug is real: "The Devil's Breath"*. At: http://kenh14.vn/kham-pha/doc-duoc-thoi-mien-co-that-hoi-tho-cua-quy-20120517025937559.chn [Date of Access: 5th Sep, 2013]

[2] Readers can review in details 114 PR tools in Chapter 4.

4) Press conference: to organize a press conference to share the official view of AS about the drug N that doesn't contain scopolamine to set people's mind at rest, as well as announcing the new wrapping to fight against counterfeit products.

Phase 2: Disseminate the dangers of scopolamine so that people would abandon the patch and switch to drug N

5) Forum seeding: to create buzz over 20 major forums on the subject of hazardous scopolamine in the patch and advise other to use drug N instead.

6) Hot blogger: to put up the narratives of 4 victims of anti-motion sickness patch containing scopolamine (accident, vomiting, blurred vision, fainting).

7) Advertorials: to publish 30 articles about the quality of drug N without scopolamine.

8) Consumer testimonials: to publish good feedback of consumers about product N of AS company.

9) Online consultant: to organize online counseling sessions on anti-motion sickness treatment with the sponsorship of AS.

10) Pharmacies activation: to promote product N in big drug stores across the country, and train staff about drug N, so they can advise consumers when being asked.

Prevention activities:

1) Prepare sufficient scientific evidence showing that drug N contains neither scopolamine nor any other substance that is able to cause similar side effects to consumers like the patch does.

2) Prepare completely business license, certificate of product quality and permit for circulating in the market.

3) Establish contacts with some influential figures (opinion leaders) and prepare response messages in case PR campaign gets reaction.

Project timeline: phase 1 (one month) and phase 2 (two months)

Budget: 150.000 USD

* Note: To protect the privacy of clients mentioned in the case study, I have changed their names and revised other details.

Discussion question:

1) Does the PR strategy above refers to a particular threat to people's health using the motion sickness patch?
2) Has the PR strategy above created a certain sense of fear in your mind, as well as given you a hopeful solution? What is that solution?

PR STRATEGY FOR SALES PROMOTION IN THE STORY-BASED APPROACH

Unlike the nature of positive PR strategy which is to offer solutions to an existing problem, and that of negative PR strategy is to scare people with a hidden disaster, the nature of story-based PR strategy is *storytelling*.

A story that is a valuable sharing lesson on one hand and a subtle purchasing hint on the other. Your product / service is a part of the story - that will make people want to hear and remember.

If comparing the 3 types of PR strategy for sales promotion, the story-based PR strategy is the most powerful because it is always more convincing for target public groups.

– *"Why is it more convincing?"*

Because a story touches to public concerns. It satisfies information needs of listeners, not on what enterprises need to say (positive PR strategy) nor threat alerts (negative PR strategy).

Saying so does not mean that we deny 2 previous kinds of strategy, because their effectiveness depends both on the specific requirements of clients when launching the product / service.

Case study 6.3:

PR strategy for sales promotion in a story-based approach

Context:

Company BCG is in top 10 largest PR firms in the market, and it has operated over 20 years.

At present, it is facing many difficulties in business. The reason is that many enterprises do not appreciate the power of PR in the business development.

BCG's research showed that 85% of companies said PR is media relations, organizing events, creating scandals, government relations, or organizing charitable activities.

To achieve its business goals, BCG wants to promote its services of public relations consulting to foreign enterprises (80%) and large domestic enterprises (20%). BCG wants to be the consulting leader in the market to retain existing customers and increase sales by 20%.

The main message BCG want to convey: "PR is currently an indispensable activity for the development of enterprises."

Available communication budget is 150.000 USD.

Implement:

Story-based approach

"How to achieve business goals effectively by PR?"

Approach:

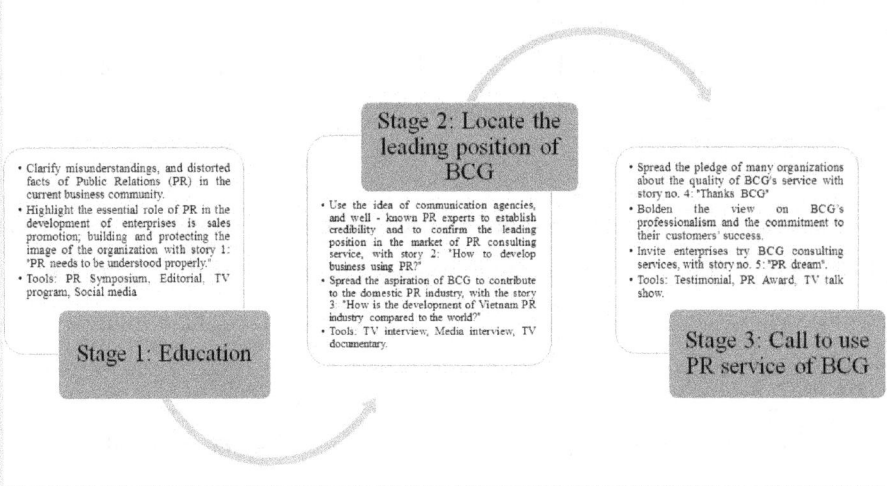

Stage 1: Education

- Clarify misunderstandings, and distorted facts of PR in the current business community.

- Highlight the essential role of PR in the development of enterprises is sales promotion; building and protecting the image of the organization with story 1: "PR needs to be understood properly."

- Tools: PR Symposium, Editorial, TV program, Social media.

Stage 2: Locate the leading position of BCG

- Use the idea of communication agencies, and well - known PR experts to establish credibility and to confirm the leading position in the market of PR consulting service.

- Spread the aspiration of BCG to contribute to the domestic PR industry.

- Tools: TV interview, Media interview, TV documentary.

Stage 3: Call to use PR consulting service of BCG

- Spread the pledge of many organizations about the quality of BCG's service.

- Bolden the view on BCG's professionalism and the commitment to their customers' success.

- Invite enterprises try BCG consulting services.

- Tools: Testimonial, PR Award, TV talk show.

* Note: To protect the privacy of clients mentioned in the case study, I have changed their names and revised other details.

C) Steps to build a PR strategy for effective sales promotion

My friend, if you are able to distinguish the three types of PR strategy for sales promotion, it will be a real party. And it will be more fun if you understand steps to build it.

Please immediately move on to the next section to learn the 8 steps that PR practitioners need to go through to build any kind of PR strategy for effective sales promotion.

> » **Step 1: Analyze public opinion**
> – *"For what?"*

To understand the current situation, prejudice, and views of the target audiences towards our products / services, so that PR practitioners can take them on to create an appropriate PR strategy.

The analysis should answer these questions:

o   How do consumers comment, acknowledge the product / service?
o   What kind of misunderstanding, and prejudice is detrimental to the product buying?
o   How do consumers understand about the product / service and its benefits?
o   What are current competitors' messages?
o   Which arguments can entice the buying behavior of consumers?
o   What communication activities are the competitors implementing? How?

   »   **Step 2: Situation Analysis**

To develop a practical and effective PR strategy, SWOT analysis about enterprises is the first thing to do, i.e. identifying their strength (S), weakness (W), opportunity (O) and threats (T).

Please note that, S and W are elements within the enterprise, and O and T are from the market.

And to support the comprehensive analysis for the identification of opportunity (O) and threat (T), PR practitioners may use PEST analysis.

PEST analysis helps identify factors that potentially have a impact on the industry that enterprises belong to, including:

o   Political factors, law - such as political stability, new legislation, trade protectionism, tax and corruption;
o   Economic factors - such as rate of inflation, interest, unemployment , GDP growth and cost of input materials;
o   Socio-cultural factors - like culture, consumption habit, education, literacy, or critical role of men and women in matters of life;
o   Technological factors - like applying new technology in manufacturing, energy saving and internet.

From findings from SWOT analysis, PR practitioners will understand the panorama inside and outside of enterprises, as well as have a lot of information to consider, create, and select PR approach.

If having great budget and conditions, PR practitioners can use market research service for SWOT analysis.

However, few companies have enough budget and eagerness to study the market comprehensively. These enterprises often do not want to pay a huge sum for accurate results similar to weather forecasts.

Because the result of the market study reflects only the past's market context, but cannot draw accurately the current picture. In addition, market researches often give incorrect results. Why?

Because when faced with the questionnaire, consumers often prefer using reasons other than the truth to answer, for when they are discussing in group to find the answer, they naturally tend to say what everyone thinks is right, they naturally do not want to be different; and in group discussion, they tend to hide their own perspectives when they see that their opinions are the minority; and whether their reasons is correct, it is just one of many elements generating the purchasing decision.

In summary, there are many reasons why consumers conceal the real motivation of their purchases, hence the market surveys are often unreliable.

> For instance. A woman praises a pink flower dress which fit her profusely because of its cool soft silk and delicate seams. She does not want to confess that it is the dress given by her husband; or
>
> A mother could list down endless reasons why she chooses formula Y for her child after learning of its nutritional components and also its potency on the other children. However, few people knows the real reason why she chooses to buy this milk due to the requirement of her hard-to-please mother in law; or
>
> A young man may explain why he only drinks beer Hanoi (a local beer), for it has the particular taste of his homeland. However, few people know the real reason why he chooses that beer because its

capacity is much larger than Heineken, and its price is much cheaper[3]and from 5th bottle onwards, when the tongue is numb, the taste of every kind of beer is the same, there is little or no difference at all.

Therefore, PR practitioners often get stuck:

o Even if they have budget to do market research, they can hardly find an accurate ground to create compelling messages and to choose media channels effectively, since market researches only reflect the results of the past.

o Not every PR project for sales promotion needs expensive and time consuming market research. Enterprises need to take full advantage of their business opportunities. They need something fast, practical and cost-effective.

o But market research is important and has its own value. Market research itself is not a random option. It is essential.

– *"So what should we do?"*

The answer to this dilemma is: PR practitioners still need to learn the market, but in ways that are faster, and more cost-effective depending on clients' years of experience or from experts and general information in reputable statistical reports.

To do so, PR practitioners need to draw a general picture of the market through answering the following questions:

Market overview of products / services at present

- For brands: is the target market a new market?

- What is the key sales channel / distribution?

- The purchasing power of existing consumers;

- The growth of the industry;

Å ——————————————————

[3] According to the survey of the average price in May 2013 in Vietnam: A bottle of Hanoi beer (450ml) costs 8,000 VND (nearly 0.4 dollars), while a bottle of Heineken beer (250ml) costs 22,000 VND (about 1 USD).

- The potential development of the industry;

- The media situation of competitors;

- The intervention, domination of law / state;

- The domination of current economic, political and social situation.

Overview of products / services being promoted

- The life cycle of products (new products, growth, regression ...);

- Recent feedback of clients, or media about the product / service;

- What are the advantages of products / services of enterprises when compared with opponents?

- How are they?

- Does it have anything disadvantage or shortcoming to avoid ?

- What are the convincing reasons to make consumers buy our product / service?

Learn about competitors

- What are their current products / services?

- What are their competitive products/ services?

- Market share;

- Sales distribution channel of competitors;

- Competitive level of their product / service (price, promotion, after-sales services, distribution channels);

- What is their message? Is it based on what facts?

- What are their communication channels?

- What kind of communication campaign they have been using or about to use?

- Who does PR consulting for them?

Other common understandings

- Does this project have any relationship with the running projects, or previous ones.

- Which timeline does PR practitioners need to pay attention to?

- Do enterprises coordinate with other agencies, or partners in implementing this project?

- If any, how to check and divide the budget consistently?

- Can this desired communication project be able to cause public opposition? Have we prepared the response?

» **Step 3: Set the goal**

This step helps PR practitioners determine what enterprises need to achieve in PR strategy for sales promotion. This is the foundation for evaluating the effectiveness of the entire PR program.

Below are some popular suggestions.

PR goals: What is the desire of enterprises using this PR campaign?

- For reputation:

    a. Improve the prestige of product / service on the consumption market.

    b. Reinforce the company's position as the leader in the field of insurance / consumption / education / food...

    c. Elaborate the image of enterprise to potential investors.

- For the community:

    d. Strengthen the relationship and build goodwill, as well as mutual understanding about enterprises.

e. Promote product / service with the main mission is to make a better life.

f. Create an exchange playground for learning, building a rich and useful source of information of a social issue, such as health care, child care, career counseling, job training…

Branding goal: What is the branding goal that enterprises want to achieve by this PR strategy?

- To ensure sales volume increases x%.

- To minimize the number of customers switching to competitors' products / services.

- To introduce new features, new wrapping to prevent fake goods.

Final destination: What is the final destination of this PR strategy?

- Consolidate / strengthen its position as a leader in this sector.

- Customers stay committed and loyal to the product / service for a long time.

» **Step 4: Identify target public groups**

We should be aware of target objects through following questions:

Who are our target consumers?

- Age

- Occupation

- Qualification

- Income

- Consumer Insight

- Geographical location

- Information channels that they often keep up with.

Do we need to target to:

- Press agencies

- Government, authorities

- Professionals, doctors, pharmacists, celebrities, vicars, priests, elders

- The masses

- The world

What do we want them to do?

- Consumers: to buy and to be loyal to the product / service;

- Press agencies: publish news, articles, and protect enterprise's reputation;

- Specialists, doctors, pharmacists: to promote products;

- Community: love, trust and support.

How can we convey the message to them?

- Consumers: transmit messages directly through seminars, trade fairs, contests, or indirectly through the press, TV, internet. But which newspapers, radio channels, web pages do they often check?

- Press agencies: convey the message directly through meetings, or indirectly via press releases, phone, email;

- Specialist, doctor and pharmacist: usually transmit messages directly through meetings, seminars.

- Community: usually transmit messages through mass media, TV, social network;

By defining the right target audiences and what they are looking for, PR practitioners will know how to create a persuasive message, and choose appropriate PR tools to transmit it to them in the most optimal way.

» **Step 5. Create compelling messages**

The art of creating messages were dissected very carefully in Chapter 3. It does not need to be repeated. And to ensure the message is suitable for PR strategy for sales promotion, you should determine what you need to convey through the following 4 suggestions:

- What is the best feature of the product / service?[4]

- What do we want to confess / send to target audiences (the general public / consumers / authorities / the press)?

- What do we want them to understand?

- Why do they have to act according to our call?

» **Step 6: Choose PR tools**

At this step, you start to realize that you are completely confident to choose and combine PR tools to convey the message with a far-reaching impact to influence the crowd's behavior (after studying Chapter 4)

This is very encouraging. And we also need to explore the *4 key elements* and *the coincidence between the target audiences* before making a final decision.

Table 6.1. Factors to be considered when selecting PR tools

4 KEY FACTORS	OVERLAP BETWEEN TARGET AUDIENCES
News channels of target audiences	Internal staff
Caste and segmentation of customers of product / service	Clients
Airing areas of messages	Share holders
Budget	Members of social organizations

Å ————————————————

[4] Author's note: A product / service can have many positive features, but to ensure a maximum media effectiveness, the message should focus on the most unique advantage of products / services compared to their competitors.

⅄ News channels of target audiences:

The budget is not infinite. It is limited. Therefore, to avoid waste, we must specify what customers usually watch, read, or listen and at where, when.

To do this, PR practitioners often estimate based on personal experience and the information gathered from newspaper ads (such as coverage, target readers, period release, circulation, broadcast time, broadcasting frequency ...).

PR professional need to conduct interviews with each typical customer groups to learn their habit of looking for information and their attitude towards each media channel they have approached. Then he would have many advantages of choosing the right media channels to spread his inspired message.

⅄ Areas to air of messages

Depending on the target market, PR practitioners will decide the channel that the message will go viral.

At the basic level, if enterprises have identified target markets which are the 6 major cities of the country, PR practitioners will strive to disseminate, and scatter the message on 6 local television stations, newspapers and websites, along with national coverage.

On a higher level, if the product / service is a common commodity, it should be widespread, but if you have not known where you should strongly focus on, PR practitioners should study the database of important customer groups - who create the majority of revenue for the organization. The PR practitioner needs to determine where this important customer group is as well as study their personalities, attitudes, lifestyles, ways of thinking, income and favorite information. They need to be taken care of and be constantly exploited.

⅄ PR budget

Comprehensively information coverage on the market, including the most remote corners, and alleys is the dream of PR practitioners. They feel happy to see their messages appear everywhere. But this cannot happen. The budget is finite and even more so, limited.

With a budget of 0, which PR tool should be chosen to call for fund to rebuild a dilapidated school located deep in a remote mountain?

With the budget (2 million USD) equivalent to the price of 4 million packets of noodles, what kind of PR tool that PR practitioners must choose to help instant noodles company get $ 4 million and a better sale condition?

Through these 2 examples, we can realize the importance of using PR budget effectively. It's really very practical.

- *"But how to optimize the PR budget?"*
- *"Convey convincing messages to the right target audiences through appropriate media channels with the lowest cost."*

For this, PR practitioners need to be clearly aware of the coincidence between target audiences.

⅄ *Recognize the coincidence between target audiences:*

An individual can be:

- an employee of an enterprise,
- a client of the enterprise,
- a shareholder of the enterprise,
- a member of a social organization.

For instance. A woman works for a confectionary factory, she is an internal employee of that firm. She purchases the company's products to consume, this means, she is also the company's consumer.

She is allowed to buy company's shares and to get dividends, this means she is a shareholder.

She is also a member of the local Red Cross, i.e. she belongs to a social organization. Her home is near the confectionery plant, i.e. she is a neighbor of the company, ie she can file a lawsuit against and request the factory to stop its operation…

There are two important things that are needed to be discussed here:

⅄ First off, people can be members of multiple groups.

This natural coincidence, in theory, allows PR practitioners use a few PR tools to get the view, and the awareness of all the individuals in any group, because of the existing coincidence.

But in fact, if the product / service is for people from all walks of life including many target groups, classes, ages (like toothpaste, soft drinks, mineral water, coffee, powdered milk, instant noodles...), its target customer groups are almost entirely belong to the general public group.

Therefore, PR practitioners prefer media channels aiming at the general public group, rather than splitting them into separate customer groups.

If the product / service is exclusively for a particular customer groups (for example, sea transportation, registry of ships, container leasing, fumigation), PR practitioners should select specialized media channels for this particular client group. What would we think if there is an article published in a daily newspaper for the masses telling "launching of ship building services from 100,000-150,000 tons?"

    ⅄ Secondly, the coincidence between target groups is inevitable, but that in itself implies a positive value for PR practitioners and enterprises.

When a person belongs to many groups, his discrepancy in this group will be broken when he is affected by the reason of another group.

For instance. The woman above will not file a lawsuit requiring the relocation of the plant because of noise, for this will make her lose her job. She will cool her family before the pressing issue, she will restrain the attack of her neighbors... to make time for the response from the board of directors. Thus, her belonging to many groups that interact with the company has converted this women from having this response to a different one, from criticizing to protecting it.

   » **Step 7. Budget and project timeline**

o Budget planning: there are 2 ways to plan

    ▪ First, ask directly, "How much is the budget for PR activities?"

    ▪ Secondly, plan it out based on the cost needed to achieve PR goals.

- Project timeline:
  - How long does it take to prepare the proposal?
  - How long does it take for customers to approve it?
  - How long to run the campaign?
  - How long to report, collect and close the project?

» **Step 8. Implementation and evaluation**

- Do PR programs need the sponsorship of professionals, government, or prestigious social agencies?

- The sphere of influence: international, national, regional / provincial, intra-enterprise?

- Which PR tools are mandatory?

- Mandatory pictures: logo, brand, social activities and charity?

Dear friends, after answering those 8 steps above, you will definitely make an excellent PR strategy for sales promotion as expected. This is a great excitement.

In addition, the most effective PR strategy for sales promotion depends on some conditions and criteria that you need to grasp.

- *"What are they?"*
- *"There are 3 conditions and 5 criteria."*

3 conditions:

- Condition 1. PR strategy will have a great effect if the leader has a "strong support" from the mass media. This means, its story still remains a priority despite the social context have generated many other hot stories.

- Condition 2. Each sector has its own characteristics. When practicing PR in many industries, you will notice that each sector has a specific strategy template using familiar PR tools.

↟ Condition 3. The participation of people in charge of the product in building a PR strategy for sales promotion is indispensable, because they had deep understanding about the strengths and weaknesses of the product / service, and customers and competitors' mind. Do not keep relying on PR consultants of PR agencies, they are just outsiders.

5 criteria:

My friends, no matter what industry you are practicing PR in, you should also pay attention to the following 5 criteria in developing a PR strategy to promote effective sales:

↟ Criterion 1. You must know the real problem of enterprises (bad products, high price, low sales, criticized, ostracized, misunderstood...) and must choose the most serious problem to solve.

↟ Criterion 2. You need to study Chapter 5 again to search for good ideas, because the source of big ideas for PR strategies is from that and also because the art of adjusting human behaviors supports greatly the construction of PR strategies.

✓ Criterion 3. For a brand new product / service in the market, an effective PR strategy is to focus on the messages about its features, uses, and benefits as well as to explain clearly the reasons why customers must buy it rather than sublime ideas.

✓ Criterion 4. PR strategy must revolves around the business philosophy of the enterprise. Often a business philosophy reflects the dream, mission, vision and experience of the founder.

✓ Criterion 5. PR Campaigns need a good human story to touch the crowd's hearts. We should understand that, once emotions touch emotions, suspicion and judgment disappear. Then there will be only support and backing left. Then the act of purchasing products / services that they like is always happens.

In summary, if these 8 steps are executed well, 2 conditions and 5 criteria are respected, I believe that you will get enough information to plan an excellent and standard PR strategy for enterprises' sales promotion.

6.2. Strategy of managing the mutual relationship between an enterprise and its target public groups

Dear friends, though the explanation in Chapter 2 (Section 2.3 B), you have understood why enterprises need the support of the crowd to survive and to develop sustainably.

Therefore, how to gain the support of target public groups is a key problem to be resolved this section 6.2.

According to the general philosophy, an enterprise will gain public support and sympathy when it meets their expectations in the long term. And because each target group has different expectations, to find out what their expectations are, we need to build a strategy on managing the mutual relationship between an enterprise and its target public groups. It consists of 5 steps:

» **Step 1: Determine target public groups**

Because of its production activities, enterprise must interact closely with many public groups - those who are likely to cause problems and affect their survival and development.

– *"Who are they?"*

They are

Customer	Producers	Enablers	Limiters
Current customers	Investors, shareholders, donors	Authorities	Competitors
Potential customers	Internal staff	Media	Opponents

Secondary customers	Suppliers	Experts	
		Alliances, distributors	

» **Step 2: Survey the outside context of the enterprise**

Learn the current situation:

↟ How do the media and the people recognize the industry that they belong to?

For instance. During Sep - Dec / 2011 in Vietnam, many mainstream newspapers reflected fiercely the fact that the infant formula's price had been increasing continuously, although the price of raw materials strongly had decreased, while the article said that milk was an essential good. The price was unfair to consumers and it seemed that consumers were pickpocketed by dairy companies.

So how should dairy companies react? What should PR practitioners advise the leadership? How should the message protect enterprises from being drafted?

↟ Determine the internal situation within industry.

Have enterprises belongs to this industry joined into an association to establish code of conduct?

Are members in solidarity for positive reaction to the negative media attack, or public opinion?

Is there any member playing dirty tricks on each other and who are whose victims? What PR practitioner has reacted?

↟ Define the enterprise's rank in the market.

Learn the forthcoming trend of public opinion:

↟ Learn the forthcoming trend of public opinion by Media Intelligence (see chapter 4)

- Learn the state administration policy, as well as advertising law, and bills by Authorities relations.

- Study the growth of the economy in the future, and difficulties that businesses will face (such as inflation, rising gas prices, raw materials) by authorities relations tool.

- Learn the causes and motives of the 'limited groups' against enterprises by using 5 defense tools.

The information gathered will be very valuable in planning communication strategies for enterprises.

» **Step 3: Survey the context within enterprises**

Understanding the information within the enterprise (about product / service, superiors' support, hidden obstacles) would be very useful for PR practitioners to suggest, and to deploy activities building organization's image.

- Learn the current quality of the product.

  PR practitioners should understand the quality of current products / services, the level of satisfaction of existing customers to recommend new improvements.

  If the product / service have a low, or medium quality or they have nothing special, enterprises should temporarily cease their promotion to focus on R & D activities.

- Define the uniqueness of products / services.

  We have to reveal all of the benefits that the product / service can bring to customers. Determine the kind of proud, satisfied, and comfortable feeling, or utility that only our product / service can provide consumers.

- Determine the power of PR department in the organization structure.

  Determining the position and power of PR department is quite important. It allows PR practitioners to foresee the pros and cons when submitting proposal, budgets, and resources for implementation, hence allowing them to prepare internal steps accordingly.

⋏ Analyze hidden obstacles

It is to define internal barriers influencing the effect of PR strategies. The two biggest obstacles are the lack of knowledge and the lack of commitment of the board of directors to PR activities.

Most leaders are often very adept in a certain profession, but it does not mean that they are excellent in all fields. An excellent sales manager has many opportunities to be promoted to general director. To run the business well, he must have a thorough knowledge of finance, research, production and development, marketing and PR...

When he attempts to get beyond his field of sales to other areas, he surely will face a state of "lacking of knowledge". His lack of PR knowledge will create understanding problem for him, thus he does not support PR practitioners.

If the power of PR department is inappreciable, if the general director does not understand the importance of PR activities, this planning should stop immediately in this step.

» **Step 4: Determine the goals**

⋏ Managing the mutual relationship between enterprise and its target audiences.

⋏ Building the support toward the enterprise in these important target public.

» **Step 5. Strategies for each target object group[5]**

FOR CUSTOMERS

Customers include: existing customers, potential customers, customers of customers.

Å ————————————————

[5]These following strategies will answer Case study 2.1 (Chapter 2).

a. Existing customers

» *Purpose 1*: build corporate image as an active and friendly member to the public through programs contributing to education and community development.

» *Tactics 1*:

⅄ Implement social activities beneficial to the community as charities, scholarships for poor students; long-term funding for shelters for orphans and the elderly; free products / services for the poor who do not have enough money to pay for products / services (drugs, special formula milk);

⅄ Sponsor (by cash or products) for campaigns such as environmental protection, safety in traffic, saying no to tobacco, blood donation, saving victims of flood, building bridges , or building schools in remote mountainous areas;

⅄ Hold a contest associated with the business name on a national scale aiming to praise the beauty of traditional culture, organizing training courses and job placement for workers, or walking for the green environment in the foundation day.

» *Purpose 2*: build business name by providing consumers products / services of high quality, improving the comfort and quality of life of the community.

» *Tactics 2*:

⅄ Convey useful information to customers about the product / service;

⅄ Create the experience using the product by offering free samples, holding seminars to disseminate the benefits of the product for consumers' daily basics;

⅄ Create a more frequent contact between customers and enterprises via a round communication channel, such as 24/7 hotline, forums, clubs, as well as company tour, sightseeing the manufacturing process and checking product quality at the factory.

b. Potential customers

» *Purpose*: Attract, seduce potential customers, competitors' customers.

» *Tactics*:

⅄ Enterprises can attract more potential customers thanks to the value added of the brand and attractive incentives.

⅄ Establish consulting channels, sources of data, or samples for those who have demand for such types of product so that they can easily interact, and learn about them.

For instance, dairy companies have a team of national consultants are ready to answer the questions of moms about nutrition for new born babies; the studying abroad company is always ready to provide instruction on how to get visa to study abroad or how to choose an appropriate country to study; or technology companies always have booths displaying products for customer to experience the sample.

⅄ For children's products, enterprises should give stimulating intelligence toys as a special offer along with products. For education service and health care, enterprises should offer trial vouchers, tuition vouchers, and free services vouchers to attract new customers.

c. Secondary customers: are potential clients introduced by existing clients.

» *Purpose*: take advantage of the relationship with existing clients to entice new customers.

» *Tactics*:

⅄ Set up *Appreciation and Recognition Policy* for any existing customer that can provide information of their relatives, or partners that have the demand for the product / service. The merit can be in form of supermarket coupons, vouchers, voucher for free products / services.

FOR PRODUCERS

This group includes: investors, shareholders, donors; internal staff; suppliers.

a. Investors, shareholders, donors

» *Purpose*: continue to keep their belief in enterprises.

» *Tactics*:

⅄ Establish communication channels to update accurately, completely, specifically, and timely for the investors, shareholders and donors about the operation of the business. Common PR tools are investor news release, PL reports, Q & A meeting, and Annual Report (see Chapter 4).

b. Internal staff

» *Purpose*: build the loyalty of employees and encourage them to maximize their strengths and talents to contribute to the organization.

» *Tactics*:

⅄ Acknowledge all the efforts whether big or small, as well as motivate and reward timely the initiatives, or ideas beneficial to the enterprise, using extra Benefit, BOD & employee meeting.

⅄ Consult Human resource department (HR) for timely adjusting the mechanism, or remuneration policy consistent with the market in order to retain talents.

⅄ Recognize and reward employee's initiatives in improving business efficiency of organizations.

⅄ Put their images on all publications to make them happy. They will show these glory articles, and videos (of the company) with their participation to their relatives and acquaintances.

c. Suppliers

Suppliers here are known as agencies providing freight, construction, fitting production systems, raw materials, legal advisory, finance (banks), compensation (insurance), or import and export...

» *Purpose*: encourage long-term collaboration with suppliers.

» *Tactics*:

⅄ Acknowledge all of the contribution of suppliers for the production activities of enterprises, using partner conference, and troop Ceremony (see chapter 4).

⅄ Learn, and study quotations to create negotiation strategies, adjust service charges, avoiding under coercion of suppliers and too high input cost.

<hr>

FOR ENABLERS

<hr>

> This includes: government, state management agencies; media; experts; alliances of distributors, dealers, department stores, shops.

a. Government and state management agencies

» *Purpose*: build and strengthen the relationship between enterprises and the government to become a relationship of management, cooperation, support and mutual benefit.

» *Tactics*:

⅄ Hangout at the right time to increase goodwill, and mutual understanding between enterprises and the government to promptly adjust the inadequacies in management policies.

⅄ Regarding the deployment, look back to 5 PR tools for the government, and state authorities, presented in Chapter 4, Section 1.4.

b. Media

» *Purpose*: build mutual understanding, as well as strengthen ties of cooperation, and support for the media source.

» *Tactics*:

⅄ Develop the knowledge of the press about the production of enterprises through tools of media tour, and press conference.

⅄ Establish mechanisms providing hot, new, and valuable information to readers of the newspaper by tools of press release, media briefing, and 24/7 hotline.

⅄ Support social programs organized by the newspapers.

c. Experts

» *Purpose*: Take advantage of their reputation to highlight the advantages of the product / service, or their support in situations of crisis communication.

» *Tactics*:

⅄ Develop their knowledge about the mission, structure, operation, products / services of enterprises through tools of expert tour, meetings, and expert product trial.

⅄ Establish mechanisms providing information to experts by tools like press release, expert tour, expert meeting, or 24/7 hotline.

d. Alliances of distributors, dealers, supermarkets, shops

» *Purpose*: maintain good cooperation between enterprises and Alliances of distributors, dealers, supermarkets, and shops to help bring products to consumers extensively and effectively.

» *Tactics*:

⅄ Identify specifically consistent provisions in the Alliances to ensure favorable and timely condition for the circulation of goods in the market and to avoid opponents' dirty tricks.

⅄ Regarding distributors, enterprises will review and appreciate their efforts of safe and intact delivery to the hands of each consumer, through tools of partner conference, and troop ceremony (see more in Chapter 4).

⅄ Research, and issue appropriate policies of commissions presenting enterprises' goodwill of long-term cooperation; as well as observing and acting against those who want to distribute similar products of competitors.

FOR LIMITERS

This group includes: competitors; objects against the existence of enterprises.

a. Competitors

» *Purpose*: to protect the growth of sales.

» *Tactics*:

⅄ Applying the 5 defense tools, enterprises keep track of competitive actions and determine whether they are healthy competitions or unhealthy ones.

⅄ In the spirit of "more friends and fewer enemies," enterprises call opponents to sit together in an alliance to fairly discuss about a game in the market that could bring mutual benefits.

b. Opponents

» *Purpose*: to protect the existence and growth of enterprises.

» *Tactics*:

⅄ Applying the 5 defense tools, enterprises find out reasons why our existence is the obstacle to the existence of opposition parties.

For example, the Hindus would not accept the success of enterprises producing drums, handbags, and leather wallets from cow hide; local people cannot accept drinking from the river that enterprises discharges toxic waste into.

Understanding their mentality and opposing actions, enterprises will wisely find out how to respond in time, such as explaining the misunderstanding, asking the government for help, or relocating the factory.

⅄ Enterprises should coordinate closely with the authorities to resolve satisfactorily any destruction of hostile parties, such as burning and destroying the plant, intimidating employees, or disseminating bad rumors ...

Transition:

To effectively apply the Strategy of managing relationship successfully, you should refer to PR tools in Chapter 4.

What is coming next will continue to bring you many valuable experiences on techniques of defending against negative effects from the market that are detrimental to enterprises' survival and growth.

-     *"What are unfavorable situations?"*
-     *"How can we retaliate in unfavorable situations?"*

If there is a negative information disseminated to cumber the purchasing decisions of consumers, if there is something that should be removed to give enterprises a favorable sales condition again, if there is a distortion of the information that need clear explanation, or if there are efficient defense strategies that must be implemented in the first place to prevent an escalation leading to a boycott of enterprises on a large scale, the below 7 defense strategies are the satisfactory answer for them.

There are hundreds of books, hundreds of seminars talking about crisis management every year, but it seems that everything is not enough, because crisis is a very difficult concept to grasp and it is constantly changing.

Obviously there is not a crisis similar to another. It diversifies in each case, person, specific context, culture, and nation.

Anyway, the nature of communication crisis management remains a combination of a series of timely actions to troubleshoot and to minimize the damage in both finance and reputation of enterprises; and the nature of defense activities is to defend themselves against an accusation, an attack, or an adverse criticism at the marketplace.

To fight back the accusation, attack, or criticism, according to the general philosophy of the media, enterprises need to make information transparency.

In other words, it's necessary to make the public understand what is happening, it's right or it's wrong, as well as how to explore and to overcome it, for the only sake of preventing a crisis.

Hereafter, you will be offered the 7 powerful defense strategies (to be concluded based on personal experience, studies, and application of communication crisis management over many years), including *strategy to prevent bad situation, strategy to retaliate, reactive defense strategy, diversionary strategy, strategy to express empathy, strategy to fix mistakes and strategy to keep silence.*

237

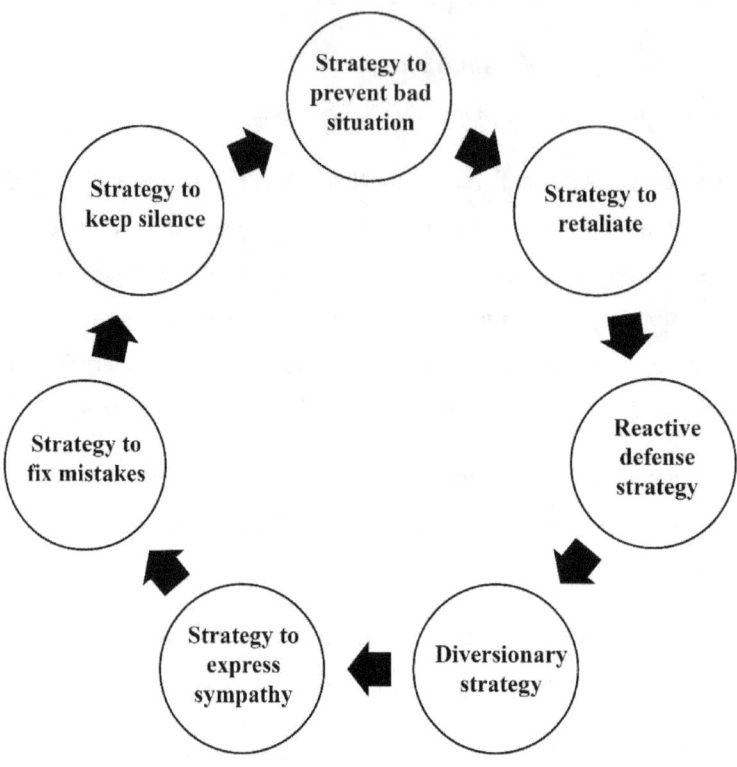

Picture 6.1. Seven defense strategies
Copy right. Le Tran Bao Phuong

1. Strategy to prevent bad situation

The philosophy of this strategy is "those who speak first will get the upper hand and the first viewpoint will eventually wipes out what goes next." It is especially useful when bad news about the enterprise are going to be viral.

This is a valuable lesson that I have learned from the children in the kindergarten.

When two children fight, we must explain to the teacher. But the one that proactively explains to her about the situation, with reason and sincerity will have more opportunities to receive forgiveness. The interpretation of the other child will obviously be taken lightly. Active voice of sincerity before errors is always perceived as a sign of ethical standards.

And now comes a situation applied this philosophy in business.

> *Context.* A woman plays as a mistreated customer calls the hotline
> of the nutrition company X to "make it clear."

> She said she unfortunately bought a cereal box with black creatures
> inside, this was extremely dangerous for her 1 year old baby and
> other innocent kids. She required to meet company's representative
> in exactly one hour...

With many indications showing that this was a situation of unhealthy competition, the "victim" probably needed to take a picture of the broken product and the representative of company X to use as an evidence for accusation, hence PR practitioners of company X had to use strategy to prevent unfavorable conditions.

He arranged two journalists to accompany the representative to work with the "victim". During the discussion, the journalists quietly observed, recorded the conversation, took photos of the woman and recorded the incident.

In the next morning, two major newspapers made the headlines with two articles criticizing dirty tricks in competitive activities and ingeniously said that "that cereal box" was just an excuse of dark PR. Then what happened?

Two articles had paralyzed the desire of other newspapers in the exploitation of the "unfortunate cereal box", which everyone had known was a slander, and an extortion. How could such creatures survive in the strict process of more than 2,000 stages of independent quality checks. And why there was only one unfortunate cereal box is with strange creatures among a thousand of other boxes.

As a result, company X has just overcome a disaster, as well as has built themselves a solid layer of defense against malicious rumors like that in future. How ingenious they were!

2. Strategy to retaliate (or Tit for tat strategy)

Enterprises need to fight back the adverse situation by *attacking, threatening, destroying enemies and becoming victims*. Tit for tat Strategy reflects the defensive strength of enterprises.

Attacking: is a defensive reaction of enterprises before allegations (such as delinquency, disregard of consumers, or business ethics violation) of the opposing forces trying to demolish their reputation.

To defend themselves, enterprises need to attack by encouraging opponents to retreat in order to preserve their honor before bringing allegations to the light of the law with the intervention of attorneys and police. Enterprises can use this strategy if adverse information is still half right half wrong.

Threatening: is to give off affirmation bringing enormous damage to the honor and money of those who slander or spread adverse rumors.

The affirmation is expressed by immediately suing, accusing libelers, slander who are detrimental to enterprises.

This strategy should only be used when there are many evidences that the enemy has flaws and irrational proofs for their accusations. Use tools of lawyer and press conference for this strategy.

Destroy the enemies: is to weaken their influence and prestige by using a third party to disclose the truth about their shame in the past. It strikes at the enemies themselves rather than their reasoning for accusations.

Despite its remarkable strength in protecting enterprises from the disadvantages caused by the enemies, it is considered to be a pure dark strategy in the field of PR.

In quite a few projects, I have tried to avoid using this strategy because it is a double edged blade. On one hand, it kills the enemies by destroying their reputation. On the other hand, it destroys the martial spirit of enterprises in case people realize that it manipulates this dark tactic.

Becoming a victim: is to officially state that enterprises are the victim of a dirty competition in the market, in order to gain the community's sympathy and to invalidate the allegations about their delinquencies.

This strategy should be used when enterprises find many evidences of a deliberate attack of rivals or absurdity in their allegations. This subtle and astute strategy should be implemented by experienced PR experts.

Case study 6.4:

Strategy for attacking and retaliating "becoming a victim "

Context:

A has been a well-known formula company in the world for over 100 years. But recently, the quality of their products has been constantly stigmatized on the internet by extremely negative articles of blogger X.

The bad news are quickly spread on the Internet and has caused extreme annoyance in the community of moms. They motivate and persuade each other to boycott products of company A.

A company's PR department has analyzed, and has found many evidences showing that the allegations of bloggers X (about the quality of the milk products of company A) has many contradictions, and also discovered indications that bloggers X is manipulated by someone else behind the scene.

Before this situation, company A decided to "Become the victim".

Goals:

» Warn journalism community to be careful in selecting and handling sources of information from bloggers, avoiding inadvertently abetting them to attack other enterprises.

» Widely spread the message "dairy company A is a victim, stigmatized by rivals on the internet and the authorities have also known this."

Implementation:

Company A organized a seminar with the participation of the representatives of the Ministry of Justice, Ministry of Information and Communications, lawyers and enterprises that are the victims of competitors' dirty tricks to achieve the 2 goals above.

» Location: Office of the Ministry of Information and Communications

» Time: 09-11am on 12.05.20xx

» Attendants:

▪ Representative of the Ministry of Information and Communications

▪ Representative of the Ministry of Justice

▪ 25 journalists, 5 TV stations

▪ 5 attorneys

▪ Representatives of enterprises that have been a victim of online stigmatization.

Content:

▪ 8h30 – 9h: Welcome guests

▪ 9h – 11h: The program took place, including 5 parts

Part 1:

- MC stated that enterprises suffered great losses from being attacked on the internet and forums by slanderous information.

- Representatives of the organizing committee spoke about the reasons of the seminar and declared the upcoming information was accurate and complete in order to help enterprises avoid the damage caused by unhealthy competitions.

- The negative news attacking enterprises are from journalists, bloggers, that were accidentally or deliberately released to the market with certain purposes.

- There are many situations showed that some enterprises have used such unfair competitions in order to cause damage to their opponents.

Part 2:

- MC invited the representative of the Ministry of Information and Communications to give a speech on measures to manage the information on the internet.

- MC invited the representative of the Ministry of Justice to speak about the articles of law, or the laws governing this matter.

- Discussion: the need to have strong sanctions against this problem.

Part 3:

- MC invited the representatives of the victims of dirty tricks to speak about the damage they suffered because of such malicious allegations.

- MC raised an accusation in which company A is the victim and invited a lawyer to talk about this issue through the sanctions and the right to sue of company A to protect their reputation.

- Discussion: The opinions of the speakers and participants.

Part 4:

- Journalists and bloggers would share the process of handling information, blogging as well as the process of censoring and self-censoring before making it public.

- Through those stories, journalists, bloggers raised the awareness of practitioners on how to handle information in a right way.

- The representatives of the Ministry of Information and Communications gave recommendation how to deal with those dirty tricks on business.

- The lawyers gave more ideas on how to handle, and face this kind of problems.

3. Reactive defense strategy

Reactive defense strategy presents a less intense reaction from enterprises before negative information, including *denying responsibility, apologizing, and making excuse.*

Denying responsibility: is the strategy in which enterprises refuse to take responsibility for a certain mistake, because they confirm that the error had not occurred, or it is unrelated to them. They are innocent and misunderstood. Whoever has caused it need to take responsibility for it.

> *For instance.* For consumption goods such as canned food, powdered milk, or soft drinks with objects, or are musty, curdy or damaged, it may be the fault of the carriers, and is not related to the production process, packaging of the factory.
>
> They produce hundreds of thousands of products each day, it's impossible that only quality of a few products are damaged. In addition, the survival of enterprises with the history of over 100

years in more than 60 countries depends on the quality of its products.

In summary, although they are not involved with defective products, but they will endeavor to coordinate with the analysis center, and authorities to investigate the causes of defects, as well as to learn about opposing activities.

Wise enterprises will not use this strategy if there is an existing evidence proving that they are completely wrong. It will cause an opposite effect and will drag their reputations in the market through the mud because it will create the image of an irresponsible organization in public's eye..

Apologizing: is to minimize the loss of business reputation over their faults or to get forgiveness for the poor product / service that they provided. There are 4 ways to say sorry, which are due to force majeure, the lack of control, unexpected accident and misfortune.

Force majeure aka having no choice, enterprises are forced to make mistakes.

An example of this narrative is that enterprises feel regretful for not paying to thousands of poor workers since their strategic partners go bankrupt.

The second excuse is *the lack of control* of enterprises over the attitude of the staffs that have offended customers. The third one is the request for forgiveness for a poor, and tardy service attributed to an unexpected catastrophic accident.

Finally, the defense of the board of directors for the losses, or the delay of launching unique new products is that they are affected by the fault of former leaderships, which is also the fourth way to apologize called *misfortune.*

Making excuse: is a strategy that enterprises admit their mistakes to maintain their reputation.

There are 3 kinds of making excuses: *spin the situation, good-or-bad is the matter of perception and fault mitigating attribution.*

Spin the situation: The pilot controlling the plane of US Airways has been honored as a hero for preventing a horrible accident and saving 155 passengers on board. He refused to share the cause of the accident. People said:

> "He is very careful about what he says. I think this is a qualification of a veteran pilot. He does not speak at random". Many people expressed their admiration on Facebook just hours after the urgent landing, "Let's look at his mastery, his experience. He did the right thing to save many lives. "[6]

Then the cause of crash was announced due to a bird strike damaging both engines. The clarity in the response of this airline helped them dispel a dangerous infant crisis. Whether the cause was true or false, in fact the media crisis was reversed ingeniously.

Good-or-bad is the matter of perception: is there any mother dares to change the type of formula that her little baby is familiar with? Surely it is rare, because the majority of moms believe that other milk products would harm the absorption of their children. The absorption of the child can be disturbed. Therefore, in maternity hospitals, dairy companies has actively offer free powdered milk to new moms.

– *"What is the purpose of their generosity?"*

Do big dairy companies want to help poor moms who cannot afford good formula milk to their babies? Or do they intentionally force new born babies to pursue their dairy products from the first spoon of milk through their moms?

Good-or-bad is the matter of the perception of each person, but this reflects how clever dairy companies are in manipulating this astute strategy.

Fault mitigating attribution: is the confession of the fault of an enthusiastic trainee. This may not represent the whole organization. Along with the promise to make good, the fault mitigating attribution has much chance to win customers' heart back.

Å ————————————————

[6] Dantri.com. (2009). *Pilots landing the plane on the river is a "hero".* At: http://dantri.com.vn/the-gioi/phi-cong-lai-may-bay-ha-canh-xuong-song-la-nguoi-hung-303730.htm [date of access Jan 16th, 2009].

4. Diversionary strategy

This is to turn the public's attack away from a negative problem related to enterprises.

Diversionary tactics include 4 forms such as *give in, distract, separate from mistakes and rename.*

Give in: is the effort to rebuild reputations affected by faults by accepting the demands of the opposition on the principle of mutual benefits.

> For instance. An MSG company who was detected discharging their waste to the river causing environmental pollution for years has agreed to pay compensation to all households that rely on the river.

> This compensation, on one hand, made up the losses of the people, while it also recovered their sympathy and brought the company another opportunities to carry on their business.

> If their concession held them back from damaging the company's reputation, then time would be a miraculous partner, erasing all mistakes. Everything would eventually be forgotten as time goes by.

Distract: is the strategy to mislead the public, making them gradually forget the attack and accusations. This is a challenge to the professional ethics of PR practitioners.

A typical example of this strategy is the activities diverting public opinion towards pole sexual scandals of celebrities. They distract the public by raising fund for charities to help the poor. They shed tears of admiration before the extraordinary willpower to overcome difficulties of unfortunate people. They create good events to attract public's attention from the old, ugly events.

Distraction is different from making concessions since it does not provide adequate answers for the questions of the opposing parties, but creates charity events to hush up an old ugly scandal.

In the field of politics, it is a powerful strategy to preserve the prestige of presidents before sexual scandals. You should watch the movie "Wag the dog" to know more about this strategy.

Separate from mistakes: is to split enterprises from incidents caused by their employees to prevent an attack from the public.

> For instance. According to Genk / Cnet (2013)[7], just a few days after Apple introduced the iPhone 5S with the 64-bit A7 processor, the marketing director of Qualcomm, Mr. AC told IDG News that Apple's 64-bit A7 processor was more of a marketing stunt than a technical enhancement and thought it would not deliver any benefits to smartphone users.

> Immediately, Qualcomm had to "fight the fire" by denying all of Mr. AC's statements, they said that his comments of Apple's 64-bit A7 processor was incorrect. The 64-bit A7 processor offered "desktop-class architecture" to users. Hardware and software ecosystem was aiming at 64-bit platform which was an irreversible trend.

> They denied earlier comments of Mr. AC who was then transferred to a new position at Qualcomm.

Their quick response has timely separated them from the dangerous mistake of the marketing director, keeping the company away from public concerns about their vision for future technologies. Obviously, this strategy has helped Qualcomm avoid a premonition disaster.

Rename: the rename strategy is to refresh enterprises by changing their brand name and identity, all of the other things (human resources, processes and products), have no considerable change or remain unchanged. Just like "new wine in the old bottle".

Å ————————————————

[7] According to GENK/CNET. (2013). *Qualcomm's marketing director was removed from office.* At: http://news.cnet.com/8301-13579_3-57609038-37/after-apple-64-bit-a7-criticism-qualcomm-exec-reassigned/?part=rss&tag=feed&subj=News-Apple [date of access Oct 27th, 2013].

Enterprises generally apply this *rename strategy* when: (1) the cost of compensation and fixing the damage in the crisis is much greater than the current value of their brand name, (2) the ability to recover their image or public trust is zero. In those two situations, renaming is a miracle solution helps enterprises reborn from the ashes.

When writing this text line by line, I feel very excited recalling the time when I worked in the field of agriculture and real estate. I've seen companies produce fake fertilizers with poor quality used this strategy very proficiently in 3 steps:

- First, they organize seminars and give free products to farmers to test the effectiveness of a new fertilizer on their plots.

The results is always perfect, plants develop very well. This is understandable since the sample usually has very high quality, even more than the normal standard.

- Second, they re-organize a seminar to announce the practical effect that their product brings to the land on which they are standing.

With an attractive promotion "buy 1 get 1", they stimulate farmers buying 10-20 boxes to store for long-term use. And these products are in low quality, or fake, this is the stage bringing them maximum profit.

- Third, the enterprise know that after finding out the products are substandard and knowing that they are fooled, farmers will boycott them, so they wisely rename the company, and the product to be able to sell these poor goods in another place with the new name.

Ironically, these kinds of deceptive companies have very natural advantages in businesses, because to properly assess whether a fertilizer is really efficient on crops, it takes time to observe (3- 6 months, even one year) and the result is driven by many factors such as soil, climate, weather, cultivation techniques, or even fertilizer dosage.

How can farmers assess it? Therefore, these companies easily obtain illicit profits in a long term, from one region to another. Therefore, farmers are very vulnerable[8].

Å————————————————

[8] Author's note: The story took place in 2008-2010 in Lam Dong, Vietnam.

I offer these following two examples to warn that such type of enterprises were fully identified by the public. The public will wisely judge these kinds of unethical enterprises.

5. Strategy to express sympathy

This strategy is to present the empathy and understanding of the enterprise towards customers' hurt and loss. Expressing empathy consists of the *attention, compassion, regret and recognition.*

Attention: this strategy shows that enterprises cannot ignore the causes of the misery, or the loss of customers that are not even their faults.

> For instance. In the mid 2008 in Vietnam, the robbers did not wait until the victim went out of the bank X, they rushed straight into the bank to rob. The robbery took place in the blink of an eye, so the victim could not respond. No guard was in duty and security camera system had not been working. This incident instantly went viral across the front pages of many mainstream newspapers that could ruin the trust on this bank.

> In this situation, the bank X refused to pay compensations since the property did not belong to the bank and it was not a part of the transaction between the bank and the victim.

> In addition, the lawyers said there was no legal basis regulating this issue. There was no precedent. The victim had to bear all the losses.

We do not comment on this situation as it ended in the past. But looking back, if the bank formally agreed to pay compensation to the victim, this could create a precedence encouraging same sophisticated settings in other banks.

And paying compensation for having a poor security system would ruin the bank's reputation. In this situation, the attention, or equitable negotiation between the bank and the victim about special allowances for the losses could solve the unexpected accident very well.

Compassion: enterprises deny the liability, but at the same time expressing the sorrow over the physical and mental loss, or damage of customers due to product misuse, or an unfortunate thing that no one can foresee.

> For instance. Using drugs to commit suicide; wrong dosage of fertilizers / pesticides that damages crops; students died overseas due to earthquakes, or tsunamis. That is not the fault of enterprises.

Regret: is the strategy represents the repentance, or sorrow of enterprises before an unfortunate situation related to them. Like compassion strategy, enterprises do not accept any legal responsibility.

This is a very sophisticated strategy responding to the crisis that true-false reasons were vague and the investigation results may be distorted. The attitude of regret, and repentance can alleviate the pain and hatred from the victims' families and help avoid nagging, or even annoying legal litigations.

Recognition: is the strategy to express the sympathy by frankly admitting mistakes and accepting full legal responsibility, as well as paying compensation to beg for forgiveness.

We will only use this strategy if the mistake is so obvious, or indisputable and maintaining corporate reputation is many times more important than blaming on the others.

For instance. According to AP, in Feb 2010, Mr. Toyoda – President of Toyota officially acknowledged that their cars' quality was not guaranteed with some errors such as accelerating beyond control.

Answering questions at the press conference, Mr. Toyoda said: "Trust me. We always put clients first". There were already more than 8 million Toyotas withdrawn due to the error related to the accelerator. The loss of paying compensations to consumers is over 7 billion USD.

However, it is less important than the reputation of the legendary company valued at 26 billion USD.

6. Strategy to fix mistakes

This is to positively response to the opposition and attack from the community by fixing mistakes.

This strategy includes 3 types: *investigation, repair* and *recovery.*

Investigation: is the prolonged strategy regarding public attack, promising a serious investigation about the delinquency attributed to the fault of enterprises.

This strategy can be used if there are faint evidences showing that the faults belong to them. We should not abuse this strategy to discourage legitimate complaints from consumers.

For instance. When I was a media representative for a famous American dairy company, a journalist contacted me about strange objects that had been found inside a new milk can of this company.

He immediately assumed that the product had poor quality and was harmful to children's health. He required an official explanation from the company about this issue and how consumers can continue to trust them.

For this request, I suggested that he should not do anything after getting the results of analysis, and investigation, because an exaggerated spoilt can of milk can cause negative social impacts, and other enormously unexpected outcomes that he could not even imagine.

Ambiguous information announced to the market brings no benefit to anyone. In fact, disseminating irrational bad news might cause panic, and fear in the community of moms, because their children hardly adapt with a different type of substitute milk.

In addition, groundless news may harm the sales, business reputation of the company and even the reputation of the newspaper.

I suggested sending immediately a new milk can to make up for the unfortunate milk can. I have used the strategy of investigation to extend the time to respond for the attack to cool off.

Repair: is the strategy to satisfactorily handle the problem by solving the existing discontent and preventing such incidents in the future.

Repair strategy is the pure light one. It satisfies both the needs of the public and enterprises on handling incidents.

For instance. It was my profound experience standing in front of the camera of a local TV station to answer questions about the leak of waste into the environment which caused serious impacts on surrounding communities and residents.

When I was a child, I enjoyed appearing on television, but I did not expect to be televised by hundreds of SOS letters asking for protection from households to local authorities.

The investigation showed that the system did not have any leak and the cause of the smell was from the amount of organic fertilizers spilling on the floor of the warehouse which was decomposed and then mixed with the rain water, then spilling outside to residential areas, which in turn cause floods, killing crops.

Before this situation, I used the repair strategy to solve the problem thoroughly. The result is that the problem has not recurred for many years and the local people still appreciate us. It has been 5 years now, and the local residents could have forgotten this sensational story.

For minor incidents, repair strategy would even bring much more goodwill to enterprises when they accept to take responsibility and fix it immediately whether the fault is not entirely theirs.

Recovery: is the strategy to preserve corporate reputation by accepting paying compensation for the loss of the victims, or actively covering the expenses of settle the cases quickly and with their goodwill.

7. Strategy to keep silence

This strategy is not responding to the attack by not giving any explanation, or defense.

It should only be used in special situations based on a profound philosophy be silent and then silence will answer.

For an organization that unfortunately falls into the whirlpool of attack, it should only use this strategy in the 3 following cases:

- Enterprises cannot think of any explanation that the public can accept and their prestige must be great enough to make the public completely trust their integrity. People believe that they cannot make a mistake like that. It is absurd for them.

- Enterprises explain adequately why they choose to be silent and why they do not want to push the issue so far, because it is unnecessary and not beneficial to anyone.

- Enterprises often choose the strategy of silence before accusation when they have a particular reason that cannot be reveal or are forced to keep it secret to preserve the cause or they are capable of lobbying strongly enough to make the ship of public opinion sink into the deep hole of time.

Transition

My friends, you have been through Chapter 6 with lots of valuable tips to apply into your practice. Everything in life has its price, and your great efforts will be rewarded in one way or another.

If you have understood thoroughly the 3 basic strategies on sales promotion, managing the mutual relationship between an enterprise and its target audiences, and retaliation in unfavorable conditions, then how well can you prevent potential risks and manage an communication crisis?

I often share with my students that, because the nature of commercial enterprises is to seek profit and since their profit equals revenue minus cost, crises will reduce their revenue and with many new expenses. Cost increases will lead to falling profit. This is bad, right?

Therefore, finding out hidden risks to prevent, and knowing how to minimize damages when crises occur are extremely important.

We will continue in *Chapter 7. The art of managing risk and crisis.*

- *"Ready to begin?"*

7

The art of
risk and crisis management

GENERAL CONTENT

The fifth supreme art is *the art of risk and crisis management.*

The fifth supreme art was developed from the fifth ancient ruling wisdom: "Having knowledge about a certain issue can help you gain the crowd's sympathy and support."

In the fifth supreme art:

If you are a corporate executive or a PR practitioner, you will learn techniques of self-defense for most of the potential hazards appearing inside and outside the enterprise, along with those against the poisons that can cause adverse effects on the reputation and production activities of your organization.

And if you are an ordinary person, you will understand how an enterprise reacts to a communication crisis. Hence, you will be able to engage better in the process of observation, evaluation, and requirements for dealing with the consequences of that enterprise.

The final destination of the art of managing risk and crisis is to recognize, to control and to eliminate as much as possible all the hazards that negatively affect the production or the business activities of enterprises, as well as to help them through legal problems.

Today, for a business, managing communication risk and crisis is becoming more and more essential than ever before, because:

- Requirements on the transparency and accountability of enterprises has been gaining prominence;

- The management and supervision of the government, and of the press on the activities of enterprises are strengthened and deepened;

- Communication crisis is becoming more dangerous for the survival and development of enterprises than ever before, because negative information can viral as fast as the speed of light without being limited by space and time. They create people's negative attitude towards enterprises;

- Damages from communication crisis are very large, such as stagnant sales, declined stocks, boycotted products, the loss of talents and partners...

Therefore, a comprehensive risk, crisis management plan must include 4 parts:

- Section 7.1. Set up a solid defense shield preventing crisis by approaching incidents proactively (so called proactive approach).

- Section 7.2. Predict all the hazards that may occur to prepare reaction plans through the reactive approach (so called reactive approach).

- Section 7.3. Establish public opinion monitor to report on status and preparation route.

- Section 7.4. Handle the crisis that actually occurs.

7.1. Set up a solid defense shield

My friend, in Section 7.1, we will go through 12 steps to establish a solid defense shield to help businesses prevent issues caused by flows of negative information in the market.

- *"What are they?"*

Step 1.   Establish the Task force

- Purpose: to timely prevent a communication risk that is about to turn into a serious crisis.

- The operating principle of the Task force:

    - As soon as the risk and crisis management plan is activated, designated members must gather to establish the Task force;

    - Members include elite officers from specialized departments;

    - All members are assigned tasks very specifically and clearly;

    - They should be trained structurally on how to deal with a communication crisis;

    - They can work independently or in groups and are able to make decisions quickly;

    - Members should update and exchange information to each other in time and accurately;

    - In case the problem gets worse, members of the task force can detach from their daily work to focus on crisis situations;

    - The members should keep in mind the time of regular, unscheduled or emergency meetings to fully participate in.

- Develop contact information and specific duties of each member:

No.	Name	Phone number	Email	Role	Responsibility
1	A	8498893262x	a@crisis.com	Commander in chief	In charge of the whole campaign
2	B.	8498893262y	a@crisis.com	Deputy Commander in chief	Develop strategies and manage the entire deployment of the operation
3	C	8498893262z	a@crisis.com	Members	Build alliances to achieve social supports
4	D	8498893262j	a@crisis.com	Members	Have relationship with the press and key opinion leaders (KoLs)
5	E	8498893262q	a@crisis.com	Members	lead the public opinion on social network
6	F	8498893262k	a@crisis.com	Members	Investigate and analyze social dynamics

Step 2. Build a strategic alliance

– *"What is a strategic alliance?"*

A strategic alliance is a set of individuals, groups, or organizations that have a voice or are likely to affect public opinion. The role of a strategic alliance is to support, to confirm, and to guarantee the retaliations of enterprises over any attack or accusation.

An alliance includes: professionals, leading scientists, government officials, prestigious journalists, famous bloggers and facebookers having strong influence among the netizen community.

– *"How do they support enterprises?"*

They provide advocacy ideas, and views supporting enterprises to drive public awareness to a correct direction, or to cool off opposing views of the opponents.

The contact list of a strategic alliance includes their name, position, organization / institution, phone number and notes.

For example:

No.	Name	Position	Organization	Phone number	* Note:
1	**Leading experts**				
	G	Professors			3-5 people
	H	PhD			
2	**Authorities**				
	I	Ministers			Depends on each project
	K	Deputy ministers			
	L	Spokesperson			
3	**Media**				
	Official newspapers				Over 40 people
	Online publication				Over 25 people

	TV stations				5-10 stations
	Radio stations				5-7 stations
4	**Key influencers**	Religious leaders, village patriarchies, famous bloggers			5-10 people

Step 3.   Identify target audiences of the crisis

Depending on the project, target audiences of the crisis may include:

- Government
- The press
- Local authorities
- Related organizations, associations
- Community of experts,
- Consumers / suppliers / distributors / shareholders / internal staff,
- General public.

Step 4.   Design key messages

Key messages should have been prepared beforehand so that they can be promptly used when crisis happens.

Key message is the positive contents on the prestige, policy, and perspective of enterprises on the issue of safety, environment, quality and social responsibility. It also expresses the sincere attitude, as well as the sense of responsibility of enterprises for troubleshooting.

For instance:
The message about the credibility of an enterprise
We are a trust-worthy organization in the field of industrial waste, since we
- Have been recognized for our contributions to the society through regional and international awards,
- Are highly capable of industrial waste treatment process,
- Have the most advanced processing technology in the local area,
- Have responsibility for a green planet,
- Have a history of over 100 years of development.

The message about the issue of safety and the environment

Our system is guaranteed by experts, and scientists for the security of workers and environment. Besides, we understand the geographical condition and the law of US on the issue of environmental protection.

The message about the quality of products

As a prestigious spice company, we firmly oppose counterfeit and substandard seasoning products affecting consumers' health.

Therefore, we will actively cooperate with the authorities to fight for this issue, as well as commit to provide products of the highest quality for consumers to cook delicious meals for a better health.

The message of social responsibility

We are favored by millions of families around the world over the last 100 years based on our consistent commitment of environmental protection, social responsibility and business ethics.

Step 5.   Prepare the official spokesperson

–   *"Who should be the official spokesperson?"*

In crisis situations, the General Director is often the official spokesperson, because he represents a comprehensive understanding of the issue and a legal spokesperson for any information about the incident.

However, enterprises should also prepare a second spokesperson (usually is the PR director) in reserve for the case the first one is sick, on vacation or not available.

The official spokesperson must be consulted every response plan, as well as be able to answer any question in any discussion regarding the case. He is the sole representative in all outward dispatches.

Step 6.   Issue Risk Management Manual

Risk Management Manual often includes 2 main parts:

Part one lists all the risks that are likely to occur in daily basics of each department as well as prevention methods for all staff to understand and carry out. Besides, it also lists the phone number of members of the task force to whom employees can easily contact, inform, and ask for assistance.

Part two gives guides on how to do first aid, how to denote the attitude and behavior appropriately in crisis.

Step 7.   Develop the plan to respond, answer questions

The plan to respond, answer questions of the press and related parties (such as government, investors, consumers...) must be prepared in advance, including:

- Identify parties that are likely to be interested in the crisis;
- Develop questionnaires and instructions for detailed answers (Q & As);
- Develop response strategies for each group;
- Identify the means and channels for information update for each group;
- Develop the process to monitor and evaluate the response of each target group.

Step 8.   Prepare operation facilities

- Crisis room:
- We should dedicate a room for the Task force during the crisis.
- Crisis room must be fully equipped with laptops, tablets, high speed internet, international phone, public opinion tracking software, fax machines, printers, white boards, etc.
- Hotline 24/7
- Enterprises should prepare a hotline and staff that has been trained to receive and to record every single feedback from the community about the issue.
- These data will be very useful to the Chief Commander to set response plans and to prepare for appropriate behaviors.

Step 9.   Identify priority items and time to respond

Depending on the scale of damage and the urgency of the problem, the task force will classify and commit the response time for every kind of problems.

The scale of damage

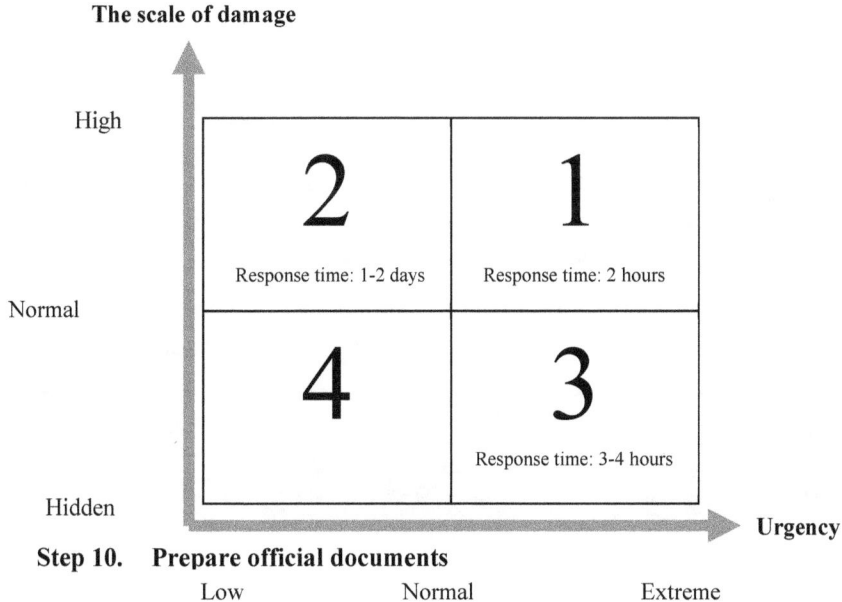

Step 10. Prepare official documents

Low   Normal   Extreme

All of official documents used to handle media crisis must be prepared in advance (in local language and English), including:

- Questions and answers (Q & As),
- Corporate background
- Policy of safety, security, and environmental protection,
- Documents describe the project, or the product / service,
- Publication of standard conformity announcement,
- Business license,
- Fact sheets

Step 11. Unify Action process

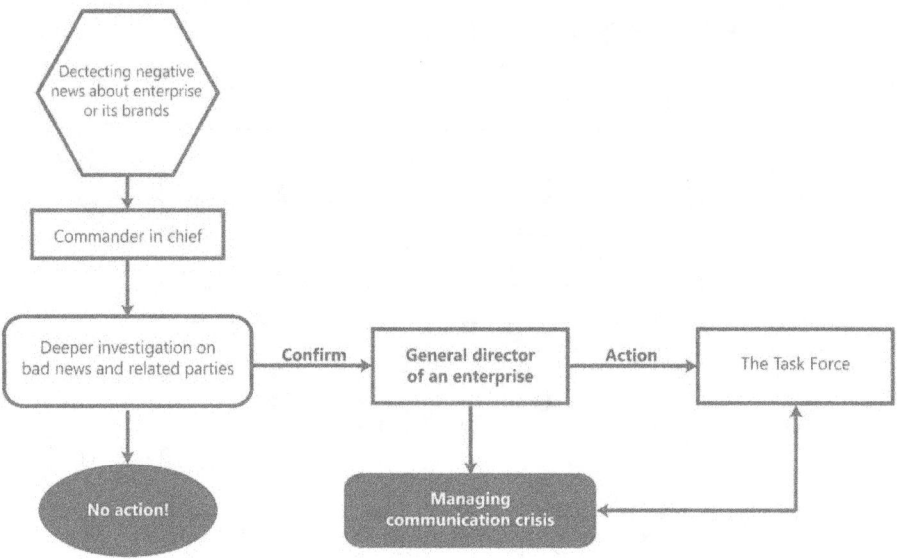

Step 12.   Evaluate the effectiveness of the crisis management

The effectiveness of crisis management will be measured in detail by the results achieved from these reactions, such as the level of understanding and sympathy of the target public, or their attitudes and perspectives towards that matter.

For instance:

Crisis	Priority	Goals:	Reaction	Outcome	Reaction Index	Result
Bank robbery	1	Explain the misunderstanding of the problem and protect the bank's reputation	Organize press conferences	The number of positive news, the number of journalists involved ...	How much The target object has understood the problem	How they have changed their initial opinion

7.2. Predict all the hazards that may occur to prepare reaction plans to deal with them

While *proactive approach* guides us how to prepare well, *reactive approach* helps us identify opposing parties, as well as potential hazards from them and suggest how to control the problem effectively.

Step 1. **Identify opposing groups**

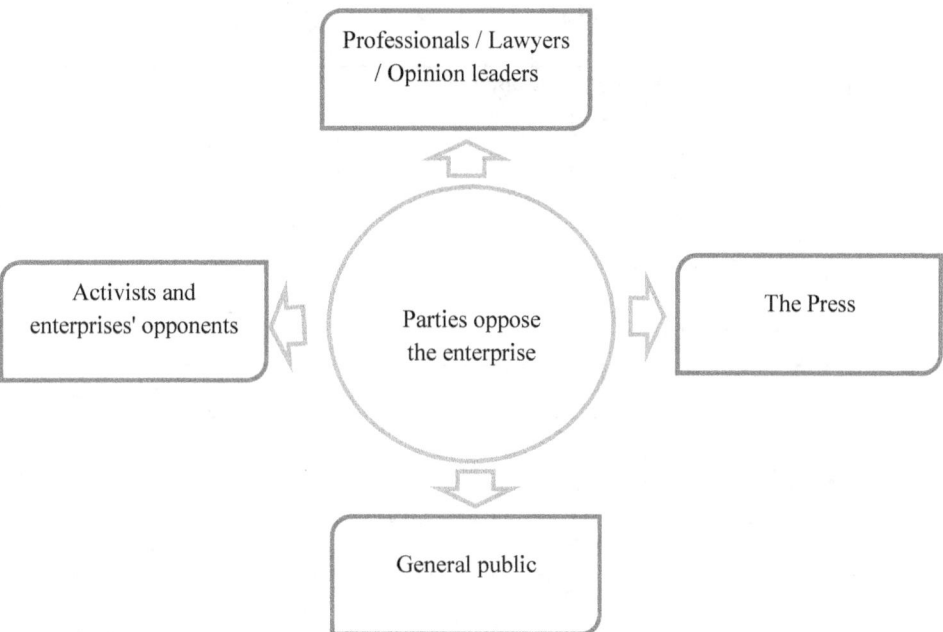

Description:

- **Professionals / Lawyers / Opinion leaders:** are people who have the voice and the ability to gain public support to create public pressure against an organization, or even a government for the claim.

- **Activists and opponents:** are individuals or organizations capable of mobilizing the government, or local people that are against the business activities of an enterprise.

  For instance: Organizations that protect crocodiles are often against companies making handbags, wallets, shoes from crocodile skin.

- **The press:** are journalists, hot bloggers and facebookers do not support enterprises.

For instance: Journalists do not support the construction or restarting of nuclear power plants.

- **General public**: are individuals or groups in provinces and/or cities in a country. They are capable of gathering together to protest against an enterprise or a special project.

Make a list of protestors[1]

No.	Name	Position	Organization	Opposing viewpoint	* Note:
1	Leaders of the opposing public opinion				
	M	Professors, Lawyers	University X	oppose the project by the points of ...	oversea
	N	PhD			
2	Opposing activists				
	U	Chairman			depends on each project
	T	Director			
3	Negative group of Journalists				
	G	Journalists			national
	Z	Journalists			international

The above list helps the Task force identify key groups that we should take care of to limit escalation of conflicts.

Step 2.   Identify potential hazards

The following 5 methods will allow us to identify potential hazards inside and outside of the enterprise. Once we understand them, we could control them.

---

[1] The information in the list is for illustration only.

⅄   **Brainstorming:** is the method to gather a group of people to record their ideas, and experience about risks that are likely to happen in the daily operation of enterprises, or in the next project.

This is a good way to gather ideas, and to maximize the imagination and experience of the members. During the discussion, the members are asked to interpret their ideas in an understandable way and obviously including the events, factors, as well as the arguments of the ideas that have been raised.

After the meeting, all agreements should not be given immediately. Let the members have time to ponder the proposals. They can continue to exchange, debate via email, phone, or direct exchange. Maybe an excellent idea will arise from it.

A next brainstorming session is held to assess and to select the best idea to apply, combining several ideas together, or disposing of all of the ideas and start all over again.

⅄   **Ishikawa diagram:** is the fishbone diagram reflecting all the causes that can lead to a certain loss. It also allows drawing the escalation from one cause to another cause.

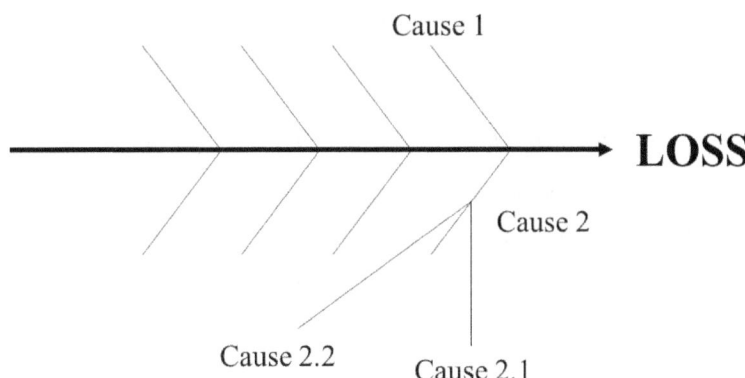

⅄   **Listing:** is a sheet that lists all the damages and lessons from losing projects, wrong decisions as well as the fraud and deception in the past project that we should learn from.

⋏ **Expert advice:** Expert advice will be very helpful for enterprises to fully identify hidden hazards in daily production activities or in potential projects. Former leader is also a source of valuable information that helps the incumbent executives recognize potential risks.

⋏ **Recommendations of State or press agencies:** when getting into new markets, enterprises should research the publication of diplomatic agencies, and industrial associations to gather necessary advice as well as recommendations.

Grasping information about the culture, tradition, way of doing business, the law, the regulations of local authorities beforehand… will keep enterprises from confusion and regrettable losses due to ignorance.

After identifying potential risks, PR practitioners must assess the extent of damage, the urgency and the likelihood of each risk to select appropriate treatments.

Step 3.   Determine how to respond to potential hazards

Potential hazard is very diverse in each company. It depends on business, and time. However, if there are groups of problems, we have 4 basic hazard groups as follows:

Group 1. The press and Advocates create the fear in the community about the product / service, or the production / business.

Example:

Story 1. Using dietary supplements for a long term could possibly lead to cancer.

- Potential communication channels: forums, online newspapers, blog, and facebook.
- The response message: based on rigorous scientific evidence, our products are certified with having natural origins, and are very safe for long term use without causing any side effect.

Story 2. The milk ingredients of cake X is bought from Chinese dairy companies that is contaminated with melamine.

- Potential communication channels: forums, online newspapers, blog and facebook.
- The response message: the type of milk that we uses to make cake X is entirely from the Netherlands, ensuring absolute food safety.

Group 2. Individuals and organizations that take advantage of enterprises' mistakes to adversely influence its growth

For instance:

The story: The product K of CK diaper company in the US is likely to be the cause of high mortality rate in children around the world, including US.

- Potential communication channels: forums, online newspapers, blog and facebook.
- The response message: the defective products have been revoked and there has not been any death. CK's product is absolutely safe for all children, including children in US.

Group 3. Local people demonstrated against a project has the potential to cause great damage.

- Protest sites: at the People's Committees of big provinces and cities, the city in which the project is implemented, the embassies, or diplomatic missions...
- Reaction:

  • Actively disseminate positive information about the project to build true understanding about the issue for related parties,

  • Cooperate with government and lawyer to resolve the problem.

Group 4. The press can exaggerate little glitches of an important project that requires high safety standard.

7.3. Establish public opinion monitor to report on status and preparation route

1. Monitor public opinion and report the situation

- Monitoring mode: daily, weekly, monthly.
- Reporting mode: report to the Chief Commander and the task force about the perspective of target objects, the increase or decrease of the level of their support, as well as the number of positive and negative information about the issue to propose appropriate response strategies.

2. Preparation route

No.	Item	Description	People in charge	Deployment time	Note
Approach the problem actively					
1	Establish the task force	Including operational principles, specific tasks and contact info	Mr. A	July, 20xx	As soon as the campaign is activated
2	Build a strategic alliance	Including professionals, leading scientists, government officials, prestigious journalists, bloggers or facebookers	Ms. C	July-September, 20xx	
3	Design key messages		Ms. D	July, 20xx	
4	Prepare the official spokesperson	(Deputy) General director of the company		July, 20xx	
5	Issue handbooks of risk management		Mr. B	July-August, 20xx	For internal use only
6	Develop a plan to respond, answer questions			July-August, 20xx	
7	Prepare operational tools	Crisis room, Hotline 24/7		July, 20xx	
8	Prepare of official documents	Information of enterprises, projects, security policy, environment, Q & A...		July, 20xx	Prepare many copies
Predict the hazards and prepare to deal with them					
1	Identify opposing parties		Mr. B	July-August, 20xx	
2	Determine how to respond to each hidden risks	4 groups of hidden potential risks	Mr. B	July-August, 20xx	

7.4 Handle the communication crisis that actually occurs

– *"What should we do to handle a crisis?"*

Unexpected incidents occur in plants such as explosion, chemical leakage, fatal accidents, broken waste water treatment system , or rumors about a product that is potentially the cause of death in consumers, or a milk can containing metal dust that cuts children's throat has create panic in public opinion ... are the first shots of a really bad crisis.

A series of articles of bad news make the situation even worse. The whole community feel insecure, doubtful and scared. Some people resents, reacts and sues.

Enterprises involved kept silent because they themselves are not aware of what has happened. The incident happiness so quickly and has an influence on the health and the spiritual life of consumers.

The press repeatedly approaches, asks and continues to exploit the story ... People waits to know the views of enterprises. Everything seems to stop to wait for someone to speak up. Someone must be responsible for this crisis.

–   *"Who will stand out to deal with this crisis?"*

–   *"Of course, that is the PR director."*

Everybody says he will judiciously deploy the crisis management strategy that has been planned before. But what should he do when the fate of the whole enterprise lie in his hand?

–   *Maybe he should tell the truth about what happened to people so they can understand.*

–   *However, it is not that simple!*

We have two things to do right away, they are: (1) Outline in detail how to respond and (2) Implement troubleshooting immediately.

1. Outline in detail how to respond

How to respond to a crisis often have 5 sections, including: *basic treatment, situation analysis, determining whether we are right or wrong and estimating the budget.*

a. Basic treatment and situation analysis

- *For crisis caused by accident, explosion or leakage*

This type of crisis often occurs in the manufacturing enterprises because of technical problems, the carelessness of the employee, or natural disasters, earthquakes, etc.

The consequences of this type of crisis are very visible such as the number of mortality, material damage, the scope and extent of pollution caused by the leakage of waste, chemicals and dust.

When the incident happens, enterprises should deploy rapidly basic treatments like turning off the circuit breaker, shutting down machines, firefighting, evacuation, rescue, fix the leakage, localizing the contaminated area, and calling the rescue team. Then they can analyze and clarify the cause of the incident.

If the damage is large, enterprises should limit the participation of the press on the process of analysis, and judgment. Because the investigation is taking place, and the conclusion is still unclear.

However, enterprises should commit to provide them the result after the investigation.

- *For the crisis occurs due to adverse information*

For multinational companies, their products have technologies with the the same origin of production, packaging, and quality inspections. Therefore, reputation crisis in one country can spread to other countries immediately. To preserve the reputation, the distribution system (ex. supermarkets, markets, dealers, department stores) will refuse to sell their goods.

The rejection of the product in question would make consumers even more fearful about it. Inquiring phone calls from journalists, consumers, and state agencies ... continue flooding the 24/7 hotline. A spark has set a whole forest on fire.

- *"If you're a respectable PR practitioner, what are you going to do?"*

The first important thing is to determine where the bad new comes from, which source, is it national or international, official or unofficial, as well as the motive, and the degree of spreading.

But please note beforehand that, whether bad news is officially or not, ambiguity always catches the attention of unknown newspapers to attract readers.

And it is noteworthy that when a newspaper has mentioned it, others will quickly take part in, generating a cruel information cyclone. The more people talks about the issue, it becomes more and more reliable, while the mass tends to believe in negative information. Therefore, they are more easily drawn into the vortex of information. Therefore, bad news will poison and destroy enterprises. The mass need to see someone punished appropriately.

b. Determining whether enterprises are right or wrong

After determining the source of bad information, the motive of the attack and the reasonable level of offensive arguments. Enterprises need to identify: whether the attack is true or false; or both.

Defining the boundary between right and wrong is very important because the attorney[2] of the enterprise must understand the nature of the case to establish a system of effective response.

In this step, before giving the advice, PR practitioners will ask business leaders the following questions:

- Where does the source of bad information come from? Who is the first one that provide information about the incident?

- Negative information about the enterprise is true or false?

- What is true? What is false? What is the justification of enterprises?

- Are there any indicators of dirty tricks, which means, are they the victims of dirty tricks in the market?

---

[2] *Author's note:* PR practitioners and lawyers share something in common. If the lawyer represents his client in court, the PR practitioner represents his company in public. If the lawyer is paid to protect the legitimate interests of his client, the PR practitioner is paid to protect the image, reputation, and sales of his client. If the lawyer can use his master of law and the art of persuasion to turn white into black, the dark PR practitioner can also use the 5 supreme arts to mislead public opinion.

- If the company is attacked, what kind of trouble and damage has it run into? For example, violations of law, business ethics, consumer rights, or losses of finance, human, and reputation.

- And does he have any solutions?

- If there isn't any attack, how can he explain / justify / deny it?

- How much had enterprise suffered from the attack?

The information is very valuable in creating the core message which will used to retaliate or alleviate the media and public opinion.

c. Estimating the budget

The cost of handling a crisis can only be estimated based on the experience of the PR practitioner.

He will assess the seriousness of the situation, compare with similar cases he has involved in to estimate the budget based on his own experience of implemented projects, or to explore how much the company can spend for this crisis.

The budget consists 2 main parts: the cost of airing advertorials and PR consulting hourly charge.

For instance: The cost of PR consulting hourly charge.

Clients	Company X		Reported for	Ms. Y
Project	"Products K is dangerous to consumers' health"		Time	28th-30th/Nov/20xx
No.	Day	Contents	Total hours 38	
			Consultant 1	Consultant 2
1	28/11	Prepare and implement a plan for handling the crisis immediately	3	
2	28/11	Trace the origin of bad news and work with board of directors, experts, doctors	3	4
3	29/11	Contact and work directly with state agencies, the General Department of Quality Measurement	4	4

4		The representatives of enterprises contact with 12 journalists		15
5	30/11	and 10 chief editors of mainstream TV & newspapers	3	
6		Work with The Consumer Protection Association	2	
Total			15	23

2. Implement troubleshooting immediately

PR practitioners often implement crisis management operations through four steps: first aid, emergency aid, treatment and recovery.

a.   First aid: Its goal is to alleviate the attack of target objects, as well as public opinion and the society.

Working with victim:

- When contact with any individual or entity that accuses the company, PR practitioners should welcome them in a professional manner.

- PR practitioners should invite the victim to the meeting room equipped with camera to record the dialogue. The victim has the right to say and PR practitioners will only listen, ask questions to clarify and the camera will record.

- Then, the victim will be asked to fill out a report on the incident (including time, location, incident, compensation, commitment, and responsibility on the testimony...).

- Then, the victim will be invited by the company's attorney to validate the testimony with the local authorities acting as the third party as. This method represents the profession and transparency of the company, while limiting any accusation with evil intentions to attack enterprises.

    You should notice that the recorded video and the report are the ground for enterprises to retaliate against the attack of bad motives against them.

- With reasonable attack on product quality, enterprises should actively contact, learn about the story, and conduct replacement of new products for customers to placate them, then withdraw defective products to analyze, and to learn the cause and solution. Contact, communicate, and compromise with victims are important steps in the process of solving the incident.

- For attacks that require compensation for damages of the victims (due to actual accidents, or explosions), enterprises need to take immediate action to support with goodwill in the first place (cost of hospitalization, and treatment) to alleviate the attack.

    Just hold off the story of "who is right, who is wrong" for a while because the victim' family is likely the source of outrage that can spread to the community, creating public opinion against enterprises, while the press is fond of dissecting stories of injustice and cruelty.

- For a reasonable attacks on violation of law, enterprises should cooperate with attorneys to complete procedures and to fix their mistakes.

- For false attacks, enterprises need to implement aggressive 'tit for tat' strategies such as assault, threaten and destroy[3].

Reassure internal staff, agents, distributors and partners:

- The next important step is to reassure internal staff, agents, distributors and partners during the crisis period, because their opinions can be cited by the press and their rumors on social media can be spread widely by netizen while their whispers with relatives and neighbors are extremely dangerous to enterprises.

    In addition, if internal staff does not understand the root of the problem, this can easily lead to misunderstanding about enterprises' information suppression. And if there is a thing needed to be hushed up, then it is definitely evil.

---

[3] Refer Chapter 6, Section 6.3. Strategy of Retaliation in unfavorable situations

Thus, PR practitioner should reassure internal staff, agents, distributors and partners immediately, by telling them what is going on, and how to solve it satisfactorily.

This makes them more optimistic about the problem, thus strengthening their trust in enterprises and helps enterprises not miss opportunities of cooperation.

Besides, when internal staff, agents and partners understand the issue, they will help enterprises minimize the spreading of fear and negative inference among the community.

Collaborate with governments, authorities:

- Collaborating with governments, authorities is a wise step showing that the company is innocent from the accusation, in compliance with government's regulations and wiling to correct its mistakes. Everyone makes mistake, but it matters to try to fix it and to be better.

- In every operation, enterprises should recognize and preserve all working records in case of necessity.

- Maintain regular contact and update the progress of the case.

Immediately launch the surveillance system of public opinion:

When using the Monitoring and Tracking tools, PR practitioners should:

- Keep track of public opinion on the press, television, radio, word of mouth and social network (facebook, twitter, youtube, forums…)

- Make sure the board of directors is always kept posted with rumors to have timely actions before the rumors turn into strong negative public opinion.

- Analyze and evaluate periodically (daily / monthly) the development of the incident to timely adjust response strategies.

- Propose 'tit for tat' strategies, timely guide public opinion to a positive direction.

- Maintain a surveillance system of public opinion until there is less or no danger.

Official spokesperson: must be ready for the content of answers, and behaviors in any discussions and interviews about the incident.

Tend the hotline (hotline 24/7):

Hotline is a 2-way communication channel and is especially important in receiving questions community and sending feedback from the enterprises.

Hotline operators must be trained on how to respond based on the Frequently Asked Questions - FAQs prepared beforehand. They are not allowed to answer unfamiliar questions or those that are beyond their scope.

Put the FAQs into practice:

The rapid and prepared response from the enterprises about the incident can reassure consumers, the press and the people very effectively.

The answers often focus on the following contents:

- The truth of the case: the accusation is true or false. Why is it true or not true?

- The view of the company about the issue;

- Expectation of the company and the victim;

- How the business is affected?

- How's about the investigation?

- Foreseen losses and the troubleshooting.

Be willing to submit press releases with unified messages:

Press releases should be prepared instantly to ensure that information is under control and to prevent crisis escalation.

After understanding the nature of the incident, depending on the accuracy of the invective, and how much have enterprises suffered from such invective, PR practitioners will choose the message to be shown in the press release, such as denying responsibility, apology, confession, defense, concession, silence ... (see Chapter 6).

But no matter what you choose to do in response, the key point of the press release is to present the reason why people should trust and support enterprises. If the given reason is not convincing, you must redesign it immediately.

b. **Emergency aid:** Its goal is to calm the public, and to dispel doubts or to intercept negative information by launching a series of positive news about the incident.

For incidents affecting a small range, PR practitioners should only explain the problem to related objects, rather than sending press releases to many newspapers, or shouting out for the whole community to know, because those things will just make the situation even worse.

As in a greater extent, if the accusation is true, enterprises should be sincere, cooperative, responsible, and willing to fix the problem once and for all.

And if it is absolutely false, enterprises must intercept it and limit the related negative information, and extensively spread positive public opinion about the case at the same time.

– *"How can we spread the positive information?"*

You can use 13 tools to protect corporate reputation in a crisis (Chapter 4) such as Letter to Chief Editor / Editorial Board of the newspaper, dispatches to Consumer Association, press conferences... to clarify the story about the incident creating the flow of positive information about enterprises.

In my experience of lecturing and consulting, I have always reminded PR practitioners of a useful philosophy in handling media crisis as follows:

"If you want to extinguish a fire, just pour a lot of water on where it burns. The water will quickly put out the fire.

And if you want to extinguish a media crisis, just create positive information to replace the negative opinion in the market. , just spread good news to where bad news comes from. Good news will surround bad news. The positive information will create a positive public opinion which is likely to dispel the panic and fear in the public."

If you apply this philosophy well, you can achieve following positive results:

- Reduce consumer's antipathy towards enterprises;

- Turn their attitude from angry, incriminate into neutral, doubtful;

- Take back public empathy if enterprises know how to make concessions, and are willing to fix their obvious mistakes.

Keep in mind that nothing is impossible to solve, the most important thing is the attitude and the spirit of cooperation.

c.   **Treatment:** The purpose is to turn public doubt into trust and support.

During this period, PR practitioners will actively post convincing evidences, and facts proving that enterprises have worked with victims, as well as the authorities in order to show their positive attitude & action towards the issue.

- Articles, interviews: have great effect in dispelling people's suspicion, and scattering doubtful information in the market and proving the professionalism and the sense of responsibility of enterprises.

- TV report, online consultation: provide firsthand evidences to convince the public, investors, and partners about enterprises' enthusiasm. TV reports will strongly reinforce partners' confidence in face of attacks, and unsubstantiated allegations of hostile forces.

During the treatment, PR practitioners should not use the word of mouth (WOM) to justify or explain about the incident. It doesn't have enough credibility to do this.

d. **Recovery:** the goal of this stage is to restore the image and reputation of the enterprise.

Based on the causes of the crisis, after the stage of treatment, we need to organize activities to recover public belief.

1. For the crisis related to legal issues or unhealthy competition, they can organize seminars for authorities, the press, victims, and witnesses to stop opposing forces from escalating to ruin enterprise's reputation (see case study 6.4, Chapter 6).

2. For the crisis of their product / service influencing consumers' health, enterprises should organize health seminars, and workshops to enhance people's knowledge to take win back their trust and that of the society (see case study 7.1 below).

Case study 7.1:

Strategies for managing communication crisis

Context:

November 9th 20xx, The Food and Drug Administration (FDA) issued warnings about tampon S of company CK that could possibly cause mortality in consumers. Also on 9th, company CK (in America) also withdrew more than 1400 products across the globe.

Just then, a series of rumors and bad news about tampon S were rampant among Vietnamese social network and in turn raised consumers' resentment. They made countless calls to the hotline of CK to express the fear at a high level. Supermarkets, distributors, and agents stopped receiving their goods. Mainstream media agencies also jumped in on the investigation, opening a series of battles against CK.

The risk of a drop in sales and prestige is real. If you are a PR consultant of CK, what would you advise them?

Goals:

» Minimize the damage and restore CK's corporate reputation.

» Restore the trust of consumers in tampon S so that CK can get back to their business as normal.

Crisis communication strategy:

Because the credibility of FDA is huge, so to defeat the fear of product S's quality in public opinion, CK should turn the story into a different direction "tampon S has been certified for their safety by prestigious inspection agencies in Vietnam. In addition, tampon S imported from England has nothing to do with that of the US. "

Step 1: First aid

1) Monitoring & Tracking: track, aggregate, measure all the negative and positive information about the incident in over 20 forums, 20 online newspapers, 10 newspapers, TV, radio, google ... during crisis treatment (3 months);

2) Press release: define key media lists and prevent them from adding fuel to the fire by sending them press releases attached with S' certification of being imported from the UK, and safety certificate from the trust - worthy local testing center.

3) Briefing: directly share and submit information and evidence to make a proper understanding of the case for the press, consumer association, distributors and agents in order to dispel their worry, as well as restraining the development of bad news, rumors.

4) Hotline 24/7: alleviate the anger of customers by answering all their questions based on the list of guided and practiced questions beforehand (FAQs).

5) Spokesman: CK's spokesman answers all the questions of the press according to a list of prepared questions.

6) Government Cooperation: cooperating with authorities is sufficient and necessary, and should not hold press conferences to avoid "making a mountain out of a mole hill".

Step 2: Emergency aid

1) Editorial / Advertorial: publish evidence proving tampon S is safe over 20 forums, 20 online newspapers, 10 newspapers ... to neutralize negative public opinion.

2) Forum seeding: retaliate stigmatized activities against CK to reassure customers.

3) Hot facebooker: post narratives of 10 hot facebookers calling for peace of mind about the quality of product S along with relevant certificates.

Step 3: Treatment

Editorial / Advertorial: posting positive articles on all channels that used to have bad judgment on tampon S in order to confirm its safety and to restore CK's reputation (according to a useful philosophy "scatter good news at where bad news are.)

Step 4: Recovery

1) Event sponsor: fund for conferences of Quality Management to prevent competitors taking advantage of the event to play dirty tricks on CK crisis.

2) Promotion: organize promotion of product S to stimulate buying habits of consumers.

Evaluate the effectiveness:

Thanks to early response and good anticipation, within a week, negative public opinion about product S was extinguished completely.

CK's business operation has gradually recovered. Their competitors cannot take advantage of this crisis to destroy them. All in all, the campaign was successful.

* Note: To protect the privacy of clients mentioned in the case study, I have changed their names and revised other details.

Transition

My friends, Chapter 7 has provided us with valuable information about The fifth art - *the art of risk and crisis management* with four core components:

- Set up a solid defense shield;
- Predict all the hazards that may occur to prepare reaction plans to deal with them;

- Establish public opinion monitor to report on status and preparation route;
- Handle the crisis that actually occurs.

Chapter 7 has comprehensively supplemented the fundamental thinking strategy of PR practitioners, from applying PR on sales promotion, building reputation, to handling crisis, and crisis. We are very happy and excited about this accomplishment.

For the next important part, I want to continue introducing the methods to evaluate the effectiveness of PR to find out how successful PR strategies have been applied in reality and what PR practitioners need to learn from them.

- *"Ready to begin?"*

8

Evaluating
the effectiveness of PR

GENERAL CONTENT

After reading from Chapter 3 to 7, you have had an idea of how to build and to deploy a comprehensive PR campaign to achieve your goal. But how do you measure its effectiveness?

Chapter 8 will answer this question. It will give you four methods of evaluating the effectiveness of PR activities, based on:

1. Anticipation;

2. The influence on public opinion;

3. The quality of the message, right target audiences and the number of coverage released;

4. Public response;

8.1. Why should we evaluate the effectiveness of PR?

That is a complicated question!

Although everyone can respond immediately that assessing the effectiveness of PR is of course necessary. We should measure to see whether it has met our expectation and whether or not the PR team has completed their task. Organizations also need to know how effective their investment in PR activities are.

The answer is very reasonable, but it is inadequate.

It only revolves around the view of the organization. An adequate answer must include the view of PR practitioners. Because the assessment of how effective PR activities are will not only help them accumulate experiences for their career, but also be a transition stage for their new projects.

Thus, we have enough reasons to realize that assessing the effectiveness of PR is very important and necessary for both organizations and for PR practitioners.

However, in the list of permanent obsessions of PR practitioners, assessing the effectiveness of PR is always ranked first. Why?

They see it is difficult to prove that the money spent on PR activities has brought good results and adequate benefits to enterprises.

- *"But why do they feel so difficult?"*

There are 5 reasons:

- First, they feel vague on evaluating PR effectiveness, ie they do not know which elements they should evaluate nor how to do it accurately.

- Second, many PR practitioners have not been trained or lack the skills of using surveys, market research and analysis of the crowd's perception.

- Third, some criteria cannot be measured accurately.

For example, how much is the value of establishing defense shield which helps enterprises avoid one or many crises? How many negative views about enterprises has been eliminated in the mind of the crowd? How many of appreciatve thoughts towards enterprises were created in the market? We cannot measure them accurately.

- Fourth, PR is a social science. It is not a science of accuracy.

Unlike finance which can be evaluated efficiently through financial figures; unlike sales of specific goods that are assessed effectively through the quantity of goods sold and selling expenses; PR is dealing with people that have diverse views, ways of thinking, behaviors, emotions, feelings, lifestyles... that are very unstable, elusive and difficult to measure. How can we measure human emotions?

- Fifth, there are many people within the company that are against PR activities. They have often rejected the contribution of PR for the development of the organization.

They may think that good sales is due to sales department, shipping department, production department and marketing department, but not thank to PR department. Does PR department have anything to do with the production, promotion, delivery, and collection of products? If anything, then it is only an indirect, and ultimate, a negligible contribution.

It seems that you really want to see the practical effect of PR activities for the organization, but the evaluation remains vague. Five reasons above may have got you stuck! You need specific guidance to judge and to recognize the important role of PR, don't you?

- *"You got it! Right below."*

8.2. 4 advanced evaluation methods

They are based on:

- Anticipation;

- The influence on public opinion;

- The quality of the message, right target audiences and the number of coverage (news, aricles) released;

- Public response.

1. Evaluation based on anticipation

It is to evaluate the effectiveness of PR activities based on hunches and experience of the observer.

This method is very basic and is mainly based on the reviewer's observation results, such as: "The general director is very happy about the result of the program", "customers love to join our next programs", "everyone admits that the campaign has been successful".

Evaluation based on anticipation is quite effective for assessing communication goals to be achieved in crisis management and for establishing key relationships with target audiences.

As for PR campaign for sales promotion, this method has certain limitations because it relies too much on subjective personal attitudes and opinions. Therefore, we will need to use it along with other methods.

2. Evaluation based on the influence on public opinion

It is to evaluate the effectiveness of PR activities based on *the level of awareness, concern and the changing behavior of consumers* over the brand and the organization after PR campaign.

Regarding the level of awareness: after the campaign, evaluate whether or not customers are impressed, care, or remember anything about the brand and the product that have been promoted recently.

Deployment: PR practitioners arrange for a group of employees to contact and to interview shoppers.

Illustrated questions for interviewees:

- Do you remember any information about a certain recently promoted milk product that is good for brain development / immune system / learning ability of children?

- Or when it comes to dairy products to help children grow taller, which one do you immediately remember?

- What did you buy? Why did you buy it?

- Which characteristic of the product has influenced your decision?

Their answers will reveal the effectiveness of the PR campaign for sales promotion.

Regarding the level of concern: PR practitioners should assess the attention and attitude of consumers towards products / services after PR campaign.

Determine if they remain indifferent or have become more interested in our product / service. Do they have the desire to choose our products? When will they switch to other products?

Deployment: PR practitioners will assign people to interview customers at their own home. This will make them comfortable and more confident.

With sophisticated questioning technique that does not orientate or influence customer responses, we can collect data reflecting their true feelings, attitude, sympathy, and belief towards the product / service.

Regarding the change in consumer's behavior: their purchase is the key to assess the success of a PR campaign for sales promotion.

To measure the change in consumer's behavior, we need sales data from sales or accounting department. Such as:

- What is the increased percentage of the number of goods sold compared to the pre campaign?

- Where have they sold the most products?

- Is there any significant change in the total number of customers after the end of the campaign?

- How many new customers do we have? Are there any important customers? Did we lost existing customers?

- How many new units want to be our distributors or agents? Where are they?

3. Evaluation based on the quality of the message, right target audiences and the number of coverage released

⅄ The quality of the message:

Its quality is evaluated based on its compatibility with the planned communication goals. We can assess the quality of the message through the following questions:

- Does the article fully and accurately convey the name of company, event, date, figures, and citations;

- Does the article correctly and fully convey the inner meaning of the message in the first place;

- Is its reasoning neutral, for or against?

- Is the inner meaning of the message easy to understand and easy to remember?

- Is it attached with trust-worthy pictures? What kind of pictures is that? What is their size and position?

- How do target public groups get the inner meaning of the message?

Deployment: by using content analysis, PR practitioners compare the inner meaning of the released message with the initial expectations to determine the possible factors that cause deviation. The discrepancy may be due to the intention or misunderstanding of journalists about the issue, or the way they "write" the news etc.

⅄ The right target audiences:

Approaching correct target objects is very important. It is generally assessed based on when, and where the message is released compared to initial plan.

- For TV, and radio channels: we should check whether the program has been broadcasted at the right channels and at the right time as commited;

- For print, and online media: we should check to see whether or not the article has been properly released on the right papers, and right page sections;

- For social networks: we should check whether or not the story, and comments are posted on the right day and in the right place.

⅄ Evaluation based on the number of coverage (news, articles) released:

This method evaluates the coverage of the message in the market by statistics on the number of stories released in reality versus planned.

- Is the number of articles equal or higher than the commited number?

- Is the cost of posting within the budget?

Deployment: use media monitoring & tracking tool to count the number of stories. and then synthetize, and compare actual results with commited results.

4. Evaluation based on public response

⅄ **For small projects**

- How much traffic has the company's website gained since the beginning of the campaign?

- How many phone calls asking for additional information about the product / service through 247 hotline?

- How many letters have we received from customers? What are they about?

- How many percent of the number of complaint calls from customers has decreased compared to yesterday?

- How does the number of positive news and negative news about enterprises change daily, weekly, monthly?

Deployment: Statistics - synthetic - report.

⅄ **For bigger projects**

- How have the press, people, key opinion leaders (KoLs) changed their attitudes towards this project?

- How have the people's reasons tosupport or to oppose the project been strengthened or weakened?

- How have the images of related parties of the project improved?

- How has people changed their attitude towards the project on forums, social networks and in reality?

Implementation:

- For press and KoLs: conduct telephone survey

- For netizens: conduct online survey, or analyze their psychology through their comments and views on the forums, or social networks.

In short, PR practitioners often want to combine all 5 methods to evaluate comprehensively the effectiveness of a PR campaign, because they will support each other to generate the most objective assessment.

Transition

My friend, chapter 8 has shared with you the methods to evaluate PR efforts that are highly practical and easy to understand, and to apply.

If you are a business leader, you can request the internal PR department or PR agencies to report their efficiency based on those 4 methods to assess the effectiveness of PR.

If you are a PR practitioner, with those 4 methods, you can be completely confident to prove your productivity. The criteria of the 4 methods above are also the criteria for you to remember throughout the process of planning, implementing, leading and controlling your PR projects. We are glad to get this advantage.

My friends, so we have been through Part 2, and we have already been through 2/4 of the book. There remains only a short part before we finish the book in achievement.

We are looking forward to exploring **Part 3. Professional Ethics And Dark PR**.

– *"Ready to begin?"*

Part 3

PROFESSIONAL ETHICS AND DARK PR

Part 3 includes 2 chapters, you will learn a system of Dark PR techniques that are used to deceive public opinion and to destroy competitors effectively. It also helps you understand more about dark PR techniques to identify and to protect yourself from them, thereby enhancing your ability to control the society.

Especially, this part will contribute to help the PR industry return to its roots and its original mission: facilitating the building of a healthy information society and a transparent business environment, thus enhancing our society.

9

Professional ethics

GENERAL CONTENT

In Chapter 9, you will be provided with a detailed list of illegal dark PR strategies, from techniques to manipulate public opinion, to the dark methods to destroy the enemy.

This list is both a useful map helps avoid media traps, and a serious warning for organizations intending to abuse dark PR for their selfish and evil purposes.

Keep in mind that good fortune in the future comes from present goodness. We often get what we give others. Therefore, we should sow fresh and good seeds.

For many books, the chapter of ethics is usually the last chapter, but for me it is the opening chapter for something bigger about to happen.

In today's world, millions of people have witnessed cheap, selfish and wicked PR tricks.

We are dissatisfied with the evil. It must be condemned and rejected. Dark PR must be condemned and rejected from our healthy information life. We are not asking for anything impossible.

– *"But is it feasible?"*

"It is!" We need to do the following 5 things:

> ⅄ Create conditions for millions of people to know about dark PR techniques to help them to identify and protect themselves from it, thereby increasing the ability to control the society.

> ⅄ Create opportunities for millions of people to speak about their needs of living in a healthy information society.

> ⅄ Create opportunities for millions of people to condemn evil dark PR techniques.

> ⅄ We raise our voice but we are not waiting for the governments to sit down together to enact a set of rules for international PR practice.

> ⅄ We need to use the power of PR to achieve the 4 things above."

I'm applying Secret Power to work on the 5 things above. In fact, I have used a supreme PR tool to fight against dark PR, that is *the book that you are reading.*

With this spirit, chapter 9 will begin very intensely: exposing 11 dark PR techniques to deceive public opinion and addressing 8 dark PR techniques to destroy competitors.

9.1. 11 dark PR techniques to deceive public opinion

Below is the list of 11 dark PR techniques to deceive public opinion.

1) Use products that are about to expire for charity. It is to gain public sympathy, and to save the cost of storing, handling, and disposing expired goods at the same time.

2) Misrepresent or exaggerate the quality of products / services to mislead customers, especially in the field of multi-level marketing, health counseling, or study abroad counseling services.

3) Magnify many times the extent of damage of a particular issue (such as tooth sensitivity, cough) to spread widely concerns in society in order to create favorable business conditions for an anonymous enterprise (a pharmaceutical company that sells anti-sensitivity toothpaste and drugs help loosen up phlegm).

4) Use school, health and consumption counselling programs to promote their products / services. Promotion activities that are hidden behind the pretext of community service will become just a tool forsales activities.

5) Take advantage of the reputation of experts / doctors / journalists to promote a new product while the product itself is just a old product with a new packaging.

6) Manipulate State officials to "ignore" the law, enabling enterprises to overcome hurdles, and regulations.

7) Threaten, or recriminate valid reflections from consumers about the poor product / service.

8) Take advantage of the holidays to increase the price to avoid the interference of the press and public opinion.

9) Take advantage of the time when the press is busy with great cultural, political, and social events to silently announce bad news. For example: closing companies, the divestment of strategic partners, or the resignation of business leaders.

10) Create compelling story to deflect public attacks against enterprises.

11) Create fake stories to distort, or to bend public opinion on a certain matter.

Right below is the list of 8 dark PR techniques that bad companies can use to destroy their competitors in the market, such as:

1) Make up and incorrectly cite the views of the authorities to accuse, causing finance and reputation losses for competitors, while lowering public belief toward the government.

2) Defame or slander competitors on the internet to damage their reputation, thus diminishing their competitiveness in the market.

> Robert Greene (2000) has concluded that the evil forces often destroy opponents by damaging their reputation first, then public opinion will kill them off[1].

3) Fabricate false evidence and spread negative rumors about competitors to create resentment among consumers, thus making their product / service boycotted.

> Just sowing a doubt accompanied by evil rumors could put opponents in a terrible dilemma. Victims may deny the rumors, but the public would still be skeptical about them. This is enough for them to spend a lot of time and expense to regain the trust from consumers (Robert Greene, 2000).

4) Widely disseminate adverse information about competitors to cause them more trouble when they are in unfavorable conditions.

5) Organize people posing as consumers, using words of mouth, to spread adverse information about competitors on important sales channels such as: General Trade (including markets, retailers, dealers, and grocery stores), Modern Trade (supermarket)s, Horeca (including restaurants, hotels, and cafes), Key Account (including malls, airports, ports, hospitals, and schools), events (including fairs, seminars, conferences, and press conferences).

---

[1] Robert Greene. (2000). The 48 laws of power (pgs 37 – 43). Great Britain: Profile Books Ltd.

6) Denounce the board of directors by sending anonymous letters to the authorities, functional agencies, investors, existing customers, potential customers, or internal staff to weaken their working spirit and to ruffle their business activities.

7) Create a fake social pages (such as facebook fanpage, youtube channel), or a fake website to harm the reputation of an individual or organization.

8) Create fake accounts on Wikipedia, or Yahoo Answers to create and spread detrimental information about opponents (see case study 9.1).

Case study 9.1:

Protect the neutrality and accuracy

According to Daniel Gabis (2013), for every few months, a controversy about the role of PR practitioners in editing Wikipedia entries arises.[2]

Most recently, several documents have reported that a company specializes in editing articles on Wikipedia to create advantages for its clients .

When this fraud was exposed, many of its members were accused of infringement by the Wikimedia Foundation, the operating organization of Wikipedia.

To protect its neutrality and accuracy, Wikipedia has applied stringent rules on who has the right to edit articles. PR practitioners should note that they are not allowed to write misleading or inaccurate articles since that violates Wikipedia's policy.

Dear friends, you should note that the above are some of the typical dark PR techniques, the actual number is much larger.

I predict that dark PR techniques will continue to be applied in the future as long as business community and people are still not clear on how dark PR work .

---

[2] Daniel Gabis. (2013). Wikipedia, PR and the Importance of Transparency. At: http://www.communiquepr.com/blog/?p=5728 [Date of access: Nov 17th, 2013].

- *"So what should consumers do to protect themselves from being manipulated by the forces of dark propaganda?"*

The advice is:

As for purchasing decision: before paying, consumers should ask themselves "why I want to buy this item", or "what reason I believe in this brand?", Any explanation for it?

For advices from experts: Nowadays, many people believe in experts, because they are the representatives of real science.

Thus, we usually hear of phrases like "scientific statement" from experts, or "many people said so" on media. However, it may not be entirely true, because a single opinion cannot represent a scientific conclusion. We need a clear distinction between sharing of knowledge and the accuracy of scientific information, between rumors and objective honesty.

- *But what should enterprises do to protect themselves from dark PR techniques from anonymous opponents?*

The answer should be: they need to recruit an excellent PR consultant.

In short, dark PR is very dangerous for the development of both the economy and social life, but it can be significantly hold back if enterprises and consumers can identify, oppose, and resist them.

9.3. The reputation of the profession of building reputation

- *"From personal viewpoint, is PR good?"*

According to my researches and studies of public attitude towards PR, it is bad.

It is because of 2 reasons:

- Firstly, the majority of organizations is using PR for its self-interest.

Most PR practitioners is hired to help them build their reputations, not to disclose limited values. Therefore, the messages that PR practitioners release are often incomplete and do not reflect the truth comprehensively.

- Second, people does not fully understand, or have negative views towards PR.

They see PR as a dark tool to manipulate human perception, leading them to path of losses unconsciously.

This is understandable because PR is so powerful that it can easily be condemned as a propaganda tool to suppress the human mind. That is the consequence of taking advantage of PR for sensitive purposes in a long time, which causes it to has a bad reputation (see case study 9.2).

Case study 9.2:

Sensitive PR activities[3]

Historically speaking, establishing agencies to control the flow of information and to manipulate public opinion has been a longstanding tradition.

Markus Sabadell has taken two examples to illustrate this tradition. They were the effort of the Catholic Church to control Gutenberg printing technology and Nazi's propagation.

This tradition still continues til today. We are not surprised to learn that the dictatorships are still trying to maintain their power by controlling the spread of information, nor the fact that information technology and communication activities have become powerful weapons of all parties in the media front.

According to Evgeny Morozov (2010), the internet is really helpful in suppressing the public rather than giving them democracy. He cited that the Iranian

---

[3]Markus Sabadello. (2011). ICTs for Citizen and Peace Journalism (pgs. 17-18).

government had officially banned Gmail and other popular Google services, replacing them with a system of domestic e-mail operated by the government.[4]

The next example to help you figure out dark PR activities is a growing use of"paid internet commentators" in a sophisticated effort to control public opinion.

According to Bristow (2008), this strategy has been used by Chinese government to create a flow of consent for their policies.

These commentators are to identify bad news and to deny them. They comment on forums and websites to turn bad news into good news in an effort to create positive public opinion.[5]

Similarly, according to Cnaan Liphshiz (2009), the Government of Israel has even recruited bloggers to comment with a second language (including English, French, Spanish and German) about the interests of Israel in an "anti-Semitic blog"[6].

Next, in the conflicts between Afghanistan and Iraq, according to Olson (2011), the US militaryhas also used a software to create fake online identities to resist its enemies's efforts to recruit the new troops. It posts false comments on blogs.

Military spokesman Michael Lawhorn confirmed that they purchased this software from Ntrepid, a security software company based in California and it is being used in Iraq and Afghanistan.

This software can be used to create virtual characters - who will comment against the support for groups that promote terrorism on local blogs.

---

[4]Morozov, E. (2010, February 20). The Digital Dictatorship. At http://online.wsj.com/article/SB10001424052748703983004575073911147404540.html [Date of Access: May 17th, 2013]

[5] Bristow, M. (2008, December 16). China's internet 'spin doctors'. At BBC News: http://news.bbc.co.uk/2/hi/asia-pacific/7783640.stm [Date of Access: May 17th, 2013]

[6] Liphshiz, C. (2009, January 19). Israel recruits 'army of bloggers' to combat anti-Zionist Web sites. At Haaretz: http://www.haaretz.com/printedition/news/israel-recruits-army-of-bloggers-to-combat-anti-zionist-web-sites-1.268393 [Date of Access: May 17th, 2013]

He added that it can not be used to trace and identify individuals. All of itsactivities has been approved to ensure that it complies with all domestic and international laws[7].

In Nigeria, Umaru Yar'Adua regime has budgeted $ 5 million to build and to sponsor 50 websites supporting a "friendly" regime[8].

* Note: the above information is summarized based on studies of researchers and scholars according to cited sources.

9.4. White and Black

– *"How can I tell white PR and dark PR apart?"*

– *"How can I support White PR, the good one?"*

– *"How can I restrict dark PR, the bad one?"*

The Power of PR (public relations) reflects the strength of education and propaganda in the society.

According to Edward Bernays (1928), education and propaganda are the black and white sides of PR. The difference between black and white lies in the way people look at things and the real motive of the users.

If we receive new information that we are willing to believe, then it is education. But if we get the information that we do not want to believe, then it is propaganda[9].

So are the teaching and preaching of catechism regarded as education or propaganda?

---

[7] Olson, P. (2011). Anonymous, The Military And Fake Virtual Armies. At Forbes: http://blogs.forbes.com/parmyolson/2011/03/17/anonymousthe-military-and-fake-virtual-armies/ [Date of Access: May 17th, 2013]

[8] Sahara Reporters. (2009). Umaru Yar'adua Regime Launches $5 Million Online War. At: http://saharareporters.com/news-page/umaru-yar%E2%80%99adua-regime-launches-5-million-online-war [Date of Access: May 17th, 2013]

[9]Author's note: This section refers the dark side of Propaganda.

The answer lies in the way how people perceives it and the real purpose of the dissemination of information. If the purpose is to enlighten human mind for a good life, it is education. But if it is to mislead the crowd for private purposes, it is propaganda.

- *"So, is PR education or propaganda?"*

Only the real motive of a PR practitioner while he is working can answer this question. Why?

Because PR professionals (at the level of enterprises) always speak well of enterprises, and they are specialized in praising their employers' new products / services - things that have never achieved public acceptance in advance.

Then how should he is viewed? Should he be regarded as a propagandist or a teacher spreading knowledge about life's useful commodity? Ask him his real motive.

In agreement with Edward Bernays, I think that PR is a holy profession. It caters for the transmission and the resonance of good things, encouraging individuals and organizations to bring benefits to the community.

PR helps spread good things as a shining example that must be replicated through various communication tools, to cover social and life information.

But how to support white PR activities? How to ensure that PR practitioners can keep their professional ethics in check under the pressure of money? How can they not use the power of PR to bend consumption demand, to create false collective hallucination, or to justify business faults...

- *"How do we to turn dark PR's cheap shots into dark clouds so that everyone can recognize them?"*

I have not found a way to convert those lost. I do not even know who dark PR practitioners are. I am so small in this vast world.

Alone I cannot do anything!

But it is possible with a united strength.

The fear of a world manipulated by dark PR is spanning across every single roads that I have the opportunity to walk by. All solutions seem to be fruitless. But I always believe that, despite my aspiration being so so unattainable and fragile, it is not easily killed.

With that belief, I spent many nights thinking, for I could not escape the thought of finding a solution to prevent people from using dark PR, and to only use white PR to bring benefits to life. The solution seems to be too big for a small individual like me to carry out.

I was wandering around a church near my home when I suddenly saw a group of first grade children playing together. A little girl, with cute littlepink hair tie , told the group that her mother said that the kid who didnt not do homework was bad. They agreed in chorus and "boycotted" the "bad kid" who was sitting among them. The "bad kid" then ran away in sadness. I guess he would not dare to miss his homework again.

Right then, I suddenly realized that, because the "bad kid" friends were educated that neglecence of study was bad, so they got together to criticize and to remind the "bad kid" to complete his homework the next time if he wanted to play with them.

I smiled because suddenly found a solution. And it is surprisingly simple!

If everyone understands what PR is and knows how to operate its power, all PR activities will be under control. It has no way but to become healthy and beneficial. Because dark PR activities will be identified and criticized by the society.

I remember Osho - an Indian spiritual master. He said that bad things are just like wet mold, it need to be covered in shade to grow. When hidden, it is growing constantly. But it will evaporate when exposed under the blazing light of the sun. Likewise, bad things will be destroyed when exposed under the light of understanding.

I have found a very efficient solution. I knew that I should share the knowledge of PR, as well as the way it is operated for everyone to understand, and to participate to monitoring this field globally.

Exactly that way!

However, does exposing the power of PR in attracting public opinion affect PR job itself? Definitely yes, but white PR could not be defeated, just as the public's need of information is unfailing, the need of interaction between enterprises and the public, and vice versa will never be lost.

  – *"Regarding this great issue, what should a PR practitioner do?"*

I have to use the 5 supreme PR tools. I have no other choice.

Actually, I have written and disseminated worldwide a book named "Secret Power: Exploring the 5 supreme arts influencing the behaviors of the crowd" to help readers around the world understand more about the power of PR and its operation in shaping attitudes and in ruling the crowd's emotions, thus leading their behavior toward the purpose of the users.

I also use *word of mouth* to spread the information of this book to you.

I am also *giving lectures* in many places, from seminars to university lectures to remind the current and future PR practitioners the importance of professional ethics.

By now, I have noticed that these 3 supreme PR tools have brought good results beyond my imagination. And it is not the end, I will continue to apply 2 other PR tools to reinforce my desire, which is the making of a *movie and* a music video *about the field of PR. I bet you will have the opportunity to enjoy it in the near future.*

We do not know what the future holds, but it depends very much on what we are doing in the present. My friend, with this book, I hope my very small effort has created a cool new breeze of fresh air for the global PR industry, allowing it to return to its roots and its original mission, which is facilitating the building of a healthy information society, and a transparent business environment, thus enhancing the society.

10

Dark PR

GENERAL CONTENT

In this special chapter, you will learn how the ancient wisdoms are being manipulated by dark forces.

You will also be surprised to find out that your behavior is being manipulated in a series of familiar daily settings.

D ear friends, this book has done its job very well to help people understand how to use the power of PR to influence the crowd´s behavior.

And with this knowledge, they can easily control the society contributing to the betterment of the industry. This is also a warning for organizations to respect the truth in their promotion activities.

10.1. A new mission

My friends, the book was received with the warmest welcome beyond my imagination.

And always, when a mission is achieved, another one opens up.

The mission of writing a book has been completed, another mission opens for me. That is the application of one more supreme PR tool, a movie, to resonate with the power of this book to scatter dark PR activities.

The tool I am going to use is a movie entitled **Dark PR**. It reveals the way bad guys are taking advantage of the ancient ruling wisdoms to achieve their evil purposes. These unethical activities are dark PR.

10.2.　How are the ancient ruling wisdoms being manipulated?

Actually, the main content of this movie is about the dark games of a Global Dark PR Organization – using the ancient wisdoms to control public opinion in many countries in order to achieve various political, economic, cultural, and social intrigues, as well as to get generous rewards.

They make up facts to control the behavior of the crowd. This regularly happens. Therefore, it was not by chance that Mark Twain said: "Truth is stranger than fiction because fiction is obliged to stick to possibilities; truth isn't".

The main Philosophy and context of the movie are:

> "A PR expert nicknamed L.T was murdered by a secret dark PR
> organization on his way home from a mini cranky supermarket at

the city's outskirt. He was killed because he had learnt many of their criminal evidences. Despite all that, they continued to kill everyone that contacted with L.T ... With the power of a secret organization, they were successful to do so, yet they lost L.T.'s eldest son B.P ."

Their power is so enormous, because they know how to fully exploit the 5 supreme arts. Specifically:

They know that word has the unique power. It is the basic element of social cohesion. Words can convey knowledge, negative thoughts, doubts to the community to shake their minds, as well as to change their lifestyle and the behavior of the whole society. They use the power of words to control people according to their own purposes.

They also realize that only undetected evil messages are really dangerous, only the type of undetected contents manipulating human behavior really has a strong power.

What goes straight to the heart without going through the judgment of human brain makes people even more confused and disorientated. Therefore, they have reached the profound level of applying words: to change people's views without propaganda, and to control their behaviors without coercion.

Next, they launch crafty PR campaigns to satisfy your desire of finding your ego, enticing you to pay for things which have been attributed with a strongly different personality, such as "It´s me, cool and outstanding."

They convince you that the product they offer will help you find out your true colors, thus getting admiration by other people. They hide the fact that your simple needs have suddenly become complicated because they have awaken and evoked them. They distort our real demands. They make us crave luxury to have us making the wrong decision. Do you still remember that feeling?

Then, they have learn that public opinion has a very strong impact on people's behavior. Why? Because when life gets rush, human mind becomes superficial. Because we are losing our inner feelings in order to adapt to a society revolving too fast around materialism.

Because our analyzing, or dissecting instincts towards every respects of life are useless before the infinity of human knowledge which make us become out of control. We become dependent on public opinion too much. We blindly believe in things that other people think are correct. We gradually lose our true colors. We have chosen public opinion over our own right to making decisions. We are influenced by public opinion.

They use celebrities like high value mercenaries in the front of scattering collective hallucinations to control public behavior. They borrow celebrities' faces in big events, media interviews, and video clips on youtube, as well as their names in the editorials, interview articles and testimonials.

They also own people who have the ability to influence many others (like politicians, priests, monks, village patriarchs, celebrities, or art idols) like "I help you, you help me ", so they can use them when needed.

They know that the internet is a hard-to-control world. Therefore, they use it to create a vibrant virtual world to attract human mind. In this virtual world, it is said that people can safely confess, criticize, and share their thoughts freely and comfortably.

They create a friendly environment for you to show your views, attitudes and making decisions. When you get familiar to this, they will connect your behaviors in the virtual world with the real world.

They also know how to put into our heads necessary stimulus to trigger whenever they want because they understand human mind is just like a simple mimicking machine.

When the machine gets familiar and reacts regularly to certain stimuli, human mind will gradually form corresponding habits. This means, they can give us the kind of stimulus that they prefer to create in each of us the responses that they expect.

They affect our wisdom like putting a CD into the player, then pressing the "play" button to have us sing after their songs. They have been successful with us because we are the victims, because they know our appearance may vary, but our cores remain the same.

To cover the eye of public opinion, they even know how to use all of the noblest truths to conceal the worst. The coward may be masked with the love for peace, the guilt may be hidden under the mask of morality, and self-interest may be disguised under the shadow of lofty humanistic activities.

They also know that deception cannot be changed, but the way people get it can be changed. Therefore, they prefer using lofty reasons to defend their deceit. They use journalists like the speakers emitting false excuses in an attempt to relieve them from violations.

They also know how to deceive the press who in turn deceives the crowd. They ask the press to relieve public opinion, or to create a diversion to confuse people about who is right and who is wrong. They create doses of poison that we swallow every day without knowing. They are the evils leading us to unpredictable consequences without knowing...

The movie continues with:

> "The oldest son was grieving his great loss in an extreme helplessness. He was alone. He did not know the origin of their power. He could not defeat this secret dark force.
>
> After many nightmares about the death of his father, BP suddenly remembered about the coded signal that his father used to ask him to remember. The coded signal deciphered the ancient wisdoms that are capable of stopping the power of dark PR. They develop a kind of opposite power against the power of dark forces.
>
> B.P overcame hardships, and escaped from the fierce hunting of the secret dark PR organization. He fled to Tibet to find an old goatskin book containing many miraculous wisdoms... Overcoming a lot of deadly traps, BP finally found the book. Fortunately, having followed his father from a young age, B.P quickly deciphered the ancient characters in the book.

The first paragraph said:

"The sun cannot be obscured by a hand. The truth cannot be concealed forever in the envelope. It will be opened through wisdom. The best way to protect yourself from temptation is to identify the purpose hidden."

Because:

"Darkness has never experienced something like light; when the light appears, darkness disappears without any confrontation. Dark PR has never experienced something like the truth; when the truth is revealed, the game of darkness itself will be over without any resistance."

Right then, BP tried to use this power to block the power of the dark force.

But he failed to do so.

After many attempts, he still failed. He could not satisfy the last wish of his venerable father. It is the common pain of people with lofty ambitions.

But he was never discouraged. He had tried his best but ultimately did not achieve anything. Something got hurt. However, we admire a person like that, because he has the same qualities like ours. He shows the quality of resilience. He is like us.

And because:

"The integration between wisdom and willingness to do right, as well as between wisdom and compassion are the foundation of greatest power."

Only after the discovery of this last philosophy, our hero knew how to use this holy power to defeat the mighty dark force.

– *"How could he make it?"*

– *"How was the war between the light and the dark?"*

You will know that after watching the movie. I'm developing this movie daily, just like I used to write this book daily.

Dear friends, I would like to see you guys again in this supreme PR tool - a movie & a book entitled **"Dark PR"**.

For now, we should systematize all the important points of **Part 4. The Summary of the 5 Supreme Arts**.

Part 4

SUMMARY OF
THE 5 SUPREME ARTS

In part 4, you will get systematized about the whole philosophy and key points of each supreme art.

11

Summary of
the 5 Supreme Arts

Dear friends, we are feeling festive since we got through the entire content of the book, through each of the supreme arts with many new things that worth considering together.

The more you read, the more valuable and useful things you learn. This worths your effort as well as your great favor for The Secret Power - *the book that everyone loves.*

To help you systematize the book, I will summarize its entire content with some key points.

Summary Of The 5 Supreme Arts

This book is divided into 12 chapters revealing the 5 Ancient Ruling Wisdoms and their application in the field of modern PR.

✿ *The First supreme art is the Art of creating messages using the power of words to establish beliefs and to induce human behavior.*

The first supreme art was developed from the first ancient ruling wisdom: "Wake up the essential human emotions - such emotions could stimulate people to carry out a certain action since most people makes decision based on emotions, yet they often argue doing based on logic."

In the field of modern PR, PR practitioners deploy this ancient ruling wisdom in form of verbal and non-verbal messages to awake emotions necessary to encourage beneficial reactions from the crowds.

✿ *The second supreme art is the Art of spreading messages using more than 100 powerful PR tools to spread your inspirational messages which has just been created in the First supreme art.*

The second supreme art was developed from the second ancient ruling wisdom: "Create in the masses a common awareness of a particular problem according to the will of the convincer to achieve a series of similar responses".

To create a common awareness, the message should be conveyed profoundly and accurately. Therefore, this book gives you more than 100 powerful PR tools that help disseminating your messages.

Hundreds of PR tools are divided into 6 groups according to the goals to be achieved when influencing the crowd's behavior, including:

- ⅄ Group one, 64 tools to create public opinion, influences awareness, knowledge and public's belief;

- ⅄ Group two, 16 tools to draw attention to a product / service and to stimulate purchases;

- ⅄ Group three, 11 tools to build trust for a product / service;

- ⅄ Group four, 5 defense tools;

- ⅄ Group five, 13 tools to protect enterprises' reputation during crisis; and

- ⅄ Group six, 5 supreme PR tools.

The name of each group has also clearly expressed its function.

✿ *The third supreme art is the art of adjusting human behaviors.*

The third supreme art was developed from the third ancient ruling wisdom: "Hit the vulnerable spots of human behaviors to create an unanimous response from the crowd".

The 3 vulnerable spots of human behaviors are *natural instincts, childhood beliefs and self-determination.*

Natural instinct is the automatic reaction of human beings to an external stimuli which leads to a corresponding action.

There are 18 kinds of human instincts that PR practitioners can exploit to stimulate their buying behavior, such as the fear, the feeling of scarcity, greedy, flattery, egocentrism...

Meanwhile, childhood belief is a factor leading to decisions that do not require much judgment, because it conforms personal prejudices, beliefs and experience. This book mentions childhood belief creation in potential customers when they are young, also known as "PR for children".

Finally, self- determination is choosing an item according to one's thinking, analyzation, comparison, and evaluation. For this third element, PR influences consumer's awareness through education, providing them with compelling evidence to evoke and tocreate in them a demand for consumption; as well as positioning products / services associated with their favorite features like classy, elegant, noble, successful, trendy ...

✿ *The fourth supreme art is the art of building a comprehensive PR strategy.*

When applying the fourth ruling wisdom in the field of modern PR, the word "comprehensive" is very satisfactory, because it describes three overarching PR strategies which efficiently support the survival and the development of any commercial organization, which are to push up the consumption of goods, to gain the support of the crowd, and to fight off negative effects of the external forces in the market.

Named according to modern style, those three PR strategies are: sales promotion strategy, strategy on managing the mutual relationship between enterprises and target public groups, and strategy of retaliation in unfavorable situations.

No matter what kind of strategies they are, they have to be guided by the fourth ancient ruling wisdom: "To be able to change the behavior of the crowd, we should be able to change their attitude first".

✿ *The fifth supreme art is the art of managing risk and crisis.*

The fifth supreme art was developed from the fifth ancient ruling wisdom: "Having knowledge about a certain issue could can help you gain the crowd's sympathy and support."

In the fifth supreme art:

If you are a corporate executive or a PR practitioner, you will learn be revealing techniques of self-defense for most of the potential hazards appearing inside and outside the enterprise, along with those against these poisons that can cause adverse effects on the reputation, and production activities of your organization.

And if you are an ordinary person, you will understand how an enterprise reacts to a communication crisis. Hence, you will be able to engage better in the process of observation, evaluation, and requirements for overcoming dealing with the consequences of that enterprise. My friend, the above summary is a big picture in itself, covering the book to helps you systematize your knowledge easier. To master each supreme art, you need to study each corresponding chapter.

In fact, the application of the power of the 5 Supreme Arts has no specific recipe. It is diverse and alternating each other. This is just like "the five elements are interdependent and opposite to one another, with non reign supreme; like four seasons take turns, without any season lasting forever; like sun 'sshade, sometimes long and sometimes short; like the moon, sometimes wane and sometimes wax[1]". This means, PR practitioners should be flexible in selecting and applying the art appropriate for their actual situation.

There is a joy I would love to share with you. Even though public relations (PR) is certainly not an easy job for people who are enthusiastic to pursue it, because it is always changing, pressurable, busy and challenging. Fortunately we have the book *Secret Power* helps us find the way to success in life.

This book is definitely a good friend that can help you save a lot of effort, limit unnecessary failure, thus making your work and your life better. That is quite certain!

---

[1] Lo Trung Kiet (translator Duy Hinh). (2008). The Art of War & 36 stratagems. Thanh Hoa Publishing house.

Ending

My friend, you may have noticed as soon as you saw The Endless Knot on the cover of the book, you were immediately attracted to it. That strong appeal is hard to explain in words, because it is the symbol with profound implications.

The Endless Knot

According to studies, the endless knot symbolizes 5 profound implications that are closely relevant to the Secret Power.

1. *It emphasizes the duality of a problem.* Every cloud has a silver lining. So is the secret power –with white and black sides.

2. *It is placed on gifts to create the link between the giver and the receiver, and to bring good lucks to the receiver.* This book is actually a gift. I believe that it will help you improve your current work results, and it will save you a lot of time to achieve your goals in your future career. It also helps you protect yourself from dark PR activities for malicious purposes.

3. *The endless knot embodies the ancient wisdoms.* I have just applied the 5 ancient wisdoms in the field of modern PR. I call them the 5 supreme arts. These arts has generated the Secret Power.

4. *The endless knot symbolizes the unity between wisdom and the right application, as well as between wisdom and compassion.* The unity of wisdom, right application and compassion is the origin of the ultimate power.

5. *The Endless Knot symbolizes the closed loop of cause and effect.* It is true that good fortune in the future comes from the present goodness. We often get what we give others. Thus, just sow fresh and good seeds. Hence, this book encourages honest and transparent communication activities.

5 sacred meanings of the endless knot are also the 5 profound implications that I have given you through the entire 12 chapters of the book, so I chose **the endless knot** as the greatest symbol for **The Secret Power.**

Thank you

Thanks again for giving this book a lot of special love.

It would be nice if you write me to share your thoughts, and your own feelings about the book, as well as to tell me about the situations that you've successfully applied the Secret Power to better your work, career, and life.

Last but not least, I sincerely wish you success and happiness in life!

Le Tran Bao Phuong
From Vietnam, August/2014
phuongpr@icloud.com